The *BIG BOOK* of POKER

Dedication

This book is dedicated to my son Neil. I especially want to thank Beth Rand for her comments and insight and for being someone I could talk to while writing this book. I also want to thank my wife Olga for her help with proofreading and preparing the manuscript. Thanks again to the other usual suspects:

Don Johnson, Biloxi, Mississippi
Jim Blecher, Wellsville, Kansas
Cody Barrett, Olathe, Kansas
Loretta Ross, St. Charles, Missouri

About the Author

Ken Warren has supported himself playing professional poker since he left the Air Force in 1987 and has parlayed that success into a career as a best-selling author of four books on poker including the *Winner's Guide to Texas Hold'em Poker* and *Ken Warren Teaches Texas Hold'em*. Warren is the best of the new breed of riverboat poker players, and has the unique distinction of playing in and winning the very first legal poker hand in Mississippi in the 20th century. That landmark hand was kings full of sevens in the big blind position.

CARDOZA PUBLISHING

The BIG BOOK of POKER

KEN ♣ WARREN

Cardoza Publishing is the foremost gaming publisher in the world, with a library of over 200 up-to-date and easy-to-read books and strategies. These authoritative works are written by the top experts in their fields and with more than 10,000,000 books in print, represent the best-selling and most popular gaming books anywhere.

SECOND EDITION

Copyright © 2004, 2007 by Ken Warren
- All Rights Reserved -

Library of Congress Catalog Card No: 2007932761
ISBN: 1-58042-219-5

Visit our web site—www.cardozapub.com—or write
for a full list of books and computer strategies.

CARDOZA PUBLISHING
P.O. Box 1500, Cooper Station, New York, NY 10276
Phone (800) 577-WINS
email: cardozapub@aol.com
www.cardozapub.com

CONTENTS

INTRODUCTION

*"There are few things that are so unpardonably
neglected in our country as poker. It is enough
to make one ashamed of our species."*

— Mark Twain

This book will tell you about the poker games played in all of the casino poker rooms, as well as most of the known poker games played at home today. If it's a poker game, and you want to know how to play it, chances are it's included in this book.

I will teach you how to play poker online, as well as all you need to know to compete in tournaments around the world—including strategies for winning them! There's also a great chapter on how to play Texas hold'em, currently the hottest poker game in the world. With the popularity of the World Series of Poker, and the fact that the $10,000 buy-in No-Limit Texas hold'em Championship event is broadcast on The Travel Channel and on ESPN2, everyone wants to know how to play the game.

There are chapters in this book that will teach you how to play five-card stud, five-card draw, seven-card stud, Omaha poker (an exciting, advanced version of Texas hold'em), Pineapple hold'em and even Liar's Poker.

If you like to play poker at home, there's a big chapter on how to organize and run a home game along with explanations of how to play some of the more popular home poker games. You'll learn how to play high-low split games as well as a couple of extremely popular non-standard poker games like Anaconda and Seven-Twenty-Seven.

For every game that you'll learn how to play, there's a section on how to apply specific advice for that game. I'll give you lots of tips and pointers that will help you be a winner from the first time you play the game. There are also separate chapters that teach everything you need to know about betting, raising, calling, bluffing, and pot odds.

This book begins with an extensive timeline of the history of poker and the evolution of playing cards. You'll learn many intriguing facts about playing cards and the game of poker, which will add to your enjoyment of the game.

Finally, there's a very important chapter concerning cheating at poker. There's little-to-no chance that you will ever see any cheating in a public poker room. If you play in a private game, however, there are some basic facts that you need to be aware of to protect yourself from the possibility of being cheated. This is not a chapter on how to cheat at poker; rather, it is an instructional guide designed to increase your awareness of the subject and to make this information available to the public. The more players there are in your poker game that know all the ways to cheat, the safer and more honest your game will be.

Why You Should Read This Book

Poker in the 21st century is going to be very different from the poker of the past. Poker is no longer associated with the undesirable elements of society. It has come out into the open where it is respectable, immensely popular across the socioeconomic spectrum, and is a valuable skill to have in many social settings.

I believe that in the coming century, it will be just as valuable for you to know how to play poker as it is for you to know how to drive a car, use a computer, or to stay abreast of current events.

There was a time when a young person could not be a great poker player because the only way to learn the game was to spend countless years playing hundreds of thousands of hands and then trying to learn lessons from the experience. But, that has changed because of the computer revolution and the fact that new information can easily be learned from poker books.

Nowadays, a young, intelligent and motivated student of poker can achieve a level of competence in two years that used to take an old-style player thirty years to achieve. In the last few years, a young college dropout and a computer geek won the world championship of poker. Let that be a lesson to you.

There's one, last reason that you should read this book and this reason is more relevant and compelling than all of the other reasons: You should read this book because all of the players that you will be playing poker against will have read this, and other, poker books. You have to know what's out there just so you can start out even with them when you sit down at a poker table.

Quotations Used in This Book

I have made extensive use of quotes from many varied and disparate sources to help illustrate a point or to make my thoughts on a particular subject more clear. I do not believe that Abraham Lincoln ever played poker, yet he undoubtedly had heard of the game either from his early years as a U.S. Army Captain during the Black Hawk War or even in his capacity as Commander-in-Chief of the Union Army during the Civil War.

You might be surprised to see that I have chosen to use a few quotes from Lincoln in this book even though I know he wasn't talking about poker when he made these statements. That's because a lot of what he had to say spoke to the universal human condition, which can be applied to poker today. Lincoln had some profoundly simple and elegant things to say about courage, patience, determination, work, justice, honesty, study, research, timing and self-reliance; all subjects that can be applied to poker.

I would feel terribly remiss and negligent if I were to know of Lincoln's thoughts on these subjects and not pass them on to you for, as Lincoln himself said, "I must keep some standard of principle fixed within myself."

I hope you enjoy reading this book as much as I enjoyed writing it for you.

CHAPTER 1

HISTORY OF POKER

"Poker and American history are inseparable."

— John McDonald

The exact date of the first game of poker remains a mystery. It is known, however, that the modern game of poker evolved from several different betting and bluffing games throughout Europe over the past four hundred years.

The evolution of the word "poker" began in the late 1600s, when a card game with rounds of betting called "Poch" was played in Germany. A similar game called "Poque" was played in France in the early 1700s. A still similar game called "Brag" was played in England. The French game of "Poque" was introduced into North America by Frenchmen living in New Orleans when France owned the Louisiana Territory. The game was adopted by the local Southerners who called it "Pokah," probably due more to their accent than a mispronunciation. The game traveled northward via the Mississippi River where Northerners called it "poker."

For several hundred years it has been universally written and accepted as a fact that poker is the descendant of the Persian (Iranian) game of As-Nas. This is categorically untrue even though this statement is made in most major encyclopedias and poker books. Even the great John Scarne got it wrong in his *Encyclopedia of Games*. There is no mention in Persian literature of any game such as As-Nas earlier than the 1700s and there are no known rules of the game in print before the 1800s. In view of the fact that "as" is not a Persian word but it is the French word for "ace," it seems most likely that the Persians adopted their game from the French, and not the other way around.

The game of poker was spread throughout the United States in the mid-1800s by riverboat gamblers who traveled up and down the Mississippi and Missouri Rivers. Soldiers who learned the game during the Civil War helped ensure that the game spread to every part of the country after the war. When the West was opened up by the discovery of gold in California in 1848, the game flourished wildly there as well.

I have made an exhaustive search of the historical record for the purpose of extracting that information that sheds light on the creation, evolution, progress and comprehensive history of the game of poker. I have organized that information and I present it to you here as a timeline of the history of poker.

The history of playing cards begins with their appearance in China in the 1100s. I have painstakingly traced the evolution of playing cards from their inception to the present day and I have culled from the historical records those notable facts that I think would be of interest to card players and poker players today. I have organized those important and notable events into a chronological timeline.

I have integrated the history of playing cards with the timeline of the history of poker and I proudly present to you, for the first time in print anywhere, the evolution of poker and playing cards. I hope it adds to your enjoyment of the great game of poker.

The Evolution of Poker and Playing Cards

1100   The earliest known playing cards came from Chinese Turkestan. The suits were coins, clubs, cups and swords.

1100s   Korean playing cards were made of oiled paper about $7\frac{5}{8}$ inches long and $\frac{1}{2}$ inch wide with a picture of an arrow on the back. There were eight suits: men, fish, crows, pheasants, antelopes, stars, rabbits and horses. There were ten cards in each suit, making a deck of eighty cards.

1190   An edict issued by the Court of Richard the Lionhearted said, "No person in the army is permitted to play at any sort of game except knights and clergymen; who in one whole day and night shall not, each, lose more than twenty shillings on pain of forfeiting 100 shillings to the archbishop of the army." This is the first known mention of money management, even though the advice carried the weight of law.

1210   The earliest known European playing cards were copied from the Chinese Cards.

1200s   Playing cards in India used a different bright color on the backs of the cards to indicate the different suits.

1371   Playing cards were introduced in Spain.

1377   Playing cards were introduced in Switzerland.

The first known civil ordinance against card playing was issued in Paris. Another ordinance was issued in Florence, Italy on March 23, 1377 (three years before the cards arrived).

1380   Playing cards were mentioned in the archives of Nurnberg, Germany.

Playing cards were first introduced into Florence, Italy and Barcelona, Spain.

1392   The French Royal Treasurer paid one Jacquemin Gringonneur, painter, for three games of cards "in gold and diverse colors, ornamented with many deuces, for the diversion of our lord, the king." This was the first documented presence of playing cards in Europe.

1430s   Meister Ingold, of Alsace, France wrote a treatise called *The Golden Game*, one of the first known books about card games.

1439   German playing cards were 7" x 4" with the suits being hunting dogs, stags, ducks and falcons. The portraits on the cards were almost always painted by women.

1440   The first known mention of the court cards—kings, queens and knaves—occurred in France.

1441   The first known mention of poch, later pochen, occurred in Strassburg, Germany.

1450s The first known Spanish playing cards were $1\frac{7}{8}$ inches by $1\frac{5}{8}$ inches—very small.

1459 Earliest known reference to card playing in England, from a private letter.

1480 The first appearance of spades, hearts, clubs and diamonds all together in one deck occurred in France.

1492 Fearful of horrendous storms, the sailors under the command of Christopher Columbus threw their playing cards overboard. Once on dry land, they regretted their decision and fashioned new cards by drawing images on wide tree leaves.

1500s Games called "Primera" in Spain and "Primero" in England were popular. There were rounds of betting and the recognized ranks of hands were, three-of-a-kind, pairs and a flux (flush), which was three cards of the same suit.

1520 *The Book on Games of Chance*, by Italian Gerolama Cardona was published. It is the first known book devoted to all of the card games of its time.

1564 The first known professional advice regarding card playing was written by Gerolama Cardona when he said, "The greatest advantage lies in not playing at all."

1590 Date of the oldest known surviving deck of English playing cards.

1610 First known use of the word 'deck' to describe what was then universally known as a pack of cards was made by William Shakespeare.

1628 A company called "The Master, Wardens and Commonality of the Mistery of Playing Cards of the City of London" was created under the protection of a royal charter. The purpose was to unify the hundreds of different card makers into a loose union to consolidate card making efforts and to prevent duplication of similar-looking cards.

1633 A Plymouth Colony record reveals that two persons were fined two pounds each for card playing. The penalty for a second offense was to "bee publickly whipt."

1700s A five-card game called Brag incorporating betting and bluffing was played in England, as Pochen in Germany and as Poque in

France. It was the French game of Pochen that is played in the French possession of Louisiana that was later mispronounced as "poker" by the Americans.

1703   Card playing was banned in Boston.

1720   Playing cards were sold in Boston and New York for one shilling per pack.

1725   The English game of Brag was mentioned by Charles Cotton in *The Compleat Gamester*:

> The nature of it is, that you are to endeavor to impose upon the judgment of the rest that play, and particularly upon the person that chiefly offers to oppose you, by boasting of cards in your hand, whether Pair Royals, Pairs, or others, that you are better than his or hers that play against you…

1732   Philadelphia printer Benjamin Franklin advertised the sale of playing cards in his first *Poor Richard's Almanach*.

1742   Edmond Hoyle's book *A Short Treatise on the Game of Whist*, was published. Actually, the complete title of his book was *A Short Treatise on the Game of Whist, containing the laws of the game; and also some Rules whereby a Beginner may, with due attention to them, attain to the Playing it well…* Incredibly, the book does not say a word about how to play the game of Whist!

1745   Benjamin Franklin used cutouts of playing cards to aid in his experiments with electricity.

1750   The queen replaced the knave as a court card in England.

1765   Playing cards were used as passes to admit students to their classes at the University of Pennsylvania.

1765 November 1st   The infamous Stamp Act levied a tax of one shilling on each pack of playing cards. The Stamp Act was repealed on March 17, 1766.

1769 August 29th   Edmond Hoyle died in London at either age 90 or 97, depending on whom you believe. Other than his book, little was known about him except that he once described himself as a "gentleman" and he was rumored to have been a barrister, or lawyer.

1770 September 5th   George Washington's diary entry read, "At home all day playing cards."

1777 May 8th   General George Washington issued the following order to his army: "...the Commander-in-Chief in the most pointed and explicit terms forbids ALL officers and soldiers playing at cards, dice or any games except those of EXERCISE for diversion; being impossible if the practice be allowed at all to discriminate between innocent play for amusement and criminal gaming for pecuniary and sordid purposes."

1790s   The lack of an index and the fact that court cards had full-length figures meant that playing cards had to be spread out with both hands for a player to know exactly what his cards were.

1795   Card playing was introduced to North American Indians by Spanish conquistadors.

1801   The first known instance in which the numbers of the cards appeared in the upper right-hand corner occurred in Spanish-made cards.

1810s   A trader at the San Carlos Indian Reservation in Arizona discovered a pack of American Indian playing cards made from what is believed to be the skins of white men.

1812   The first steamboat to operate on the Mississippi River is Robert Fulton's "New Orleans."

1814   The United States Treasury reported that 400,000 packs of playing cards were manufactured that year with a duty of 25¢ per pack.

1815   The city of New Orleans, Louisiana licensed casino gambling.

1820s   American Indians gambled profusely, betting all of their worldly possessions, their horses, tee pees and wives centuries before white men introduced them to gambling. Wives lost to gambling often nonchalantly took up residence with the winner, knowing that they would soon be lost back to their husbands.

1820   There were exactly twenty gambling steamboats on the Mississippi River.

Accounts of a game called "Whiskey Poker" were found. It is the ancestor of all modern poker games played in North America today, although the original game has long since passed out of popularity.

1827   The first known appearance of playing cards with double heads; this replaced the full-length figures.

John Davis opened a luxury casino in New Orleans called the Crescent City House, at the corner of Orleans & Bourbon Street. It is the first known offering of poker in a public cardroom. The casino was the model for Las Vegas and Atlantic City casinos built more than 120 years later.

1829   The first account of poker was written in the diary of the English actor Joseph Crowell, who was visiting America in 1829.

The first account of poker being played in the United States was revealed by Jonathan H. Green in his book *Exposure of the Arts and Miseries of Gambling*, written in 1834 but not published until 1843. The book was re-titled *Gamblers Exposed* and re-released the same year it was published. The poker deck consisted of only twenty cards—four each of aces, kings, queens, jacks and 10s.

1830   Poker players could buy a pack of marked cards advertised in newspapers and catalogues from E.N. Grandine Co. of New York for $1.25 per pack or $10 per dozen. These cards were shipped by mail and express pony to card players all over North America.

1833   The fifty-two-card deck is first used in America, taking twenty years to finally gain nationwide acceptance.

1834   Jonathan H. Green describes poker and calls it "the cheating game" in his book An *Exposure of the Art and Miseries of Gambling*.

Most poker games were dealt with a twenty-card deck. The only possible hands were pairs, trips, four-of-a-kind (no straights or flushes), and there was no draw.

1835   Casino gambling was declared illegal in New Orleans, Louisiana.

1836   American-style poker was mentioned in *Dragon Campaigns to the Rocky Mountains*.

1845   *American Hoyle* mentioned a game called "Twenty-Card Poker" and another game called "Poker or Bluff."

There were 557 gambling steamboats operating on the Mississippi River.

1846 His Honor, Walter Cotton, the Mayor of Monterrey, California issued one of the first known ordinances against gambling in North America: "A vice which shows itself here more on the Sabbath than any other day of the week."

1847 U.S. gamblers, and card players in particular followed the conquering U.S. Army into Mexico City during the Mexican War. After discovering that the Mexicans were scrupulously honest card players and knew nothing of cheating, they ordered 14,440 decks of marked playing cards from a New York supplier to introduce to Mexico City.

1848 The San Francisco Town Council passed an ordinance against gambling and card playing; however, they quickly repealed it because they needed the tax revenue card playing generated.

Mid-1800s The first true joker was added to the deck to act as the "Best Bower" in the game of Euchre, as it still is today. Poker players borrowed it, using it as any card they chose to help improve their hands. The joker does not come from the fool in tarot cards as is popularly believed.

Apache Indians created their own decks of cards by painting images on deerskin and hides. Their decks consisted of forty cards with ten cards in each of the four suits. The ten cards were 2, 3, 4, 5, 6, 7, the page (equal to a jack), knight, king and ace.

1850 A playing card manufacturer from New York featured portraits of George and Martha Washington on the ace of spades.

San Francisco gambling houses purposefully employed female dealers because they believed that outright cheating by a female dealer was more likely to be overlooked or forgiven by the male clientele.

1850–1890 Riverboat card players bought their cards from the ship's bartenders. Even though the decks were new and still in their original unopened packaging, with their unbroken seals, they were still marked. The bartenders were paid well to keep them in stock.

1850s Children as young as ten and twelve years old frequented California gambling house card rooms, losing hundreds of dollars a day.

San Francisco had more than 1,000 gambling houses where poker could be played.

A typical steamboat operating on the Mississippi River was 140 feet long, 28 feet wide, could carry as much as 200 tons (400,000 lbs) of cargo and up to fifty passengers. It could go 10 mph down the river and 4 mph up the river.

1851 One California lumber company paid its workers with vouchers that could be redeemed at local gambling houses, instead of paying them cash.

1860 There were 735 gambling steamboats operating on the Mississippi River.

1860s A deck of cards was referred to as "The Devil's Picture Gallery" by preachers and anti-gambling proponents.

The joker was more commonly called a 'cuter' or 'imperial trump' that could be used as an ace.

1861–1865 Civil War soldiers on both sides played poker but threw their cards away before a battle because they considered them to be "instruments of the Devil" and they believed it was a curse to be killed in battle while carrying them.

1862 The first known playing cards to be manufactured in Mexico were made this year.

1864 *American Hoyle* gave the ranks of poker hands as: one pair, two pairs, straight sequence or rotation, triplets, flush, full-house, and fours. Then added, "When a straight and a flush come together, it outranks a full."

1864 Oct 31st Nevada was admitted to the Union with a state constitution that permitted gambling.

1867 *Hoyle's Games* mentioned for the first time that a straight, a flush, and an ante had been added to the game.

1869 Shoshoni Indian women were voracious card players, often betting and losing their husbands' possessions.

1870 The first known mention of jackpots (requiring openers to have at least a pair of jacks) occurred in Toledo, Ohio.

1870s Wild cards in poker came about as a way to employ the blank card that came with every deck.

1872   Poker was introduced to England by the American Ambassador to Great Britain, Robert C. Schenk.

Pickney Pinchback became Governor of Louisiana. He was George Devol's black servant and cheating partner. He made so much money cheating at cards that he was able to finance his political campaigns with it.

1875   *Hoyle's Games* first mentioned jackpot poker and the use of a joker as a wild card.

Well-known, popular and highly-skilled American Indian poker player White Geese Sounding on Waters—better known as Poker Jim—issued sage poker advice: "Two pair not much good."

1876   The first time that playing cards were made with rounded instead of square corners.

1876 August 2nd   James Butler "Wild Bill" Hickock was shot in the back and killed by Jack "Crooked Nose" McCall in the Mann-Lewis Saloon in Deadwood, South Dakota. He was holding two pair—aces and 8s—and contrary to popular legend, his exact fifth card is not known today. This hand is now named "The Deadman's Hand" in memory of Wild Bill.

1877   In many poker games played in the West, the highest hand was four aces, or four kings with an ace. A straight flush was not yet universally recognized.

1880s   Professional riverboat card players resorted to dressing as common farmers, business-men, cross-country travelers or even clergymen due to their well-earned unsavory reputations.

Indexed playing cards finally become the norm although unindexed cards were still in use and could be easily found.

1885   Most of the wild, fast, and loose poker games in the East evaporated as most card players favored going west to California to take advantage of the gold miners.

1887   The joker first appeared in decks of Canadian cards made by the Union Card and Paper Company of Montreal.

1888   Instructions for using a holdout machine according to the Ohio Historical Society:

1. Practice at least three weeks a month with the machine, to get it down fine.

2. Don't work the machine too much. In a big game, three or four times a night are enough.

3. Never play it in a small game.

4. Holding out one card will beat any square game in the world.

5. Holding out two cards can be very strong but can't easily be played on smart people.

6. Three cards are too many to hold out on smart men, as a "full" [house] is too big [a hand] to be held without acting as an eye-opener.

7. Never, under any circumstances, hold out four or five cards.

8. One card is enough, as you are really playing with six cards to everyone else's five.

9. If you are an expert, you can play the machine on your own deal; but it looks better if you do it on someone else's.

1890s Apache war chief Geronimo, while interred at Fort Sill, Oklahoma, spent his days enthusiastically playing poker.

1891 Poker card machines were invented. There were more than 3,000 of them in Brooklyn, New York placed in licensed liquor establishments.

The Broadmoor Casino opened in Colorado City, Colorado, which became part of Colorado Springs in 1917. The casino drew more than 15,000 gamblers and poker players per day.

1901 Poker card machines in Brooklyn were redesigned to allow the play of draw poker.

1907 The Arizona and New Mexico Territorial Governments prohibited all forms of gambling. This was done to increase their chances of being admitted as states to the Union.

1910 Nevada closed all of its casinos.

1911 Legislation prohibited stud poker as a game of luck. The law held that draw poker, however, was legal because it was a game of skill.

1920s Prohibition led to the explosion in the number of home games as illegal gambling establishments were closed down.

1930s Entertainer, comedian, and movie star Groucho Marx got his name because he always carried his poker winnings in a "grouch bag." He was a chronic cheat at the game.

1931 Nevada legalized casino gambling.

1937 A new deck of cards with a new, fifth suit called Eagle was introduced in America. The purpose was to help stimulate the Depression-era economy by inducing the public to buy new decks of cards. It was an instant failure.

Harrah's Casino opened in Reno, Nevada.

1941 The El Rancho Casino was the first casino to open on the Las Vegas strip.

1943–1945 U.S. Navy Lieutenant Commander Richard M. Nixon won more than $6,000 playing poker while assigned as a supply officer in the South Pacific during WWII. He used that money to finance a campaign for the U.S. House of Representatives in 1946, which he won.

1945 The state of Nevada licensed casinos for the first time.

President Harry S Truman played pot limit poker with the press corps sixteen hours a day aboard ship while coming home from the Potsdam Conference.

1949 Nick "The Greek" Dandalos and Johnny Moss play a five-month long head-up poker game in Las Vegas. This game was the inspiration for the inception of what was to become the World Series of Poker.

Physicist Albert Einstein visited Las Vegas during the Moss vs. Dandalos match. He was introduced around town as, "Little Al from Jersey."

1955 Movie star John Wayne won the equally famous dog Lassie from his owner and trainer in a poker game. He later gave the dog back.

Nevada created the Gaming Control Board under the direction of the State Treasury Division.

1959 Nevada created the Nevada Gaming Commission to oversee decisions of the Gaming Control Board.

1963 Texas hold'em was first introduced to Las Vegas poker rooms by Texan Felton "Corky" McCorquodale.

1969 Nevada legalized the ownership of casinos by public corporations.

1970 The First World Series of Poker (WSOP) was held in Las Vegas. Johnny Moss won all five events, defeating a field of thirty-seven other players, and was voted champion by the other players.

There were only seventy licensed poker tables in Nevada. They took in $4,500,000 that year.

Don Laughlin opened the first casino in Laughlin, Nevada.

1971 The buy-in for the World Series of Poker was $5,000. It was a winner-take-all event.

The 2nd World Series of Poker was won by Johnny Moss.

1972 The 3rd World Series of Poker was won by Thomas Austin "Amarillo Slim" Preston.

1973 The 4th World Series of Poker was won by Walter Clyde "Puggy" Pearson.

1974 The 5th World Series of Poker was won by Johnny Moss.

1975 The 6th World Series of Poker was won by Sailor Roberts.

1976 The 7th World Series of Poker was won by Doyle "Texas Dolly" Brunson.

The first book devoted exclusively to Texas hold'em, *Hold'em Poker*, was written by David Sklansky.

New Jersey voters, by a margin of 56% to 44%, voted to legalize casino-style gambling in Atlantic City.

1977 The 8th World Series of Poker was won by Doyle "Texas Dolly" Brunson.

The ladies only WSOP event—entitled The Women's Championship of Poker—was a 7-Card Stud Tournament won by Jackie McDaniels. First Prize was $5,580.

1978 The 9th World Series of Poker was won by Bobby Baldwin, who at age 27 was the youngest-yet winner of the tournament.

Women's World Series of Poker Champion Barbara Freer was the first woman to enter the $10,000 buy-in No Limit Texas hold'em main event.

Atlantic City, New Jersey opened Resorts International, its first casino.

First year that the prize money was split five ways. The Women's Championship of Poker was won by Barbara Freer, who also this year was the first woman to enter the $10,000 buy-in No Limit Hold'em Championship Event.

1979   The 10th World Series of Poker was won by Hal Fowler, the first amateur to ever win.

The Poker Hall of Fame was founded. The first seven inductees were: Johnny Moss, Nick "The Greek" Dandalos, Felton "Corky" McCorquodale, Red Winn, Sid Wyman, James Butler "Wild Bill" Hickock, and Edmond Hoyle.

Hal Fowler was the first amateur to win the WSOP. Entertainer Kenny Rogers sang his hit song, "The Gambler" at the event. This was the first WSOP to be recorded on videotape since 1973.

1980   There were 423 licensed poker tables in Nevada casinos. They took in $50,164,000 that year.

The 11th World Series of Poker was won by Stu Ungar.

T. "Blondie" Forbes was inducted into the Poker Hall of Fame.

1981   The 12th World Series of Poker was won by Stu Ungar.

The World Series of Poker awarded prize money to all nine of the players who made the final table.

Bill Boyd was inducted into the Poker Hall of Fame.

Five of the nine players to make the final table had made it to this same final table in previous WSOP championship tournaments.

1982   The 13th World Series of Poker was won by Jack "Treetop" Straus.

Vera Richmond was the first woman to win an open World Series of Poker event—the $1,000 buy-in ace-to-5 five-card draw event.

Tommy Abdo was inducted into the Poker Hall of Fame.

Doyle Brunson became the first player to win more that $1,000,000 in accumulated total winnings in WSOP events.

1983   The 14th World Series of Poker was won Tom McEvoy.

The first year that a satellite winner won the $10,000 buy-in for the World Series of Poker Championship. The runner-up was also a satellite winner. Tom McEvoy and Rod Peate won a total of $756,000 with an investment of only $100 each!

Joe Bernstein was inducted into the Poker Hall of Fame.

The IRS seized $46,000 in poker chips from professional poker player Sarge Ferris while he was playing in a game in a Las Vegas poker room!

1984   The 15th World Series of Poker was won by Jack Keller.

Pot-limit Omaha was added to the World Series of Poker tournament schedule.

Murph Harrold was inducted into the Poker Hall of Fame.

The first book devoted exclusively to poker tells, *Caro's Book of Tells*, was published by Mike Caro.

1985   The President's Commission on Organized Crime reported that it considered gambling to be a legitimate industry.

The 16th World Series of Poker was won by Bill Smith.

Red Hodges was inducted into the Poker Hall of Fame.

1986   The 17th World Series of Poker was won by Berry Johnston.

Henry Green was inducted into the Poker Hall of Fame.

1987   The 18th World Series of Poker was won by Johnny Chan.

Walter Clyde "Puggy" Pearson was inducted into the Poker Hall of Fame.

1988   Binion's Horseshoe Casino opened their first poker room after acquiring their next door neighbor, the Mint Casino.

The 19th World Series of Poker was won by Johnny Chan.

Doyle "Texas Dolly" Brunson and Jack "Treetop" Straus were inducted into the Poker Hall of Fame.

Live poker, with a $5 betting limit, was legalized in the historic town of Deadwood, South Dakota.

1989   The 20th World Series of Poker was won by Phil Hellmuth, who at age 24, became the youngest player ever to win the tournament.

Sarge Ferris was inducted into the Poker Hall of Fame.

Iowa legalized riverboat casino gambling, with a $5 limit on bets.

1990   The 21st World Series of Poker was won by Mansour Matloubi.

Omaha High-Low Split was added to the World Series of Poker tournament schedule.

Benny Binion was inducted into the Poker Hall of Fame.

1991   The 22nd World Series of Poker was won by Brad Daugherty, the first player to win a prize of $1,000,000.

David Edward "Chip" Reese was inducted to the Poker Hall of Fame.

Television personalities Telly Savalas and Gabe Kaplan played in the $10,000 buy-in No Limit Championship Event.

1992   The 23rd World Series of Poker was won by Hamid Dastmalchi.

Thomas Austin "Amarillo Slim" Preston was inducted into the Poker Hall of Fame.

The first hand of legal poker dealt in the state of Mississippi in the 20th century was a Texas hold'em hand won by poker writer Ken Warren.

The U.S. Congress legalized gambling on U.S. flagships.

1993   The 24th World Series of Poker was won by Jim Bechtel.

Jack Keller was inducted into the Poker Hall of Fame.

1994   The 25th World Series of Poker was won by Russ Hamilton.

Russ Hamilton won an additional 330 pounds (his weight) in silver when he won the World Series of Poker. At $5.40 an ounce, that came to $28,512.

1995   The 26th World Series of Poker was won by Dan Harrington.

Barbara Enright became the first female to make the final table at the World Series of Poker No-Limit $10,000 Buy-in Texas hold'em main event. She finished in 5th place, winning $114,180.

1996   The 27th World Series of Poker was won by Huck Seed.

Julius "Little Man" Popwell was inducted into the Poker Hall of Fame.

1997 Roger Moore was inducted to the Poker Hall of Fame.

The 28th World Series of Poker was won by Stu Ungar.

Maria Stern won the World Series of Poker seven-card stud event and Max Stern won the seven-card stud high-low event. They were the first husband and wife to win World Series of Poker titles.

1998 The 29th World Series of Poker was won by Scotty Nguyen.

Casino owners in Nevada spent over $26,000,000 trying to defeat a referendum in neighboring California that would allow American Indian tribes to open their own casinos. The referendum passed.

1999 The 30th World Series of Poker was won by Noel Furlong.

The World Series of Poker had 3,456 players and paid out $11,291,000 in prize money.

2000 The 31st World Series of Poker was won by Chris "Jesus" Ferguson, the first player to win a $1,500,000 first prize.

2001 The 32nd World Series of Poker was won by Carlos Mortensen.

Stu Ungar was inducted into the Poker Hall of Fame.

2002 The first year that the World Series of Poker became a non-smoking event.

The 33rd World Series of Poker was won by Robert Varkonyi, the first player to win a $2,000,000 first prize.

Lyle Berman and Johnny Chan were inducted into the Poker Hall of Fame.

2003 The 34th World Series of Poker was won by Chris Moneymaker, the first one to win a $2,500,000 first prize.

Chris Moneymaker was the first World Series of Poker $10,000 Buy-in No-Limit Texas hold'em player to have won his entry fee through an on-line Texas hold'em tournament. His original buy-in was only $40. He was a 27-year old accountant from Spring Hill, Tennessee.

A record fifty-one players got their $10,000 buy-in into the World Series of Poker Texas hold'em No-Limit event by winning internet tournaments.

The only states to not have any form of legal public gambling or private charity gambling were Hawaii and Utah.

2004 Forty percent of the 2,576 entrants to the WSOP Championship event won their way into the tournament through online tournaments. The 2004 field had players from thirty different nations. One hundred women entered the tournament and three of them won 1st prize bracelets.

The 35th World Series of Poker was won by Greg Raymer, earning a $5 million prize.

2005 Tiffany Williams, an attorney from the United Kingdom, was the highest-placed female finisher in the WSOP Championship event—winning $400,000 for 15th place.

The 36th World Series of Poker was won by Joe Hachem of Australia, earning a $7.5 million prize.

2006 WSOP Champion Jamie Gold was not paid any of his 1st place prize money of $12,000,000 at the time of his victory pending a court case to decide whether or not he had an agreement to split the money with an alleged partner.

Fifty-one percent of the WSOP Championship event entrants earned their entries by online tournaments.

2007 A total of 54,288 registrations were received for all of the events, the largest number in WSOP history. However, due to unfriendly Internet legislation in the United States, the actual number of participants in the main event was 6,358, the first reduction in players since 1992.

The 37th World Series of Poker was won by Jerry Yang, earning an $8.25 million prize.

HOW TO PLAY

CHAPTER 2

The Object of the Game

If you ask the average poker player what the object of the game is, he would likely tell you something like, "to win money," or "to beat the other players." All of these answers appear to be logical and make sense but you must understand from the very beginning of this book that the average poker player is a lifetime loser at the game and his ideas about the object of the game are wrong.

Would you like to win pots, win money and beat the other players in a poker game? Of course you would. And the way to do that is very easy—all you have to do is to play every hand all the way to the end without folding. If you do that, you will never fold a hand that will win, you'll win every time it was possible for you to win, you'll win the money in those pots and you'll beat the other players. But you won't be a winner at poker.

The real object of the game of poker is to make the best quality decisions you can with the information available to you at that time. This book will teach you how to do that. Every time it is your turn to act you will either have to fold, check, call, raise, re-raise or check raise. Your job at the poker table is to collect information, analyze and process that information and then decide a course of action that is best for you.

Once you make a decision and then act on it, you have actually fulfilled the object of the game. This will probably surprise you, but what happens in the hand after you act is not important. It does not matter what your opponents do next and it's immaterial

> ## *FACT!*
> The real object of the game is to consistently make better decisions than the other players in the game. If you can do that, the money will come.

whether or not you win the hand. The most important thing is that you understand why you're making the play and what goal you're trying to accomplish.

The Number of Players

Poker can be played with as few as two players or as many as twenty-two players. The actual number is determined and restricted by the exact poker game being played. With only fifty-two cards in the deck there is a limit on how many players can draw replacement cards in five-card draw. A Texas hold'em game can accommodate twenty-two players because of the community cards used in the game. Customarily, it is only played with nine or ten players.

The Cards

Poker is played with a standard deck of fifty-two cards. Some home games also use one or both of the jokers that come with the deck. Playing cards can be made of paper, cardboard, or plastic. The plastic cards are the best because they last longer, they resist marking that could be used for cheating, and you can wash them with soap and water.

Poker Chips

Poker chips are used instead of cash in a poker game. Some of the advantages of chips over cash are that they are easier to handle and count, they speed up the game, they make it easier to split pots, and they make it easier to know how much money a player has in front of him at any time.

The one main disadvantage of playing with poker chips in a home game is that it is very easy for a dishonest player to bring the same chips with him to the game. He can then slip them into the game or his stack, thereby increasing his buy-in without paying for it.

Types of Poker Games

Poker is typically played as high poker, where the strongest high hand wins. There are also variations where the low hand wins, and some, where players compete for both ends of the spectrum—the best high hand and the best low hand. All these variations are considered valid and standard forms of poker.

High Poker

In high poker, the best hand, and therefore the winning hand, is the one that is highest on the traditional scale of poker hands. That scale, from weakest to strongest, starts with no-pair, then goes up through one pair, two pairs, three-of-a-kind, straight, flush, full-house, four-of-a-kind, straight flush and royal flush. Most games are played as high poker.

Low Poker

Poker that is played where the traditional ranking of poker hands is turned upside down and the lowest poker hand wins. Straight and flushes are considered to be irrelevant and it does not count against a player if he has a straight or a flush. In fact, the best possible low hand is a 5-high straight (5432A) which is also called a **wheel** or a **bicycle**. This is a less popular form of poker but still enjoyed by many players.

High-Low Poker

This is a form of poker where players look to have either the best high hand, the best low hand, or the best of both. With two different ways to win, these games tend to be wilder with a lot of betting. Typically, the best high hand wins half the pot, splitting that amount with the best low hand. If the player has the best high and low, he wins the entire pot. Or, in certain variations, if a player *declares* that he is going for both, he must win both or he loses the entire amount, even if he has a strong hand on the high or low side.

Wild Card Poker

This is a type of poker game that allows a specific card, or cards, to take on the value of any other card in the deck. This means that the highest possible poker hand is now five-of-a-kind when wild cards are in play. There are two types of wild card games. The first is where the wild card may actually be any other card in the deck and the second is where the wild card may be used only as any card needed to be an ace or to complete a straight, a flush or a low draw.

Ranking of Poker Hands

Poker hands are ranked the way they are because of one cold, hard fact: The more difficult it is, statistically speaking, to be dealt a particular poker hand in five cards, the higher it ranks on the scale of poker hands. Thus, the strongest hand, the royal flush, is listed first and the weakest, high card hands, are listed last.

So you will see that a flush is stronger than a straight, which is stronger than a three-of-a-kind hand.

Royal Flush and Straight Flush

There are 2,598,960 different ways to be dealt any five cards from a deck of fifty-two cards. Only four of these hands are a royal flush:

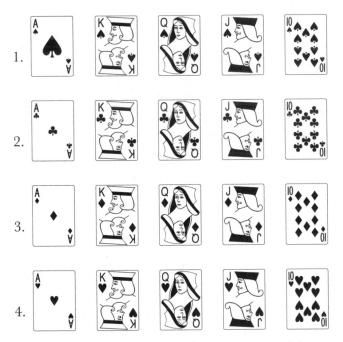

A straight flush is any five cards in sequence of the same suit. A Royal Flush is also a straight but since it is the highest possible straight flush it is called a Royal Flush because it contains the court cards with an ace. There are nine other straight flushes and they are the 5-high through the king-high straight flushes.

Four-of-a-Kind   Four-of-a-kind is four cards all of the same rank, such as

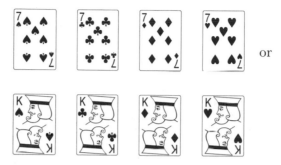 or

At first, you might think that since there are thirteen ranks of cards there must be only thirteen different four-of-a-kinds. There are actually 624 of them! That's because a poker hand consists of five, and not four, cards. Each of the thirteen four-of-a-kinds can combine with each of the remaining forty-eight cards in the deck to make that complete poker hand (13x48=624).

Full-House   A full house is a five-card hand consisting of three-of-a-kind and one pair, such as

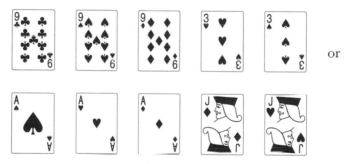 or

The value of the full house is determined by what the three-of-a-kind is with the higher three-of-a-kind beating the lower one. You are said to be "full of" whatever your three-of-a-kind is and the full houses shown here are "9s full of 3s" and "aces full of jacks."

Flush
A flush is any five cards of the same suit that are not a straight flush. For example,

When there are two or more flushes in a hand, the flush with the highest card is the winner. If they are the same, then the second-highest card determines the winner and so on down to the fifth card.

Straight
A straight is any five cards in sequence that are not of the same suit. The highest straight is an ace-high straight, which is AKQJ10 of mixed suits, such as

It is also called a Broadway. A king-high straight is called an Off-Broadway. The lowest possible straight is a 5-high straight: 5432A of mixed suits and is also called a wheel or bicycle. Straights may not wrap around the ace, for example, QKA23 is not a straight, but merely an ace-high hand.

Three-of-a-Kind
This hand consists of three cards of the same rank with two other cards of different ranks, such as:

      and

are two examples.

Three-of-a-kind is also called **trips**.

Two Pair Two pair is two cards of the same rank and two other cards of the same rank, along with another card that does not match the two pair. When announcing two pair, the higher hand is mentioned as being *over* the lower pair.

is two pair; called "aces over 4s," or "aces and 4s."

One Pair One pair is two cards of the same rank with three other cards of different ranks.

is a pair of Kings.

High Card A high card hand is one that cannot make any of the above hands and is known by the highest card in the hand.

A hand consisting of

would be called "queen-high."

Betting Basics

Most games, whether home or in a casino or cardroom setting, require some form of forced betting. It can be an **ante**, a forced contribution into the pot required by all players before any cards are dealt, or a **blind** (as in a *blind bet*) a forced bet required of the first one, two, or sometimes three players in the first round in a game. Blinds are typically associated with hold'em and Omaha, while in stud games, the first player to act in the first round only is often required to *bring it in*, which means to make a forced bet to get the action going.

A blind or bring-in bet must be made regardless of a player's hand and it forces all subsequent players to make some sort of bet or they must fold—there is no checking possible. Antes, on the other hand, are made before the cards are dealt and don't affect any player's options of checking, which he may do if he is first to act and there is no other forced bet required.

Antes

An **ante** is a uniform bet made by all players before the cards are dealt. When there are no forced bets, such as a blind or bring-in bet, antes are usually used in games to "sweeten" the game, give the players something to compete for.

Antes in Home Games

Imagine you're in a home stud or draw poker game with five other players. Each player has to ante a quarter or a dollar or whatever one chip is worth. Imagine that everyone's having a good time—drinking, talking, walking, not paying attention—you know, like most home games go. There's always somebody who forgets to ante before each hand and it's always a different player. The antes are always one bet short before the start of each deal and nobody can figure out who the short player is. Honestly, this really does describe how most informal home games go.

LINGO

Board: The cards that are turned face up in a flop game and belong to everybody. Also called community cards.

A solution has evolved to solve this problem. It's simple. All you have to do is have the dealer ante the six chips out of his stack and *voila!*—everybody's ante is accounted for. No one puts up any ante money except the dealer. This works because every player then antes when it is his turn to deal and since the deal rotates and everyone deals the same number of times in the long run, it averages out. It eliminates all the confusion over who didn't ante and it greatly speeds up the game. It's similar to the blinds rotating in flop games like Hold'em.

The above accurately describes the most preferred and most common way of anteing in home games today. I would be remiss to not recommend it to new players and if I don't mention it in the book, I'll get emails that start out with, "Hey, don't you know about …"

Antes in Casino Games In casino games where there is an ante, every player is required to make his own ante bet. This will be supervised by the dealer who will not deal the cards until every player has contributed the proper amount.

How to Play Poker

Of course, when you have dozens or hundreds of different poker games, the exact way to deal each game varies with the specific game in question. All poker games follow a simple pattern of play:

1. The dealer shuffles the cards and the player to his immediate right cuts them.

2. There is an ante bet made by all of the players. In the old days, each player was responsible for placing his own ante into the pot before the deal. That practice has now evolved so that the dealer makes the total ante bet for each player out of his own stack of chips. This greatly speeds up the game, avoids confusion over who didn't ante, and since the deal rotates through all of the players anyway, the ante expense averages out in the long run so each player pays his fair share.

    In community card games like hold'em there is a small and large blind posted by the two players to the left of the dealer instead of an ante.

3. The players receive their initial cards.

4. There is a round of betting where each player may in turn bet, call, fold, raise, re-raise or check raise.

5. The players either draw a replacement card, more up cards, or community cards. There are more rounds of betting until the game is over.

6. There may be several rounds where players receive more cards, and thus, additional rounds of betting again, de-

pending on the game. After the last round of betting is completed, the player with the best hand wins the pot and the game is over.

7. The deal rotates one player to the left of the previous dealer and the next game begins.

Specific advice about poker etiquette and how to handle common dealing situations will be covered in the chapters on each specific game later in this book.

How Play Begins

Once the cards are dealt to all players, the player to the left of the dealer gets to act first. If the dealer is not an active participant—such as in a casino or cardroom setting—then the player to the left of the dealer's position acts first. In stud games, where some cards are dealt openly on the table, the cards showing will determine the first player to act rather than a player's relative position to the dealer.

What to Do When it is Your Turn to Play

In a way, poker can be very easy to play because when it is your turn to act there are only five options available to you. You can either check, fold, bet, call or raise. That's it. That's all you can do. World champion poker players who have been playing for decades can't do any more than you can when it is their turn to play. Now, of course, poker can be very difficult because knowing which one of these options to choose and why is the hard part that requires some skill and takes some time to learn.

Let's go over what these options mean.

Checking

If it is your turn and no bet has been made yet, then you may "**check**." Checking means to make no bet and pass play on to the next player while remaining active in the hand.

Folding

Folding is the act of surrendering your hand instead of putting money in the pot. If another player has made a bet and you do not wish to match that bet, you may fold your hand in lieu of playing this hand any further. If you fold, you are out of the hand until the next hand is dealt.

Betting   A **bet** is a wager. It is an amount of money that you may put into the pot when it is your turn to act on your hand. When you make a bet, your opponents either have to at least match it or fold their hand. If no one chooses to match your bet then you win the pot.

Calling   **Calling** is what happens on the other end of betting. Poker is all about putting up your money in an effort to win the pot. If another player has made a bet and you wish to continue to play your hand and contest the pot, then you must match the initial player's bet with an equal amount of money of your own to stay in the hand. This is known as "calling."

Raising   **Raising** is the act of increasing the amount of the bet you have to call by an amount equal to the size of the original bet. This is for the typical structure of poker. (There are poker structures were your raise can be for a different amount.) If a player bets $3 and you want to raise, you may do so by adding another bet to the call, thereby raising another $3. Any player behind you now either has to call the $6, or raise, or fold. If he has already called the original $3 bet or was the one to make it, he is now due just the $3 extra you raised.

What Betting is All About

In poker, you compete for the **pot**, the accumulation of monies bet by all the players, which is kept in the middle of the table. Players will make bets for two reasons:

A. They feel their hands have value and they want to induce other players into trying their luck against their cards, or

B. They want to force opponents out of the pot so that the field is narrowed or completely eliminated and they can win the pot uncontested.

The Five Options Looked at More Closely

Sometimes you don't even have all of those options available to you because the action of a player before you can eliminate one or more of those options.

For example:

If You are First to Act...

You can only bet or check. You don't need to fold because there is no bet due to you, nor can you raise, as there is no original bet to raise. If you are playing a game where there is a forced bet on the first round of play—as in many games where the first player to act is required to make a bet—you will have no choice but to make that bet. But if no bet is required, you have the two choices: betting or checking.

If Another Player Checks to You...

There is no bet required to play so you can either bet or check, and pass the decision on to the next player. If all players in a round check, either a new round ensues, or if this is the last round for that game, then all players reveal their cards to see who has the best hand and is the winner.

If Another Player Bets...

You can only fold, call or raise. You can no longer check. As they say, make a move or get off the pot. Here is where you have a big decision. Are your cards worth the money? If you don't bet, you must fold. If you bet in this situation, known as *calling the bet* or simply, *calling*, you also have the option of *raising* and making the game more expensive for the other players contesting the pot. Now they have to decide if this new cost is worth it to *them* to keep playing.

We'll look into strategies for the different games later to give you insights into how to approach all of these options so you have a sense of what to do.

If Another Player Raises...

You can only fold, call, or raise again if there has not yet been a maximum number of raises for that round. Typically, raises are restricted to three times in any one round, unless the game is head to head (just two players), where an unlimited amount of raising is allowed between the two players.

Learning the Options is Easy

These options and the limitations on the options are the essence of how the game is played. Fortunately, they are not difficult to learn because they will be repeated in every round of every game of poker you will play. You will learn them easily and quickly through the strength of sheer repetition. It doesn't take more than a few minutes and a few practice hands to learn what your options are.

How a Betting Round Ends

Once all bets have been called by the various opponents who have not folded, there can be no raises or reraises in a round. For example, if there is an eight-handed game (eight players), and Player 1 bets $5, Player 2 calls the $5 bet, Players 3, 4, 5, 6 and 7 fold, and Player 8 calls the $5 bet, the betting for this round is over. When play comes around to Player 1, he cannot raise his own bet. Since all bets in this round were called, the betting is over for the round.

However, let's say that instead of calling, Player 2 raises the $5 bet with another $5 bet. Player 8 must now pony up $10 to play (calling the original $5 bet and the $5 raise) or he must fold. He may also raise it $5 more, making it $10 more to Player 1 (Player 2's $5 raise and Player 8's $5 raise).

But lets say Player 8 folds. Now there are just two players left competing for the pot: Player 1, the original bettor, and Player 2, who raised that bet. Player 1 has the choice of calling Player 2's raise and completing betting for this round (Player 2 may not raise his own bet) or Player 1 may fold, whereupon Player 2 wins the pot by default since no other opponents remain. Player 1 also has the option to reraise and push those options back to Player 2—calling, raising, or folding.

Once it comes around to a player and all bets have been called, that's it. A further round of cards will be distributed and another round of betting will ensue. When all rounds have been played for the game—each game is different, as we will show later—then there is the showdown.

The Showdown and How to Win

The showdown happens when all of the rounds of betting, calling, raising and folding are completed and the hand is over. All of the remaining players left in the game who want to claim the pot then reveal their entire poker hands and determine who has the best hand. The player with the best hand wins that pot.

You win in poker either by having the best hand at the **showdown**, the completion of betting on the last round of play, or by default, if all other players have folded their hands before the showdown. Then the last remaining player wins the pot by default, even if he didn't actually have the best hand.

In poker, you have to pay to play. Any combination of betting or raising by one player along with other players feeling they have inferior cards may cause all opponents to concede the pot to the bettor (or raiser).

The purpose of this book is to teach you how to figure out what your best option is when it's your turn to act, and why.

Betting Structures Used in Poker

All forms of poker require you to either make a bet, call, or fold your hand if another player has made a bet. The amount of money you may bet at any one time is determined by the type of game you're playing.

There are three types: Limit, Pot-Limit and No-Limit.

Limit Poker

Limit poker is by far the most common type of poker played, not only privately, but in cardroom and casino **cash games** (also called **ring games**). In these games, all of the players have agreed in advance that each bet made cannot be larger than the agreed-upon amount. And raises as well can only be as much as the maximum limit for each bet.

Most limit poker games, especially if you play in a public card room, are played with a 1:2 betting ratio. This means that the size of the bets before a specified time in a game will be one unit and the size of the bets after this period will be two units.

We'll use an example of a draw poker game. In this game, the small bets and big bets (and raises) are divided before and after the draw. Therefore, in a $5-$10 game, you can only bet $5 before the draw; you cannot bet $10. After the draw, all bets and raises must be in $10 increments; you may not bet or raise $5 anymore.

In hold'em, the $5 limit applies to the first two bets—when you receive the pocket cards and on the flop—while the $10 limit applies to the turn and river. (We'll talk about what these terms mean later in the draw poker and hold'em sections.)

There are many other limits that could be found: $3-$6, $4-$8, $15-$30, $20-$40, $50-$100, and more.

Pot-Limit

Pot-Limit is the style of poker played by many skilled professionals. This means that the maximum bet allowed at any one time is limited to the amount in the pot at the time the player makes the bet. In a betting round the first player may bet the size of the pot, thereby doubling it. The next player can then call that bet and also bet the size of the pot, thereby doubling it again. If several players do this then the pot can grow in size to many thousands of dollars in just one betting round.

No-Limit

There is one more type of betting limit and that is to have no-limit at all. It's called **no-limit poker**. Two-time World Series of Poker champion Doyle Brunson calls no-limit hold'em "the Cadillac of poker games," and he's right. In no-limit, you can bet all of the money you have in front of you in one bet at any stage of the hand. This type of poker requires the most skill because, unlike limit poker, if you make just one mistake and there's no-limit to how much it could cost you. Find out more about this exciting game in the no-limit chapter of this book.

Betting Limits

The betting limits are agreed upon in advance by all of the players. Here are the usual limits for each type of game:

Five-Card Draw

Bets are made with a 1:2 ratio. That is, the betting limit before the draw is doubled after the draw.

Seven-Card Stud

Bets are made with a 1:2 ratio. The bets on 3rd and 4th Street are doubled for 5th, 6th and 7th Streets. Sometimes, by agreement, the bets may double on 4th Street if there is an open pair showing in anyone's hand.

Community Card Games

Texas hold'em, Pineapple hold'em and Omaha are also played with a 1:2 betting ratio. The bet is one unit before the flop and on the flop, and then doubles to two units for the turn and river. Omaha is sometimes played with a 1:2:3:4 or a 1:2:4:4 betting ratio, due to the very large number of cards dealt and possible hand combinations. A 1:2:3:4 betting structure means that in a $3-$6 game the progression of the bets will be $3-$6-$9-$12 before the flop, on the flop, on the turn and on the river. A 1:2:4:4 betting structure means that those same bets will be $3-$6-$12-$12.

Home Games   Any poker game can be played for any betting limit and with any ratio as long as everyone in the game agrees before the game starts.

Some Quick Terms

Here are a few quick terms that you will see used throughout the discussion of the games. Though they are in the glossary, I want you to be familiar with these terms now.

Short-Handed Play   A typical five-card draw game consists of about six players and a typical hold'em game has about nine or ten players. Whenever a game has half as many players in them than is normal, or fewer, then they are considered to be **short-handed.** This is important because the fewer number of players changes the mathematics and odds for the game being played and that means that the players must make adjustments for the way they play. Strategies and tactics that are correct and useful in a full game are not as effective in a short-handed game. Short-handed play is a separate skill in itself that takes a great deal of experience to learn.

Straight Draw   A straight draw is to have four cards in a row and to need one of the cards at either end to complete the straight. For example, you have a straight draw if you hold 6 7 8 9 because a 5 or a 10 will complete the straight.

Gutshot Straight Draw   This is a straight draw where only a card of one specific rank will complete your straight. If you hold 9 10 Q K you have a gutshot draw because only a jack will complete your straight. A straight draw while holding J Q K A or A 2 3 4 is also a gutshot draw because only a card of one specific rank will complete your straight.

Flush Draw   A flush draw is to have four cards of the same suit with more cards to come. Getting one more card of your suit will complete your flush draw and give you a flush.

Streets   Streets is the term used in stud games to identify how many cards each player has. For example, in seven-card stud, the betting begins when everyone has three cards, which is third street. When everyone gets a fourth card, that is called fourth street, and so on to the seventh and final card, which is called seventh street.

The Nuts   This term applies only to flop games like Texas hold'em and Omaha. The nuts is simply the best possible poker hand at any stage of the hand, given the cards on the board. The player with the nut hand has an unbeatable hand.

KEEPING RECORDS

"Beware, above all, of the man who simply tells you he broke even. He is the big winner."

— Anthony Holden

Poker is a game that is easy to learn, but a difficult game to master. It is estimated that of all the people who play poker seriously, only one out of twenty is a regular winner in the long run. Nineteen out of twenty players are losers at the game for life. It's not that these nineteen players are idiots, or that they can't learn the game, or that they can't read poker books to try to learn to play better. Most poker players have great intelligence and a lot of them do read poker books and magazines in an attempt to improve their game. The problem is the game of poker itself. Poker, while being deceptively easy to play, is extremely hard to play correctly all the time.

There are easily over one hundred separate skills you must master to become an expert poker player. Every skill that you master will have a positive impact on your game in two ways. First, when you possess a particular skill that you can use against your opponents, and your opponents do not have that same skill, you will win money from them (in the long run) in those situations. Secondly, when you possess that skill and your opponent does also, you will not lose any money to him in the long run when that particular situation arises. In other words, having certain skills will make you money when the other players don't have those skills and it will keep you from losing money when they do.

When you hear that a certain player has a "leak" in his game, what is being referred to is the fact that he lacks a certain important skill, and that it is causing him to lose a lot of money.

What does all of this have to do with keeping records? I have taught a lot of people how to play poker. And, of course, I know a lot of self-taught poker players. Between the two groups I know many poker players and I know who the overall winners and losers are. Most of these players are keenly interested in improving their game, and I know they work hard at it. In all my years of teaching poker, I've seen everything that a player will do to improve his game. It is a fact that the players who go on to become winners in the long run—one player out of twenty—are the ones who kept records of their poker playing from the beginning.

SAID

"Nobody is always a winner, and anybody who says he is, is either a liar or doesn't play poker."

— Amarillo "Slim" Preston

Learning any game and then practicing at it until you become one of the best is very hard. It doesn't matter if it's chess, tennis, bridge, or even poker. It requires a lot of self-analysis, self-criticism, introspection, attention to detail, concentration, and most importantly, the ability to be brutally honest with yourself and to be able to recognize unpleasant facts about your poker playing. If you keep records of your poker sessions, you'll see that those brutally honest facts about yourself will be the times that you lost at poker and then actually recorded that fact in your ledger. Players who are willing to do this are the ones that have what it takes to be winners at hold'em.

Now that you've decided you're going to be a winner at poker, what kind of records should you keep? You're limited only by your imagination and the time that you're willing to put into it. You can make them as detailed or as sketchy as you like. Here's a list of suggested categories that you can put in your poker records:

Where Did You Play?

If you're lucky enough to have a choice of casino poker rooms, note which one you played in. If you played at a private home game, note the host's name and the street address.

What Game Did You Play?

This could be Texas hold'em, seven-card stud, Omaha or any other poker game.

What Limit Did You Play?

This could be any limit but will most likely be something like $3-$6 or $1-$4-$8-$8, since you'll be playing at the beginning lower limits.

How Long Did You Play?

This is the actual time at the table in the game. Do not count that hour you went to lunch or all those excessive short absences from the table. You should make this entry in terms of quarter hours and, if you can, narrow it down to tenths of an hour. The more accurate your records are, the more valid your results will be when you analyze them later.

Calendar Date

This will always be a number between 1 and 31; some date from the first of the month to the thirty-first of the month. This will be useful for later analysis.

Day of the Week

M, T, W, R, F, S, U. R is for Thursday and U is for Sunday. This is a very important note to keep.

Time of Day

Record the time that you started playing and the time that you quit playing. Keep this number separate from the total number of hours played in #4, above. They are very different statistics.

How Much Did You Win or Lose?

This is the bottom line number that you focus on after each playing session, but it is by no means the only statistic of any use to you.

Your Win/Loss Converted Into Number of Big Bets

Experienced poker players talk about their wins and losses in terms of how many big bets they won or lost because that is really the best way to communicate all of the relevant information. If someone tells you, "I won $200 the other night playing poker," he hasn't really told you as much as he could. You don't know if he was playing $1-$5 for two hours and he was extremely lucky or if he was playing $5-$10 for eight hours and won that $200 on the last hand he played before leaving the game. Speaking in terms of big bets also allows you to more easily compare how you are doing in different games at varying limits.

Hourly Rate for this Game

Divide your win or loss for this session by the number of hours you played. If you played eight hours and won $120, then your hourly rate would be plus $15 per hour. If you were playing $3-$6 limit, this would convert to 2.5 big bets per hour.

Hourly Rate for All Games and Totals

This is the total of all the poker games you've played—regardless of the type of game or the limit—divided by the total number of hours you've played poker. You'll be mixing together all of your stud games with your hold'em games, but it doesn't matter.

 TIP

The categories listed above should be the bare minimum that you will keep records of. How much more information you want to collect is practically unlimited and, of course, up to you. Theoretically, the more information you have with which to make decisions, the better your decisions will be.

Who Else is at the Table?

If you have a few known rocks or a few habitually bad players in the game, then you know that your results may not be truly representative of an average session for you. It will make you feel better to make a note of that, especially if you had a loss that session.

Type of Table

Was it a very loose table or was it full of no-action rocks? You might want to create a rating system to help you quantify this factor. You could rate the table on a scale from 1 to 10 with 1 being the tightest table in the world, 5 being average, and 10 being the loosest game you've ever seen. Use whatever works for you.

How Well Did You Play?

Understand that this is not related to how much you actually won or lost. This has to do with how well did you played the game. Did you do your best? Did you go on tilt? How was your discipline?

Secondary Expenses

If you're going to have a hobby, you might as well know how much it's really costing you. Does it cost you anything to get to the game? Bus fare? Road tolls? Valet parking? If you play in the Chicago area, this might be a regular expense.

Dealer Tokes

You'd be amazed at how much this can add up to if you give it a little thought. If you play forty hours a week, dealer tips could be as much as $8,000 per year, depending on your style of play and what kind of tipper you are. Whatever it is, I strongly recommend that you keep track of your tokes. Apart from being a losing player, this is the single biggest drain on your overall bottom line.

Cocktail Waitress Tips

This can be a big expense for some people. These tips come out of the stack of poker chips that you have in front of you, so write it down.

Narrative Remarks

This is anything you want to say about the game that cannot be reduced to numbers or it can be remarks used to expand upon and explain any of the above entries. I use it as a diary-like entry so that I can give each poker session its own unique characteristics. This is so that, after reading everything I have on a session,

I will be able to remember actually playing that session, even if it was several years ago.

Tournament Results

Poker tournaments are very different from regular ring games. These records should be kept totally separate from non-tournament records. Be sure to record all the information that you do for your regular games, being sure to keep it in a separate ledger or file.

How often you take notes is up to you. I would say that the best guideline is: Write it down before you forget it. Some people take notes and update them every time they get the dealer button. That's about once every twenty minutes. Some players take notes during the time the dealer is being replaced by a new dealer. That's exactly once every thirty minutes. Most players wait until after their playing session is over and then take their notes when they get home, either the same day or the next day. Do whatever works for you.

If you play in a private home game, this will probably work best for you. Taking notes openly in front of your fellow poker players usually has a chilling effect on the game. It will cause them to play better against you because you're obviously taking the game more seriously than they are. You always want your opponents to think that you're a loose, carefree and unsophisticated player. This will cause them to misjudge you, which works to your benefit.

I recommend you carry a pen and small writing tablet with you at all times. There are poker rooms that don't allow electronic devices to be used at the table. This includes pocket calculators, voice recorders and palm-sized electronic notepads. I personally use a small, state-of-the-art digital voice recorder that I step away from the table to use when the dealers are changing. I know another player who sets up a laptop computer on an unused nearby poker table so he can update his notes every hour or so. Incidentally, this player is far superior to me in skill so, while you're taking advice from me, maybe I should take advice from him. Couldn't hurt.

Future Records

If you're going to be a winning poker player, or at least a serious poker player, you'll need to take a lot of notes. However, this book is intended for beginning and novice poker players. You might feel that constant notetaking is a burden or nuisance that you really don't care about. I want to assure you that as your skill at poker increases, and your desire to excel makes you want to be an even better player, you will be glad that you kept detailed records.

When you pass the stage where you are no longer a beginner and you approach the point where you are a solid, advanced level player, you'll see that the statistics you've kept will be even more useful to you than you could imagine right now. You will be able to calculate standard deviation, confidence intervals, bankroll requirements, chance of going broke, expectation, standard error, variance and several other things that may not mean anything to you right now.

My advice is: Keep the detailed records now, even if you don't understand it all, because one day you will understand and you'll benefit from the records.

Give yourself a break. Decide how long you want to take as your learning period and concentrate on improving as a player; don't worry too much about the results. Of course you'd like to see an upward trend after a while but you should be more concerned about increasing your understanding of the game. Give yourself whatever period you like and then, when you feel like you're no longer a beginner, start your records over with a zero balance, as if you had never played before. And have fun!

Hourly Rate

Once you've played a few sessions you will see that your poker playing is worth so much per hour to you. All you have to do is divide the amount you're winning by the number of hours you've played and that will tell you how much per hour you're winning—or losing. The only statistic that really matters is your hourly rate, which is just another way of restating what's called your bottom line. All of the other statistics you keep are interesting, and some are just plain fun, but the one thing that they all have in common is that they are intended to help you improve your hourly rate.

> **SAID**
>
> "Keep in mind that poker is a war fought over the course of your life, not a battle won or lost today."
>
> — Roy Cooke

Once you become known as a serious poker player one question that you'll hear regularly from your well meaning friends is, "How'd you do last night?" You know that how you did last night is of little consequence because your hourly rate is how you measure yourself as a poker player. Besides, it's no fun to say, "I lost a hundred dollars," if you had a losing session. I recommend that you take the time and effort to educate your family and close friends to the fact that how you do in any one particular playing session is not necessarily indicative of your overall skill as a poker player. I've been asked that question many times and I've found that the best answer is, "I have a good hourly rate." I think it will work for you, too.

>  **TIP**
>
> Don't forget that you're just a beginner. Don't be too hard on yourself. When you start playing poker seriously and you're keeping records, you might get discouraged when you have to record loss after loss. This might keep you from wanting to play the game at all. So, what I want you to do is allow yourself a training period where we will agree in advance that your results don't matter. After all, it's a training period and nobody can expect to be a big winner while they're learning, no matter what it is they're learning.

You should create a file, folder, ledger, logbook or notebook for keeping your poker records. It can be anything from a memo pad with just the basics or it can be a computer file with every conceivable category you can imagine.

If you don't have any idea how you want to do this, then I suggest you use an 8½"x11" notepad. Following the 18 categories listed above, number your lines 1 through 18 and fill in the blanks. Use the rest of the page for narrative remarks

I have provided a sample record sheet for you on the next page.

Perhaps one day in the future you might decide to convert all of your old handwritten notes over to computer files (or you can have your kids or grandkids do it for you). I can tell you, in advance, that the more information you have to put into those files for computer analysis, the more you will be able to learn about yourself and the game.

Sample Record Sheet

DATE_____ DAY OF WEEK_____ TIME_____ -- _____

OF HRS_____ WHERE_____ GAME _____

LIMIT_____ $W/$L_____ $W/$L #BB _____

$W/$L DIVIDED BY # OF HRS_____

#BB DIVIDED BY # OF HRS_____

WHO DID YOU PLAY AGAINST? _____

TYPE OF TABLE _____

HOW WELL DID YOU PLAY? _____

2ND EXPENSES_____ $ DLR TIPS_____

$ WAITER TIPS_____

_____

_____

_____

_____

_____

CHAPTER 4

FIVE-CARD STUD

"Poker is a tough way to make an easy living."
— Poker Wisdom

Five-card stud is the first true all-American poker game played in the United States. It is the game from which all other forms of American-style poker have evolved. It was first played in the United States in the mid-1830s and for a while was the only game in town, or on the riverboat.

Play of the Game

The game is very easy to deal.

Each player begins by placing his ante in the pot. The dealer then deals one card face down to each player and then one more card face up to each player.

Now the action begins. Starting with the player who has the lowest (or in some games the highest) card showing, players check, bet, fold, call and raise in turn. After each round of betting is complete, the dealer then deals every remaining active player another face up card. There is another round of betting. This continues until each player has a total of five cards—one face down and four face up.

After the action is complete on the last round of betting, all of the players who want to claim the pot reveal their hole cards to determine who has the best poker hand. The highest hand gets the pot. The player to the left of the dealer is the new dealer (the deal rotates clockwise) and a new game begins.

The Strategy

The strategy for five-card stud is very easy to understand and to put into practice. And that is: Fold if you can see that you are beaten. That's also called "beat in sight."

If your highest card is the in someone else's hand and you can see the

FOLD

If your highest card is the and you see a higher card than that in another hand

FOLD

If your hand is

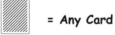 = Any Card and you're looking at

FOLD

You get the idea.

What a great game! If only all poker games were this easy to play. As you can see, it's not hard to become a good five-card stud player. Any time you have the best hand showing, it's correct for the other players to fold almost all of the time, with one exception: If a player can obviously see that he's beaten, there are more cards to come, and the pot is big enough to justify his continuing to play.

For example, if you have A♥ K♣ Q♠ and your opponent has ▨ 5♣ 5♠, you are beaten in sight. You have two more cards to come with which to catch an ace, king or queen, and possibly pair whatever you catch on fourth street if it's higher than a 5. You have about a one in six chance of finishing with a hand that can beat a pair of 5s and if the pot is offering you the right odds, you can continue playing.

There's only one real opportunity to bluff, to read your opponents, to outplay your opponents or to try to insert any advanced strategy at all into the game. This opportunity occurs when your opponent bets on the last card with a hand that you can beat in sight. Or, conversely, when you bet on the last card with a hand that does not (in sight) beat your opponent's. For example, you have J♥ 10♦ J♣ K♣ 7♠ and your opponent has ▨ 10♠ 9♣ 3♥ Q♥, and he bets into you, even though you have him beat in sight. You have a pair of jacks and obviously, his hole card must be exactly a queen for him to bet and win the hand.

This is where the strategy comes in. Did the Q♥ on fifth street pair his hold card? Or is he bluffing? What does he read you for having? What are the pot odds? Players who became experts at the game were capable of correctly folding whenever they thought they were beat, whether they could see it or not.

This example points out several problems with the game of five-card stud. The first and most obvious is the fact that your opponents have only one card for you to deduce. If you know your opponent's habits and style of play and you follow the action as each card is dealt, you can usually know with a great deal of certainty where you stand in each hand you play.

Against just a few players, any pair and any two high cards will often win without improving, especially if one of those high cards is an ace. Against five or more players, it's advisable to fold unless your first two cards add up to nineteen, twenty or twenty-one. Obviously, your hand is much stronger when you pair your hole card rather than one of your other up cards.

One of the few real skills that you can use in the game is to keep track of all of the cards that have been exposed, whether you need them for your hand or not. This will help you figure out if future exposed cards helped your opponents. Knowing the likelihood that a card did not help your opponent and knowing the pot odds will help you play more correctly than the player who doesn't watch these things.

Oh, there is one other "strategy" you could use in the play of the game and that is to cheat. Since the entire game centers around the rank of one unknown card, all kinds of methods have been created to find out what that card is. I've always been proud of the fact that there never was a problem that good ol' American ingenuity couldn't solve.

When riverboat gambling on the Mississippi and Missouri Rivers was at its height in the late 1800s, cheating was the order of the day. There were about 7,000 regular gamblers on all of the waterways and, by mutual consensus of those 7,000 poker players, only about four were honest players all of the time!

Five-Card Stud Probability of Pairing Your Hole Card (or Any of Your Up Cards)

All Odds Are Given in Percentages
(< = less than, > = greater than)

	THREE CARDS TO COME		
NUMBER OF CARDS SEEN	HOLE CARDS EXPOSED		
	0	1	2
3	17.6	12.0	6.2
4	18.0	12.2	6.3
5	18.3	12.5	6.4
6	18.7	12.7	6.5
7	19.1	13.0	6.7
8	19.5	13.3	6.8
9	19.9	13.6	7.0
10	20.4	13.9	7.1

TWO CARDS TO COME

NUMBER OF CARDS SEEN	HOLE CARDS EXPOSED		
	0	1	2
5	12.5	8.4	>4.3
6	12.8	8.6	<4.3
7	13.0	8.8	4.4
8	13.3	9.0	4.5
9	13.6	9.2	4.7
10	13.9	9.4	4.8
11	14.3	9.6	4.9
12	14.6	9.9	5.0

ONE CARD TO COME

NUMBER OF CARDS SEEN	HOLE CARDS EXPOSED		
	0	1	2
7	6.7	4.4	2.2
8	6.8	4.5	<2.3
9	7.0	4.7	>2.3
10	7.1	4.80	<2.4
11	7.3	4.92	>2.4
12	7.5	5.0	2.5
13	7.7	5.1	<2.6
14	7.9	5.3	>2.6
15	8.1	5.4	2.7

These tables might at first look a little difficult to use but they are easy if you follow the little three-step procedure. This is really three tables in one so the first step is to determine how many more cards are left to come (it will always be 1, 2 or 3) and go to that section of the table only.

Now determine how many total cards you can see face up in the game. Include your own hole card and any cards that have been folded, because you did see them. Look down the page for that number in the far left-hand column.

Next, determine how many of the target cards you can see. It will usually be an ace or the highest card in your hand. Look to see where the left coumn, *Number or Cards Seen*, intersects with the three possibilites, 0, 1 and 2, at the top column, *Hole Cards*

Exposed. That number will be the percentage chance that you will pair the card you are looking for by the end of the hand.

For example, if you have (A) J for your starting hand and you can see seven total cards, and no other aces are showing, you have a 19.1% chance of pairing your ace before the hand is over.

If you have (A) J 9 K and you've seen thirteen cards and two of them were aces, then you have less than a 2.6% chance of pairing your ace.

Variations of Five-Card Stud

Deuces Wild

This makes the game a little more interesting. It is almost always necessary to throw your hand away in five-card stud when one of your first two cards is a deuce. To encourage players to play a few more hands than usual and to add a little more action to the game, you can agree that deuces are wild for everyone.

You must also agree in advance of the exact definition of wild. Typically, a wild card can be used to fill in for whatever card you need to make a straight, a flush or can be used as an ace.

This means that if your first two cards are 2♣ A♦ you have a pair of aces because the deuce is wild. If your final hand is 2♣ A♦ 8♦ 3♦ Q♦ you still have the pair of aces but you also have four diamonds showing and the wild card you have in the hole can also be used as a diamond to make the flush.

If your final hand is 2♣ A♦ K♥ Q♣ J♠ then the deuce can be used as a 10 to make the straight. If your hand is 2♣ 5♠ 6♣ 7♥ 8♦ then you can use the deuce as a nine to complete the straight.

Occasionally there is a difference of opinion when it comes to using the wild card as a substitute for any other card in the deck. For example, if your hand is 2♣ K♥ 10♣ 8♠ 3♠ the question is if you can use your deuce as a king to make a pair of kings. It is best to determine this in advance because your hand will only be ace-king high if the deuce is not truly wild.

When the deuce is used as a true wild card, it can take on the value of any card at all, to your best advantage.

CHAPTER 5

SEVEN-CARD STUD

"It's not the hands you play, it's the hands you fold that determine whether or not you'll have a positive bottom line."

— Doyle Brunson

The earliest known reference to a stud game played with seven cards was in Hoyle's Games in 1867, although it seems most likely that the game was played earlier, by soldiers during the Civil War, before it officially made it into any book about card games. The use of a fifty-two card deck and the fact that it was so easy to cheat at five-card stud lead to the creation of seven-card stud. To make it more difficult to know a player's hand, he was given two down cards to start with and another down card at the end of the hand.

For the first twenty years that it was played, seven-card stud was known by it's more common, popular name—"five-card stud with two extra cards."

Play of the Game

Every player puts an ante into the pot. In some games, the dealer antes for everyone. This eliminates any confusion or problems over trying to figure out who's the last player in the game to not ante. Each player is dealt two cards face down and one card face up to start the game. There is a round of betting. The person with either the highest or the lowest card showing is forced to start the betting. After the forced bring-in bet, players may fold, call or raise.

A fourth card is dealt face up to each remaining player. Everyone now has two up cards. There is another round of betting. A fifth card is dealt face up to each remaining player. Everyone now has three up cards. There is another round of betting. Traditionally, and in most games, the maximum bet allowed doubles on this round. A sixth card is dealt face up to each remaining player. There is another round of betting. A seventh, and final, card is dealt face down to each remaining player. There is a final round of betting.

After the betting is completed, there is a showdown among all active players who wish to claim the pot. The highest standard poker hand wins.

The Ante

Seven-card stud is a game where the structure of the game has more of an impact on playing style than most other poker games. That's because the size of the ante in relation to the size of the bets dictates what your style of play should be.

When the ante is very small compared to the bet size, you can afford to sit back and play very few starting hands by being selective about which hands you want to get involved with. You can afford to wait for the best, premium starting hands because the size of the ante is so small that you can recoup those antes just by winning one decent-sized pot.

On the other hand, if the ante is big in relation to the size of the bet, you will find yourself losing your buy-in because you'll be putting big antes into the pot and then not playing any hands if you play too tight. When the ante is big you have to play with looser starting hand requirements and you have to play a little more liberally than the tight player. Tight players prefer to have a small ante.

Another factor that affects your playing style is whether the high card showing or the low card showing has to bring in the first bet. Some games require the low card to bring it in because this helps get an additional player in the game, thereby increasing the action and the pot size.

Good players prefer to have the high card showing bring in the first bet because it's more likely to help make a high poker hand and it might be a hand with which he would have called with anyway. In other words, a tight player who is forced by the rules to make the first bet is a lot happier if his up card is the K♦ than the 2♣.

Starting Hands

The greatest bit of starting hand advice is this: The best hand at the beginning (third street) figures to usually be the best at the end of the hand (seventh street). For this reason, wait until you think you have the best hand at the beginning of the hand before you decide to play. This means you should be selective and you have to be aware of what your opponents have.

There are two other principles that go hand-in-hand with the above advice. Keeping in mind that everyone gets four more cards after looking at their first three, the additions to the above advice are:

> **LINGO**
>
> **Chasing:** Calling or trying to make poker hands that are longshots or statistically improbable.

• It's okay to start with a hand that you know is not the best at the moment, but has a chance to beat the current best hand before the game is over.

• Drawing hands to a straight or a flush are good hands if certain other conditions are also met.

All of this taken together means that if you don't start with the best cards, you can play other hands if you have a good chance to catch up by seventh street.

Types of Starting Hands

There are five types of starting hands:

Premium Pairs: That would be aces, kings, queens, jacks and 10s.

Drawing Hands: That would be three cards to a straight, preferably connected, and three cards to a flush. All three of the straight cards have to be 9 or higher and the flush draw has to be ace-high.

Small Pairs with a Big Kicker: The kicker must be bigger than the highest up card of any of the other players who call the initial bet.

Split Pairs: This is a hand like (Q♣ J♦)Q♥.

Concealed Pairs: This is a hand like (Q♣ Q♥)J♦.

Third Street Strategy

Know the opposition.

There's no substitute for being able to predict ahead of time how a certain player will play a particular hand. This saves you time, conserves your mental energy and allows you to devote your attention to other parts of the game.

Understand that seven-card stud is a game of high cards, live cards and big kickers.

Your cards are going to have to be consistently higher than the other players' in the long run. You can't habitually play low cards and be a winner at this game.

Having **live cards** means that you don't see the cards you need to make your hand in the hands of the other players. If you start with three hearts, you don't want to look around the table and see the A♥ in one player's hand, the J♥ in somebody else's hand and still yet, the 4♥ in another hand. This means three of your hearts are dead. If you start with three hearts, you don't want to see other hearts face up around the board.

Since two pair is a common winning hand in this game, you need to think ahead and be sure that any two pair you make is going to be big enough to win. Remember that any small two pair only makes a small full house. If you start with a hand like 4♥ 5♣ 4♠, you are doubly handicapped, even though you might have the highest hand at the moment. You have a low pair, you have a low kicker and if you make two pair, it will only be 5s and

4s. If you see another 4 or 5 around the board, you are really in trouble. Most good players pass hands like this most of the time.

When you have the best starting hand, you want players out rather than in.

If you start with A♠ Q♣ A♦ you will most likely finish with two high pair or trips. With a hand like that you want to play against fewer players rather than many. Too many players like to limp in with this hand because they think they'll win a bigger pot with more players in the hand. This is wrong!

A lot of players in the hand increases the likelihood that someone will make a straight or a flush against your two pair or trips. You should always raise to give the drawing hands the wrong odds to play against your premium pair. If you raise, the only hands that should be able to call you will be other pairs. This is good for you because you will win these contests most of the time.

It is better to win a small pot than to lose a big one. The biggest benefit of raising with an ace showing is that in the future, you won't always have that pair of aces. Sometimes you'll have two other high cards that are overcards to all the other up cards on board. Sometimes you will have a pair in the pocket and sometimes you will have a three-flush in the suit of your ace.

This means that when you raise with the ace showing, your opponents won't know if you have A♦ J♥ A♣, K♥ Q♦ A♣, 5♠ 5♣ A♥ or 9♣ 3♣ A♣. This adds an element of deception to your play and makes it harder for the others to read your hands. This in turn causes them to make mistakes when playing against you and this leads to profits for you.

Always raise when you have a concealed pair and the highest up card.

If you have 7♥ 7♦ Q♥ you should raise if you don't see any other up cards higher than your queen. This gives you the best chance to win the hand.

Conversely, when calling a raise, your own side card is very important.

You can call a raise with J♣ 8♥ 8♠ if the raiser has an up card lower than your jack but you should fold if his up card is higher than your jack.

When you have a split pair such as (J♠ 6♣) 6♥ you can raise against one higher up card but not more than one.

A player showing an ace, king or queen won't always be paired with that card and he will often fold, making your hand high. This is not a profitable strategy if you're facing more than two up cards.

Don't forget to look around the board for your opponents' up cards. If you have a pair of kings and you see three aces up on third street, it's a good bet that no one has the other ace to make a pair to beat you.

A pair of 10s is a much better hand to start with than a pair of 9s, even though they are as close as can be in strength.

That's because you need a 5 or a 10 to make a straight and if you have two 10s in your hand that greatly reduces the chance that someone will make a straight to beat you.

Small pairs are not a strong hand to bet on early in the game.

Their strength comes from the fact that they have deception value if they are concealed and it is easy for the other players to misread your hand. If you have 4♥ 4♣ K♣ and you get another four, your hand will be very well disguised.

Do not play small straight draws.

If you do, it means that you started with three small cards and making the straight will usually be your only way to win the hand. That is not going to happen often enough to justify playing those low cards. Most of the time you will end up with a small pair or two and that will make you a loser in the long run.

Some players like to limp in when they start with the best pair, usually aces or kings.

Take the time to remember who they are because this will help you read their hands later. When you can positively put a player on a specific pair or two pair, you can make a lot of money from him by knowing when to raise and check-raise. You also know when his cards are live or dead and he won't know that you know that.

Three big straight flush cards are a great starting hand, but remember, you will not actually make the straight flush 98% of the time.

You have to pay a little more attention because now you must look not only for flush cards and straight cards, but your high cards as well.

When the game gets (or starts) short handed, remember that the value of all pairs goes up while the value of straights and flushes goes down.

That's because you will usually not get the right odds to draw to straights and flushes and when you miss, anyone left in the hand with a pair will pick you off.

Not all drawing hands are equal.

Whether or not you should draw to a straight or flush depends on your position, the pot odds you're getting and your door card. If you are to the left of the highest card on board, you will usually have to call a bet to draw. If you are head-up, you won't be getting the correct odds to play. If your **door card**, your first face-up card, is dead, the other players will correctly deduce that you might be on a draw.

Ante stealing is a big part of the game when the ante is big compared to the size of the initial bet.

If this is the case, you should raise a lot more often on third street with any playable hand if you are the first to enter the pot. The bigger the pot, the more correct it is to play looser. That means you can raise with hands you would usually call with and you can call with some hands that you might often fold.

Fourth Street Strategy

After the smoke has cleared on third street and you see who has survived the initial betting round, you might have an idea of what some of the other players have started with. And maybe not. The card that comes on fourth street will give you a clue about everyone's hand because you will get to see how it relates to their first up card and how they feel about that relationship. This is the beginning of being able to read the other player's hands.

They will be looking at you and your cards too. This is how you should proceed on fourth street:

Do not draw to an inside straight unless everyone else has smaller cards than you.

As an obvious example, it does not pay to draw to 4♠ 5♣ 7♥ 8♦ when the other player is showing 10♠ J♦ Q♥ K♣.

If you do draw to a gutshot straight, all four of your cards must be live.

Three live cards is not enough. The reason is, if you're playing high cards, your opponents will be, too. If you need a big card to make a straight, there's a good chance one of those cards is already in the hands of your opponent, even if you don't see it. If you actually see one of your **out cards**, cards that will actually improve your hand, on board, then it's very likely that there are two of them out—one seen and one unseen by you. That means you really only have two outs and that's not enough.

If you started with a small pair and did not make two pair or trips on fourth street, then you need to have picked up a straight or flush draw to continue playing.

This is one of the most common and costly errors that most stud players make. If you start with 3♠ 3♣ Q♣ and get the 7♥ on fourth street, you have missed and you should fold. In this example, you needed a queen, a 3 or a club to continue playing.

Once you make a great hand on fourth street, say two big pair or trips, your strategy changes from wanting to get players out to wanting to keep them in.

Your chances of winning the hand just shot way up, especially with three more cards to come. With a big hand on fourth street you can now tolerate having a lot of players in the hand trying to draw out on you. This becomes truer as there are fewer cards yet to come.

Keeping the above advice in mind, you do want to raise to get the stragglers out when you have the two big pair.

Two pair is more vulnerable to a drawing hand than trips are. To improve two pair, you must get exactly one of the four remaining cards of your pairs. To improve trips, you only need to pair any card in your hand.

If you have a hand that needs protecting, players who missed what they were hoping for on fourth street usually need to be eliminated. A raise from you will take care of that.

Two small pair are much worse than they look.

They will fill up (make full houses) only 12% of the time from here and they cannot beat most other two pairs. Most good players actually fold if they make two small pair on fourth street and there's a bet due them.

If you make an open pair on fourth street and it gives you trips, you should usually not go for the check-raise.

Even though it's a good idea to bet for value and try to build the pot, it gives away your hand too soon. Your hand will be too easy to read and that kills your action. You should wait until fifth street to check-raise. The pot will be big, the other players will be more committed to calling anyway because they only need two more cards, and the bets double on fifth street.

You do not always need the best hand to bet.

If you have any kind of hand at all and there's a chance that you could eliminate players or win the pot right there you should not give any free cards. Betting on fourth street can actually be a defensive (rather than offensive) move because it might induce everyone to check to you on fifth street where the bets have doubled.

You should often raise on fourth street if you are on a draw or have a weak, but playable, hand.

That's because the other players will often read your raise for strength and check to you on fifth street. You can then check right behind them, thereby saving one-half of one big bet. These saved half-bets add up over the course of a playing session.

Fifth Street Strategy

This is the real time to fold if you don't have the best hand or a draw to the best hand.

You might have made a loose call on fourth street when you missed but now the bets have doubled. If you missed on two cards in a row, this is the time to get out.

On the other hand, this is also the time to bet and raise to eliminate stragglers, small pairs, busted draws and weak hands.

You're a definite favorite against any one of these bad hands alone. The problem is that you're not a favorite against all of them collectively at the same time. So you can't let that happen if you have the best hand. Raise.

When you've made a hand on fifth street that you're sure will win the hand on seventh street, you might want to wait until sixth street to raise.

If you're sure that it won't hurt you to give everyone another card, you can wait to trap them for an extra bet. Since they also know fifth street is the time to fold bad hands, you might let them stay in for one more card, and they will call a raise on sixth street because they need to see only one more card.

If you have the second-best hand, it is often correct to raise if you believe it will get you head-up with the best hand.

This improves your chances of winning the pot because you now have to beat only one player instead of two or three.

Remember, a straight is the lowest ranking of the completed hands.

If you have a straight on fifth street and someone else makes a completed hand by seventh street, you may not win the hand. For this reason you should try to win the hand right here if it looks like you're facing any other drawing hands. The only straight I really like is the ace-high straight because it takes a flush or better to beat it. I don't like making a straight only to lose to another straight.

How do you play one pair on fifth street?

This is a good question because you will often be in this situation. You should not automatically fold every time. You should think about playing your pair against one other player if you think you have a chance to win. That depends on how high your cards are, what your overcards are and if the cards you need are live. You should usually not play your one pair against two or more players past fifth street.

If you call on fifth street, it should usually be with the idea that you will play to the end of the hand.

It is usually wrong to call on fifth street and then fold on sixth street. Players who do this make a mistake because that means their hand was not strong enough to call with on fifth street. Fifth street is the time to either cut if off or play to the end.

Sixth Street Strategy

This is the time to raise, check-raise, get in extra bets and do whatever you can to build the pot if you have the winning hand.

The other players are more likely to pay you off because they need to see the last card to know if they have a winner or not. Make them pay for that curiosity.

If you're still on a draw, you should be sure you will win the hand if you make it.

Seventh Street Strategy

By the time you've come this far, your hand will play itself.

Your best guiding principle is to be direct, straightforward and uncomplicated, even if it makes you feel like you're giving your hand away or you think what you have is obvious. You should bet when you have the best hand, raise if you think it will win you more bets and call if you think that will win you more bets.

Forget about bluffing, for the most part.

Unless you have some very specific reason to think that a bluff attempt will work, you should usually just check and fold if there's a bet. That's because most players will call you with anything in this game, just to see what you have.

If you have a good hand, do not bet into what you think is a busted straight or flush draw.

Since this player cannot call a bet on the end—the last card—you won't win any more money when you bet.

You should check to him with your good hand. Now there is the chance that he will try to bluff you. If he bets, you've got an extra bet in the pot from him that you could not get in there if you had bet first. At this point there is no harm in raising because now he will either call or fold.

If you check first, hoping to induce him to bluff, and then he checks right behind you, you do not have to feel bad about it. That's because he could not have called your bet anyway and you have not lost anything.

> **SAID**
>
> "Never interrupt your enemy when he is making a mistake."
>
> — Napoleon Bonaparte

Strategy Summary

The key to winning at seven-card stud is simply to start with the best hand or a draw to the best hand and then to protect and improve that hand as the game progresses.

If you are not a winner at seven-card stud, there's a good chance it's because you're not aware of the above advice. Perhaps you are ignoring or deliberately violating some of the above guidelines. Chances are, you have the typical beginner's weakness of needing to "see just one more card." If this is you, then stop that! I can tell you that that strategy has already been tried by millions of players and it has conclusively been proven that it doesn't work.

There is no need for you to try to reinvent the wheel. All you have to do is periodically review the above strategy guidelines and follow them as best you can. The only acceptable reasons for losing a hand at seven-card stud are either you didn't make your draw that would have won the hand or you had the winning hand going into the last round and someone drew out on you. If you're losing for any other reason (other than being cheated) all you have to do is follow the above strategy advice.

19 More Strategy Tips

What follows is some general advice that will help clarify some of the strategy guidelines mentioned above. This will make the game a lot easier and more fun to play.

1. The single most important decision that you will make in any poker game is whether or not to call that first bet. You don't have a lot to lose when you don't have anything invested in the hand.

   A bad decision here will usually cause you to chase your money and your draws when you should not have even played to begin with. For some players, a decision to call that first bet automatically means they will call all the other bets as well.

2. You not only have to remember what cards everyone called the initial bet with, you have to remember which cards were folded at the beginning of the hand. It's really helpful when you see an open pair in someone's hand and you remember that both of the other cards of that rank were seen and then folded.

3. There are two advantages to having a lot of players in the hand. This first applies to all forms of poker: if you win the hand, you will win a bigger pot.

   The second advantage applies only to stud. The more players that receive up cards, the easier it is for you to determine how many outs you have and to know if your cards are live or not. If two players play to fourth street, then you will only see eight up cards. If six players play to fourth street, you will all see twenty-four up cards. That makes computations easier and more accurate.

4. A raise on third street usually means the raiser has a split pair. That means he has a pair of whatever his door card is. In the absence of any other information, this is what you should take it to mean until you can determine otherwise.

5. A player who re-raises on third street usually has exactly what it looks like he should have. If he has (X X) A♣ you can be sure it's a pair of aces. Don't overlook the possibility that he could have rolled-up trips. Even though it's statistically unlikely (424-1) that anyone will be rolled-up on any one hand, a player who re-raises is more likely than that to have it.

6. A big pair played head-up against a single player with a straight or a flush draw is a favorite to win the hand.

7. A player on fourth street or later, who pairs his third street card is very likely to have made trips. That's because two out of three pairs on third street will be split pairs.

8. A player who pairs his fourth street card more likely has two pair or just the one open pair instead of trips.

9. You cannot make a straight or a flush in four cards. So, that's the time to make the straight and flush draws pay to beat you. They don't have a hand yet and they're going to have to pay for the privilege of drawing.

10. It is not profitable to draw to a straight when another player is obviously drawing to a flush. There are four possible outcomes in this situation:

A. You miss/he misses

B. You miss/he hits

C. You hit/he misses

D. You hit/he hits

Of the four possibilities, only one is good for you, and not consistantly good at that. That's because you won't always win the hand when you make your straight.

Your hand is better when two players are obviously drawing to a flush in the same suit. The worst case scenario is when two or three players are all trying to make a flush in different suits while you're drawing to a straight.

11. The weaker your hand is or the more vulnerable it is, the happier you should be to win the pot early. Do not be disappointed if you win just a small pot before all the cards are out.

12. If you are on a draw, think about how you can win the hand if you miss the draw, because that's what's going to happen most of the time. That's why it's good to always start with high cards because this gives you the option of pairing them if you don't make the draw.

13. A player who raises or re-raises on sixth street with a pair showing almost always has a full house. Ask yourself if this player would play his hand like that if all he had was trips or two pair. Most of the time the answer is, "No."

14. If you have two pair on sixth street, you will not make a full house on the end eleven out of twelve times. And that's if all four of your outs are live. That's why you need to start with high pairs.

15. When the action begins on seventh street, you should recall who had to make the bring-in bet on third street. You'd be surprised to see how much this helps you read his hand by seventh street.

16. A player who raises and re-raises strongly on seventh street with no apparent straight or flush draw almost always has a perfectly hidden full house. If his board is (X X) K♦ 9♥ 7♣ 3♠ (X) and he obviously really likes it, it's a full house. This is a good time to try to account for his out cards.

17. A player who makes a flush will usually make it in the suit of his door card, which is the first up card. That's because most flush draws start out with two or three cards to the flush. It's mathematically difficult to start with two spades and a diamond and end up with a diamond flush. (But it happens.)

18. When two players have the same hand or the same type of hand, who wins? Often, both players will have been on a draw and they both missed. The pot usually goes to the more aggressive player who made the last bet.

19. If you play seven-card stud in a public poker room, you should try to move up in limit as soon as you are able. Do not let the slightly higher limit intimidate you. You are more than compensated by the fact that the players are a little better and therefore easier to read. They usually play the cards they're supposed to play, they play the way they're supposed to, and they often have the hand you think they do. Also, the rake is a smaller percentage of the pot and this increases your profits.

Variations of Seven-Card Stud

For a good, solid one-hundred years from the 1870s to the 1970s, seven-card stud was the most popular poker game in the world. That presented quite an opportunity for a lot of players to think about how they would change or possibly improve upon the game if they could. That led to the creation of a lot of variations of the game. Here are the most popular:

Baseball   Modeled after the actual game of baseball, this game is dealt like the traditional seven-card stud game. This modification is that the 3s and 9s are wild and if you get a 4, you immediately get an extra card. It usually takes a straight flush or five-of-a-kind to win.

Deuces Wild There are only four of them, so having one of them is a huge advantage. A player who has two deuces can usually make four-of-a-kind or better. You need a pair of aces or better or a deuce to call the third street bet in this game.

Dr. Pepper Named after the popular soft drink, 10s, 2s and 4s are wild. Dr. Pepper advertising suggests you have one of their sodas at 10am, 2pm and 4pm. This sounds like a lot of soda but this ad campaign originated when the sodas came in 8-ounce bottles. Since there are twelve wild cards, you need two of them to play and the average winning hand is a high five-of-a-kind.

Eight-Card Stud The only change from the regular game is that everyone gets three down cards to start instead of the usual two. This makes straights and flushes more likely.

Follow-the-Queen This is regular seven-card stud except that the card dealt face up immediately after a queen is considered a wild card. If you get the queen, the first player on your immediate left gets the wild card. If two queens are dealt in succession, the next card that is not a queen is wild. If another queen is dealt after the wild card, then the wild card changes to the card that comes after the second queen. If a queen is the last card dealt face up, then there are no wild cards for that game. The playing requirements for this game are about the same as those for deuces wild, except you don't know for sure what the "wild card" is until after sixth street is dealt.

High-Low Spade This is also called High Chicago or Low Chicago. It is regular seven-card stud except that the pot is split two ways between the highest poker hand and the hand that has the highest or lowest (as called before the hand is dealt) spade face down. You can bet on a sure thing when you can see that you have the best spade face down in your hand. If you have the A♠, you have a guaranteed winner. If you have the K and the A is face up on the board anywhere, you have the same guaranteed winner.

High-Low Split This is seven-card stud except that the highest poker hand splits the pot with the lowest poker hand. Be careful if you are playing for high because some hands that start out going for low can end up making a straight or a flush. For example, a player who starts out going for a low hand with A♥ 2♥ 3♥ may make a 5♥ and end up with a flush.

Joker Poker The joker is added to the deck to make either a wild card or a bug. It is traditionally used as a bug (good for aces, straight or flushes only) since one completely wild card is too much of an edge to give just one player.

Low Hole Card Wild Everyone's lowest face down card is wild and all cards of the same rank that they have in their hand are also wild. This is a popular action because everyone gets to have a wild card and the average winning hand is a straight or better.

Six-Card Stud Cards are dealt one down, four up and one down. The high pairs and trips go way up in value as the lack of a seventh down card makes straights and flushes more difficult.

Woolworth This is regular seven-card stud with the 5s and 10s wild. Fold if two of your cards aren't wild. You need two wild cards to call the first bet.

Quick Six This game is played only in public poker rooms with a bad beat jackpot. Everyone is dealt his first three cards in the traditional fashion. Then, everyone calls the initial bring-in bet, usually one dollar. Next, everyone checks on fourth, fifth and sixth streets, regardless of what poker hands they make. At this point all of the players are still in the game, they all have six cards and they all have invested only $1 each in the hand. Betting doesn't start until after the seventh street card is dealt.

The purpose of playing like this is to get as many of the cards as possible in the hands of as many players as possible to increase the likelihood that someone will make a full house of aces full of jacks, or better, and then lose the hand to four-of-a-kind or better. This is what it takes to win the bad beat jackpot.

FIVE-CARD DRAW

CHAPTER 6

"A priest rebuked a gambler for
the time he wasted at play.

'Yes,' replied the latter, 'There is a lot of
time wasted shuffling the cards.'"

— Charles William Heckethorn

One of the earliest poker games played in America was a game called Whiskey Poker. It was popular in the 1820s and 1830s. It was played with a twenty-card deck, the standard deck in use at that time. Each player was dealt five cards, there was a round of betting and then there was a showdown. The highest hand won. There was no draw. I suppose another name for the game could have been five-card no-draw.

Shortly after the fifty-two-card deck was introduced into North America in 1833, new card games came into existence. Old games were changed. The new deck changed Whiskey Poker because there were now enough cards in the deck to allow players to draw more cards in an effort to improve their hands. It also created a little more action because it allowed for one more betting round after the draw. This new game was called five-card draw.

How to Play Five-Card Draw

Five-card draw can be played with as few as two players and as many as eight. As a practical matter, it is best played with five or six players.

Every player in the game is dealt five cards face down, one card at a time in a clockwise manner. There is a round of betting in which players may fold, bet, raise, re-raise or check-raise. After all of the action has been completed, players discard the cards they want to get rid of. They are then dealt a number of replacement cards equal to their discards, so that they all again have five cards in their hands. There is another round of betting.

When the action has been completed, all active players who want to claim the pot show their hands. The highest hand wins.

Helpful Hints for Playing

- Agree on how many raises will be allowed. Only three raises are allowed in most poker games; however, since there are only two betting rounds in five-card draw, some games allow for a four- or even a five-raise limit.

- Always cut the cards before the deal. There must be at least five cards in the stack of cards lifted for the cut.

- A card accidentally turned face-up by the dealer is considered to be a blank piece of paper and will not be used for this deal. The dealer continues to deal until all players have their cards. This is so that each player will receive the cards he was going to get if the card had not been exposed. After the deal is complete, the dealer then deals a replacement card to the player whose card was dealt face-up. The dealer then places the bad card on the top of the deck, to be used as a burn card. Assurances that a flashed card was not seen by any of the players are meaningless.

- A card accidentally turned face-up by the player must be played by that player.

- No player, including the dealer, or even a spectator is allowed to go near or touch the discard pile while the game is still in progress.

- You should decide ahead of time how many cards a player is allowed to draw. There are sometimes objections to allowing a player to draw all five new cards, which is called *taking a book*.

- Always burn the top card on the deck before dealing replacement cards.

- You must agree on what to do when the deck is depleted before all the players have drawn their cards, if that happens. There are two common solutions:

  A. Shuffle the discards, cut, burn a card and then finish dealing

  B. Determine that the deck is of insufficient number to deal everyone's replacement cards before you deal any replacement card to anyone. You then limit everyone to drawing two or three cards.

- The winner of the pot must have five cards in his hand.

- The winner of the pot must show his hand unless his bet is not called by anyone.

- If the winner of the pot is called, any player in the game may ask to see the winning hand.

Strategy Guidelines and Tips

1. **Five-card draw is traditionally played with a bug in the deck.**

   A bug is a joker that can be used as an ace or to help make a straight or a flush.

   For example:

   If your hand is

   then you have two pair: Aces and 3s.

If your hand is

you can use the as a to complete the straight.

If your hand is

FACT!

The joker is not wild and cannot be used as any card; it can only be used to make aces, straights or flushes.

then you can use the as a to complete the flush.

If your hand is

then your hand is **two pair**: queens and jacks.

2. **Five-card draw is traditionally played with the requirement that a player has a pair of jacks or better in his hand in order to start the betting after the deal.**

A player may have a hand like 5♦ 7♦ J♦ A♣ Joker, thereby having a pair of aces for openers and a 4-flush to draw to. If he opened the pot and wants to draw to his flush, he must then turn his A♣ face-up and put a chip on it in front of him, while declaring, "Splitting openers." If he wins the hand, he better have another ace or joker in his hand to prove he did, in fact, split openers.

When a player splits openers and you play until the showdown, don't throw your hand away until the opener shows openers, because the second-best hand wins the pot if he doesn't have them.

3. **Position is very important.**

The player under the gun—first to act after the dealer—should have at least a pair of aces or better to open the betting. He may open if he has jacks, queens or kings; however, it would be unwise to do so. The reason is that with many players still left to act behind him, he does not figure to have the best hand to begin with.

Only as your position improves can you open with weaker hands. The fact that players in front of you have not opened indicates that it is more likely that one of the few remaining players has the best hand at this point, even if it's only jacks or queens.

4. **Reading hands before the draw is very important.**

It is true that the best hand before the draw is usually still the best hand after the draw. For that reason, you should have a good idea of what your opponents' minimum opening requirements are.

If you know for a fact that a player would not open in early position unless he had aces, then you should not call him with a smaller pair. On the other hand, if you know he opens with anything, in games where jacks or better are not required to open the betting, then you can call him with kings or queens.

5. **If a player in front of you has opened, you can raise immediately if you have aces.**

This will cause some players to fold and will also give you the best chance of winning the hand.

6. **If you have two small pair, you obviously have openers because you can beat the opening requirements, which is a pair of jacks or better.**

Surprisingly, the best play is to not open the pot! If you open in early position with two small pair and draw one card, you will not improve your hand and still have two small pair after the draw eleven out of twelve times.

Two small pair after the draw is a weak and vulnerable hand and is one you should not bet on or have to defend in this position. The best way to play the hand is to check and wait and see if someone else opens the pot behind you. Then, when the action comes back around to you, you will have much more information with which to decide how to play the hand. Most of the time the best play will be to fold, but it will be more clear to you why if you wait and see.

7. Be more inclined to call when your opponent drew one card than if he drew two or three cards.

If he drew two or three cards, then he's likely holding a pair—a pair with an ace kicker or trips. If you call, then you know you have to beat at least one of those hands.

If he draws one card, he is most likely drawing to a straight or a flush and he'll miss his draw four out of five times. If he always bets after drawing one card, he's bluffing about 80% of the time. Call more often.

Also, if you're first to act and you intend to bet, you should consider checking and letting him try to bluff you. If you always bet, he'll only be able to call about 20% of the time. If you check, he'll bet almost 100% of the time and you will win about 80% of those bets.

8. Raise before the draw with aces, but not kings.

Even though they are right next to each other on the strength chart, kings are much weaker than aces. If you have kings, you have two disadvantages. The first is, the aces are unaccounted for and someone could be holding a pair of them. The second disadvantage is that a player who holds only one ace can easily draw another one to beat your kings. kings usually have to improve after the draw to win pots in this game.

9. Bluff less in a low limit game.

With almost all of the deck in the hands of your opponents, someone will always have some hand to call you with, even if it's only a pair of deuces and they're calling because they can beat a missed straight or flush draw. Play your game in such a way that you expect to be called when you bet. That means you should have a hand.

10. Realize that aces are the key cards in this game, for two very good reasons.

The first is, there are five aces and only four of the other ranks of cards. The second reason is that aces will win all contests of like hands: pair, two pair and trips. Adding a bug to the deck has the following implications for the odds:

A. It increases the total number of poker hands from 2,598,960 to 2,969,658—an increase of 10.42%.

B. You are 53% more likely to get a pair of aces than any other pair.

C. You are 2.4 times more likely to get three aces (trips) than any other trips.

D. Open-end straight draws are 10.16% more likely to be completed.

E. The odds of completing a four-flush draw go down from 4.2-1 to 3.8-1 against.

F. In a six-handed game, someone will have the joker in their hand about 80% of the time.

11. Usually draw three cards to a pair.

The only time to keep an ace kicker to your pair is when you know that you will have to beat kings- or queens-up.

"Should I keep an ace kicker with my pair?" is a very common question among beginning five-card draw players. The answer, as is the answer to almost all poker-related questions, is, "It depends." The short answer is that keeping a kicker improves your chances of making two pair while decreasing your chances of making trips. You should keep a kicker only when you know two pair will win if you make it. Otherwise draw three cards. Here are the exact odds:

FINAL HAND	DRAWING 3 CARDS TO A PAIR	DRAWING 2 CARDS TO A PAIR & KICKER
Two pair	0.160	0.172
Trips	0.114	0.078
Full House	0.010	0.008
Four-of-a-Kind	0.003	0.001
Total	**0.287**	**0.260**

12. A corollary to the above advice pertains to keeping a king kicker with a pair of aces.

The only time you should ever do this is if you somehow know that your opponent also has a pair of aces before the draw (perhaps he opened under the gun or re-raised and then drew three cards) and you feel that two pair—aces and kings—can win the hand. There's also the possibility that you both do not improve on the draw and your pair of aces with a king kicker wins the pot. Do not keep a kicker with aces against more than one opponent, as you should always be drawing to your best hand unless you have some specific reason not to.

13. You should usually draw two cards to trips because that gives you the best chances of improving the hand.

You have some slight advantage because some players will believe that you're drawing to a pair with a kicker. The only time you should draw one card to trips is if you're trying to convince a before-the-draw raiser that you're drawing to a straight or flush. He will often check to you after the draw.

14. Sandbagging is very common in five-card draw.

Sandbagging means to check a good hand in hopes of being able to raise with it later in that round. You can also sandbag to disguise a very powerful holding for deception purposes. I think there is more of this going on in draw than in any other poker game.

15. The joker (bug) improves the game.

Adding the bug means more pots get opened, pat hands are more common and easier to be dealt, and more draws get completed. All of this increases the action and the enjoyment of the game.

Variations of Five-Card Draw

Canadian Draw Instead of requiring jacks or better to open, you may open the bidding with a four-card straight draw (also known as an open-end straight draw) or a 4-flush. An open-end straight and a 4-flush beats a pair and the 4-flush beats the open-end straight.

Double Draw This is a game where there is a second draw of cards with another round of betting after the first draw. Everybody gets to draw twice. This usually means that you will have to shuffle the discards.

Flush The only poker hands that exist in this game are the flushes. The best five-card flush wins. If no one has a five-card flush, then the best four-card flush wins and if no one has that, then the best three-card flush wins.

High-Low Split The best high hand splits the pot with the best low hand. The best low hand is 5 4 3 2 A, using the California Lowball scale. Straights and flushes do not count against a hand when you're going for low.

Jacks Back This requires jacks or better to open, and if no one can open then the game is played for low. If that happens, you should be aware that the low hands will be better than average, since everyone has already indicated that they don't have a high hand. If you like, you may also decline to open with a low pat straight so that you can play it for low.

Pass-Out If you can't open, you must fold your hand and you're out of the game until the next deal.

Pip Poker The traditional poker hands do not count in this game. The values of the cards are added up to arrive at a point value for your hand. The ace counts as one point, the kings, queens, jacks and 10s count as ten points and all the other cards count as their face value. The game is usually played high-low split. A perfect high hand is a fifty point hand and the perfect low hand is four aces with a Deuce.

FACT!

The odds of being dealt a fifty point hand are just slightly less than that of being dealt a pat flush.

Progressive Poker This is jacks or better to open and if no one can open, the hand is redealt and queens or better open. If no one can open with queens or better, the hand is again redealt with kings or better to open, and then aces if kings are unsuccessful. If no one can open by then, the openers go back down the scale. The pot builds and no one can win it until the pot is opened.

Rembrandt All of the face cards are wild. That might sound pretty outrageous but there are only twelve of them, just as in Dr. Pepper (where the 10s, 2s and 4s are wild).

Shotgun Poker Deal three cards and then have a round of betting. Deal a fourth card, followed by a round of betting. Deal a fifth card with another round of betting. Everyone can then draw cards with a final round of betting. This can be played high-low split if you like.

Spanish Draw The 2s, 3s, 4s, 5s and 6s are removed from the deck. Players are limited to drawing three cards due to the smaller deck. It is harder to make straights and flushes in this game but it is a lot easier to make trips, full-houses and four-of-a-kind.

Spit in the Ocean Deal four cards to everyone and then put one card face-up in the middle of the table. This card belongs to everyone.

Wild Card Draw You can make the deuces wild, you can make everyone's lowest card in their hand wild or you can name any other card you like as a wild card. At the showdown, players must call their own hand. Their declarations are binding if they call a hand that can be made with the cards they're holding. Make sure everyone agrees before the game starts on what the ranks of the poker hands are. If you're playing with wild cards, then five-of-a-kind beats a royal flush.

Median Hands

One interesting mathematical aspect of five-card draw poker concerns the situation when you know that a player has a particular hand in his first five cards.

For every five-card poker hand, there is a median hand. That means that half of the similar hands will be lower than the median hand and the other half of the like hands will be higher. For example, if a player has five cards, his median hand will be a pair of deuces. Half of the poker hands will be higher and half will be lower than that. Here's a table of interesting median hands:

IF A PLAYER HOLDS...	THE MEDIAN HAND WILL BE
Any five cards	Pair of deuces
Exactly one pair	Pair of 10s
Jacks or better	Pair of aces
Aces or better	10s-up
Exactly two-pair	Jacks-up
Two pair or better	Aces-up
Jacks-up or better	Three 9s
Aces-up or better	Three 9s
Trips or better	Three kings
Three 6s or better	Three aces
Three jacks or better	7-high straight
Three aces or better	10 high straight
5-High straight or better	King-high straight
Any flush or better	Ace-high flush
Any full-house or better	10s-full
Aces-full or better	Four 5s

TEXAS HOLD'EM

"Aces are larger than life and
greater than mountains."

— Mike Caro

Betting Limits

Texas hold'em is played for a wide variety of limits. All of these limits have the same betting structure, which is a 1:2 betting ratio. The bets before the flop and on the flop will be exactly one small bet, the lower betting tier, and the bets on the turn and river will be exactly one big bet, the higher betting tier, which is twice the small bet.

The most common betting limits are $1-2, $2-4, $3-6, $4-8, $5-10, $10-20, $15-30, $20-40, $30-60, $60-120, $100-200, and $300-600. Since you must bet exactly the predetermined amount, Texas hold'em is known as a structured game. You are not free to bet, for example, $4 or $5 in a $3 to $6 game.

There is another betting structure that is common at the lower limits called **spread limit**. It allows you to bet any amount you choose at any time as long as that amount is within the preset minimum and maximum. The most common spread limit is $1 to $5, meaning that you can bet any amount from $1 to $5 and, as in all other poker games, a raise must be at least the amount of the previous bet.

Another betting structure that is very popular is called $1-$4-$8-$8 limit. It is part structured and part spread limit. This means you may bet from $1 to $4 before and after the flop and from $1 to $8 on the turn and the river.

Number of Players

Texas hold'em can be played with as few as two players and with as many as twenty-two players. The most desirable number of players is ten and many Las Vegas poker rooms play eleven-handed. I believe that the best number of players to have at the table is eight or nine, as I will explain later.

High Hand Wins

Hold'em is played for high hand only. Standard high hand wins. There are no wild cards. Remember, the final poker hand is made up of exactly five cards.

Small Blind and Big Blind

The blinds are used to force action from the first two players to the left of the dealer by having the two players put money into the pot before the cards are dealt. The big blind is always the same amount as the small bet and the small blind is one-half of the big blind. For example, the blinds in a $4 to $8 game would be $2 in the small blind and $4 in the big blind. In a game where the small blind cannot be exactly half of the big blind, it is usually rounded down. For example, the blinds in a $3 to $6 game should be $3 and $1.50 but, since a half-dollar is not a betting denomination, the blinds are $3 and $1.

The purpose of having two blinds is to create a situation where two of the players will have random hands. The hands are random because the players put their money in the pot before they saw their hands, and the other players will have voluntarily entered the pot after looking at their hands. This mix of totally random hands versus hands that other players knowingly play against them is designed to create a contest for the

LINGO

Little blind: The smaller of the two blinds in hold'em, posted by the first player to the dealer's left before the hands are dealt.

pot when the flop comes. Because of this two blind feature of the game, there is no ante in Texas hold'em as there is in stud or draw poker.

Play of the Game

Each player is dealt two cards face down. These cards are called the pocket cards. Do not show these cards to any other player since this constitutes your entire private hand. Starting with the player to the immediate left of the big blind, and moving clockwise, each player has the option of either folding, calling, or raising. Folding means to throw your hand in the discard pile, or the *muck*, and to forfeit all interest and claims to the pot for that hand. Calling is to match another player's bet without raising.

If no one has raised by the time the action comes back to the small blind, he can either fold, call the remainder of the big blind bet, or raise at least the amount of the big blind. For example, in a $1 - $4 - $8 - $8 game where the big blind is $2, a raise of $1 is not permitted because all raises in poker must be for at least the amount of the previous bet. In a structured game, ($3 to $6 or $5 to $10) the raise must be exactly the small-tiered amount. Since the blinds had to put their money in the pot before they saw their hands, they have the option of raising themselves. If no one has raised by the time the action gets back around to the big blind, he then has the option to raise. The dealer will ask him, "Option?" and the big blind has to answer with either "Check," ("I bet nothing") or "I raise."

The Flop

After this first betting round just described above, the dealer burns the top card, removes it from play, and turns the next three cards face up on the board. This is the **flop**. There is a round of betting, with a small bet and a three raise limit. This round of betting begins with the small blind, or the first player in the hand after the small blind if he has folded. Players may check and pass on to the next player until someone bets.

Once a bet is made, however, players must either call the bet or raise, or they must fold and go out of play for the remainder

CARDOZA PUBLISHING ◆ KEN WARREN

of the hand. Checking is no longer possible once a bet is made. This is true on this and all future rounds of play. Some poker rooms have a four raise or even a five raise limit, so it is wise to ask what the raise limit is before you start playing.

The Turn

After the flop, the dealer burns another card and then turns the next card face up on the table. This fourth community card is called the **turn**. A round of betting among the remaining players follows, only this time you can bet from $1 to $8 in the $1-$4-$8-$8 game or the higher tiered amount in the structured game. For example, in a $3-$6 game you must now bet or raise in $6 increments.

The River

After the action is completed on the turn, the dealer burns the top card and turns a fifth, and final, card face up on the board. There is a final round of betting according to the same guidelines as on the turn.

The Showdown

After all the action is complete, there is a showdown. All the active players who want to claim the pot then turn their hands face up. Using each player's pocket cards and the five cards on the board, each player (with the dealer) then determines what the best poker hand is. High hand wins.

The dealer **button** then moves one player to the left marking the new dealer's position. The blinds are posted by the next two players, and the game begins all over again.

This is the structure and format used to deal all flop games such as Texas hold'em, Omaha, Pineapple, Cincinnati or any other flop game you can think of.

The Importance of Position

The number one thing that distinguishes flop games from stud games is the fact that your position relative to the dealer does

100   THE BIG BOOK OF POKER

not change during the hand. If you're first to act before the flop, you'll still be first to act on the flop, turn and river.

The rule of thumb for playing position is to play very tight in early position and to only loosen up your requirements a little as your position improves. The number of players who have already acted on their hands in front of you indicates the chance of a raise behind; the more players who have acted on their hands, the less chance of a raise. The object is to be able to see the flop for only one bet when you don't have a raising hand yourself.

FACT!

You will be dealt an ace about 15% of the time. That's about one in six hands.

The hands you play in early position should be high cards, high pairs and hands that have a good chance of winning without improving too much. You should play lower ranking cards and purely drawing hands only in later position.

Starting Hands

One of the keys to being a consistent winner at hold'em is knowing which cards to play and which ones to fold. You will have the best chance of winning and avoiding traps and pitfalls if you stick to high hands and hands that have a good chance of winning in the long run.

The three categories of starting hands that I recommend you play are:

Pocket Pairs

Always raise and re-raise before the flop with aces and kings. See the flop with pocket queens, jacks and 10s. You can play pocket 9s down through 2s if there are at least four other players in the hand with you. This will give you the best odds of showing a profit with these lower pairs.

Twenty or Twenty-One Count Cards

These are cards that add up to twenty or twenty-one, with the ace counting as eleven. These are the top five cards (with the exception of A 9. You will usually be a favorite to win the hand with these cards and you will show a profit with them in the long run. You can determine the point value of your hold'em hand by adding the two cards together. Aces count as eleven points, face cards are worth ten points and the pip cards (2, 3, 4, 5, 6, 7, 8, 9 and 10) are worth their face value.

Suited Aces Any time you have an ace and another card of the same suit, you have a hand that you can see the flop with. You can't ordinarily play A 8 or A 2, but you can if it's suited.

Once you loosen up and start playing too many more hands than the ones listed above, you will start having big swings in your bankroll and you will usually end up a loser. Hold'em is a game of position and high cards.

Choosing a Game and a Seat

If you're lucky enough to be able to play in a public poker room with more than one game in progress, you have a decision to make. You want to choose the game that will be the most profitable for you. Generally, you want to see a lot of action, a lot of loose players, some drinking going on, happy, cheerful players who aren't paying attention to the game and of course, you'd like to see a lot of money on the table.

Once you decide which table to sit at, you need to give some thought to which seat is best for you. There are certain types of players that you would rather have sitting on your right, so that they can act on their hands before you do. Those players are:

Loose Players This is so you can trap them for an extra bet when you raise with your quality hands. You know they will always call when they shouldn't.

Very Aggressive Players This is so you don't get trapped for an extra bet. Let these players raise before the action gets to you.

The Money By this I mean the player who has the most on the table. That's because it usually means he's the best player in the game and you always want to know what he's going to do before you have to act on your hand.

There are two types of players that you'd like to have sitting on your left. They are:

Passive Players   You can always count on them not to raise after you've called a bet. After all, if you wanted it raised, you could have done it yourself first.

Maniacs   These are players who bet, raise, and re-raise every hand regardless of the strength or merits of their poker hands. This is helpful to you because you can always count on them to bet for you when you want to check-raise.

Bluffers   If the player on your immediate left missed his draw and you bet into him, you will not win a bet from him because he will have to fold. However, if you know he's a frequent bluffer, you can check your winning hand to him and he will then put another bet into the pot when he tries to bluff you.

Most of the information that's valuable to you comes from players on your right. If it's not possible to determine where you'd rather sit, you still have one other option. That is to sit in the 3 or 8 seat at the hold'em table. That way all of the other players will be in your field of vision at once. This gives you the best opportunity to pick up tells, which will be covered in great detail in another chapter.

The Importance of Raising

This might surprise you, but it is true that in all forms of poker where you have an option to either call or fold, raising might be the best move of all. So many more good things can happen when you raise rather than just call or fold. There are five major reasons to raise:

To Eliminate Players   The best feature of this raise is that it dramatically increases your chances of winning the hand by knocking out the other players from the very beginning.

To Get a Free Card   In games when the bet doubles—either on fourth street in hold'em or on fifth street in stud—a raise is profitable because it often induces the other players to check to you on the double-bet round. You can then also check, thereby saving one-half of a big bet. These one-half bets really add up over the course of a playing session or a lifetime of playing.

To Gain Information How a player reacts to your raise gives you a lot of information about his hand if you know how to interpret what you see. This is valuable to you because the earlier in the hand that you know what the other players' cards are, the more profitable the hand can be for you.

To Get Value From Your Hand This is when you have a sure hand and you raise to get the other players to put money in a pot that you know you're going to win.

To Bluff or Semi-Bluff Betting as a bluff is a big part of the game and will be covered in detail in a later chapter. However, raising as a bluff, especially on the river, is almost never seen in a lower limit game.

When you raise, especially before the flop, you have a lot of hidden power because your opponents will never know for sure which one of the five reasons to raise it is that you have in mind.

If you raise to eliminate players, you might also get a free card, gain information and get value from your hand. If you raise to gain information you might also eliminate a player and get added value from your hand. If you raise to get value from your hand, you might eliminate a player and gain some information. This is powerful stuff!

Playing in Late Position

The biggest advantage to being in late position is that you will be the most informed player in the game on every betting round. All of the other players will have acted on their hands before you and you will have that information with which to make your decisions.

Another advantage to being in late position is that you will be able to bet with weaker hands if the other players have checked to you. You will be able to win pots by betting in late position that you could not win if you were in early position.

This also means that a raise from you in late position is going to force players to fold their hands more often, which means you will be able to steal the blinds. Do not be disappointed if you raise in late position and all you win is the blinds. This is a good win because it gives you the chips you need to be able to post the blinds yourself and play another round.

An additional advantage to being in late position is that a raise from you before the flop will sometimes enable you to see the entire rest of the hand for free. Here's how it works: You raise in late position, you get callers. The flop comes and everyone checks to you because your preflop raise showed strength. You also check. The turn card comes and everyone checks to you again, assuming that now you'll bet because the bets have doubled. You surprise everyone by checking again. Now the river card comes and no matter what happens, you've just seen the flop, turn and river without putting any bets in the pot. And it all happened because you raised in late position.

It's nice to be last to act but you must keep in mind that being last cannot turn garbage hands into winners just because you're last. Being last to act is a small edge that builds up over time. Don't fall into the trap of playing every hand in late position just because you're in late position.

You should be aware that if you're raising in late position to steal the blinds that your probability of success will be due more to the personality types of the players in the blinds than to your position or cards. If you're going to try to steal the blinds, you'll have a lot more luck if you know that the players in the blinds are tight and will not defend their blinds by calling your raise. If the player in the big blind is a loose, habitual caller you should not try to steal his blind. If you raise him before the flop it should be because you have a good hand.

Playing with an Ace

You will be dealt an ace about 15% of the time. That's about one in six hands. How you play these hands is very important because you have an opportunity to lose a lot of money if you don't play correctly.

The golden rule about playing aces is: Every other player at the table also gets an ace one out of six hands. Getting an ace is no big deal, so there has to be something special about yours.

Here's a few quick tips to keep in mind when you're thinking about playing just because one of your cards is an ace:

1. In a ten-handed game, about 13% of the time no one will be dealt an ace.

2. In a ten-handed game, if you get an ace, no one else will get one about 25% of the time.

3. In a ten-handed game, if you don't get an ace, no one else will have one about 15% of the time.

4. Generally, if you get an ace, you should play only if your other card is a 10 or higher or of the same suit as your ace.

5. If you must play a low card with your ace, the one to pick is A 5. That's because you can make a straight using both of your hole cards. A 5 is more valuable to you than A 6.

6. If you're going to play an ace solely for the purpose of trying to hit a jackpot you should make sure the jackpot is over $15,000 and you are at a full table. Otherwise, the mathematics of the jackpot don't justify it. See the chapter on jackpots for a more detailed explanation.

Overcalling

Texas hold'em is a game that allows you to make informed decisions based on the prior actions of the other players. One area where this is really true is the subject of overcalling.

Overcalling is simply calling a bet after another player has already called that bet. For example: Player A bets and Player B calls that bet. Then you also call. Your call, since it was made after there was already a bet and a call is an overcall.

It is profitable to understand how to analyze this situation because it occurs so often and the entire pot is at stake every time. Chiefly, all you have to understand is that the first player could have bet with anything or nothing. He could have a great hand or a busted draw and is now betting as a pure bluff. Sometimes you just can't know what he has.

What you do know, however, is that the first player to call that bet has to have some poker hand to speak of. This knowledge helps you evaluate your chances of calling both of them and winning the pot. The first caller is the key player in this situation. If you can determine what he thinks the bettor has and then adjust your calling requirements based on that, you will probably be saving a lot of bets on the end.

Dominated Hands

Because of the community card feature of Texas hold'em, it is relatively difficult for a weak hand to beat a better hand. Whenever a player has a pocket pair higher than his opponent's, or when he has two cards higher than his opponent's, he will always be about a 4-1 favorite over the weaker hand.

This is important because many hands will be played head-up in hold'em. If your opponent has given you a clue that he holds higher cards than yours, then you will win the hand only about one time in four. In the long run, to be able to show a profit in this situation, you have to have pot odds of better than 4-1, and that simply doesn't happen when there's just the two of you in the hand.

It's a difficult thing to do, but often the best move is to fold when a single opponent raises and you can see that you'll be playing the hand head-up. This means that you will sometimes fold better than average hands, but that's what it takes to be a winner.

Playing on the Flop

When you see the flop you will, of course, instantly know if you missed your hand, made a good draw or made a good hand. The rule for playing past the flop is:

You should have flopped the best hand, or a draw to the best hand; or, you should have flopped the best probable hand, or a draw to the best probable hand.

Deciding what constitutes the best probable hand or a draw to the best probable hand is what all the difference of opinion is about. It is simply not profitable to try to play any other hand not described by the above rule.

Playing Against the Blinds

Since the blinds get their cards at random and they are already in the pot, you don't have any clues to help you figure out what they might be holding. When the flop comes and the blind bets into you, you don't have any idea what his hand is or why he's betting.

TIP

If you put the blind on a legitimate poker hand, do not play the guessing game. Give him credit for a good hand and consider folding slightly better than average hands than you would if it had been any other player who bet.

My experience has been that the blinds don't bet unless they have what they consider to be a very good hand. That's because they have the disadvantage of being in early position, they don't know what you have, there are more cards to come and they know that they are susceptible to being raised. All of this put together means that a player betting from the blind position usually has a good hand, even if it means that he has to be holding some bad cards to have hit the flop.

Reading Hands

If the other players always played with all of their cards face up for you to see, you'd always know the best move to make. And you would always know if it was okay to call that last bet on the river. You'd never have to wonder if you just lost an entire pot for not calling one last bet.

You'll never actually get to see everyone's cards before you make your decisions, but there is an exercise that you can perform to help you learn how your opponents play. It has to do with improving your ability to read hands.

When a bet is made on the river, what you should do is try to guess, estimate, deduce or determine exactly what the bettor's hole cards are and what type of poker hand that gives him. If you've been following the action you will probably have a pretty good idea what his hand might be.

When the hand is over and you see what he had, your guess will have fallen into one of three categories

1. You will have guessed that his hand is better than it actually was.

2. You will have guessed that his hand is worse than it actually was.

3. Your guess will have been exactly right on.

This is helpful to you because if you keep track of what your guesses have been you will begin to see a pattern after you accumulate a large enough sample. Most average, low limit players tend to underrate their opponent's hands. This causes them to call too often when they should be folding.

If your guesses are too high then you are giving your opponents too much credit and this is causing you to fold hands and forfeit pots when you should be calling and winning those pots.

Summary

All of the above tips have been covered in great detail in my book, *Ken Warren Teaches Texas Hold'em*. It is 33 chapters containing 28 separate lessons designed to teach you how to be a winner at Texas hold'em.

NO-LIMIT POKER

"There are only two powers in the world...the sword and the spirit. In the long run, the sword is always defeated by the spirit."

— Napoleon Bonaparte

Until the year 2003, about only one poker player in a thousand played no-limit poker. Then Chris Moneymaker won the no-limit Texas hold'em championship event at the World Series of Poker in Las Vegas that summer. In addition, two other forces—the inception of the World Poker Tour broadcasts on The Travel Channel, which attracted millions of viewers, and the rise of Internet poker—triggered a major boom in poker, particularly of the no-limit hold'em variety.

As a result of these three events, the popularity of no-limit Texas hold'em exploded. Now, the new most popular poker game in the world is $1-$2 blind, $100 buy-in, no-limit Texas hold'em, making it correct and necessary for you, as a poker player, to learn how to play this exciting game.

There are several good reasons why you should learn how to play no-limit poker, even if you have been a life-long limit player:

1. Understanding no-limit theory and practice will add immeasurably to your enjoyment when you watch the World Series of Poker and other poker events on television. You will be able to better understand what's going on in the minds of the players and why they make the decisions that they do.

2. The players you will be playing against will already be experienced at no-limit play. You need to learn what they know just so you can start out even with them.

3. The low-stakes limit hold'em games are drying up. The poker rooms are evolving in response to public demand. You may not be able to find a $3-$6 limit game as easily because everyone prefers to play no-limit.

4. There are so many new low buy-in no-limit Texas hold'em games available that a player who understands hand selection guidelines, the importance of position along with a knack for knowing how much to how little to bet can be an instant winner. And if you throw in an understanding of how to read your opponents, how to read tells and how to bluff, then you have a chance to be a huge winner.

The purpose of this chapter is to help get you started on the right track.

Advantages of No-limit Over Limit Poker

Every different poker game, every different type of betting limit and every rule has its own way of impacting how a game is played. These differences will be either advantages or disadvantages depending upon the skill levels and preferences of the players.

Some of the biggest advantages of playing no-limit are:

1. You have more control over the play of the hand and how your opponent plays.

2. You will win more often when you bet before the flop because there won't be a flop much of the time.

3. No-limit poker offers you a much greater choice of options when deciding how to play a hand.

4. Good decisions are rewarded more often in no-limit poker than in limit poker.

5. Bad decisions, careless play, leaks in your game and not knowing your opponents' playing styles is penalized more

heavily. This is simply because more money is at stake with every bet that is made.

6. It's very emotionally satisfying to win a huge no-limit pot with a hand that would have won only a few big bets in a limit game. And it's even better than that when you win a huge pot with a stone cold bluff.

7. You don't need to play as many hands as you would in a limit game. Some pros are satisfied with winning only five to ten hands in a typical eight-hour session. They wait for the absolute best starting cards and the pots they win are big.

8. You can manipulate the size of the pot much better than in limit poker. That's because when you can bet any amount you want, you can create the exact odds that you want for your opponents. You can put more pressure on drawing hands and make it mathematically incorrect for opponents to call or you can bet so little that it would be wrong for your opponent to throw away almost any hand.

9. This, in turn, means that you can protect a hand more successfully in no-limit that in limit poker.

10. There is more than one way to play a hand.

11. The strategic aspects of the game take on a much greater role than in limit poker. The player who has a superior understanding of the concepts of position, betting, raising, check-raising, bluffing, drawing and pot odds will be able to use all of that knowledge during a no-limit game.

12. There's one other skill that's essential for you to have in your poker arsenal that's not as big a factor at limit poker: The ability to fold good hands before the flop and on the flop.

The Buy-in

How much should you buy in for when you're going to be in a game where you can bet and possibly lose it all in one hand? In some cardrooms, this question has already been answered for you. Sometimes the house rule is that you can buy-in for only $100 or $200 in the $1-$2 blind game. In some places the limit is $500, the rationale being that that's the standard buy-in for a $10-$20 limit game, and players are used to that. I played in one cardroom where the floorman had to first count down the one player at the table who had the most money and then tell me that I could buy-in for as much as half of what he had.

It's either a forced decision imposed by the cardroom or a personal decision based on your available bankroll, your personality, the level of the competition, your skill level and your tolerance for loss. I have found that a $200 buy-in for the $1-$2 blind game is enough to accomplish your goals. It's enough to give you a good shot at winning and not so much that it would keep you from pulling out more cash if you lost it all to a bad beat.

Keep in mind that the size of the game is really determined by the size of the blinds. When good players play their hands correctly and make sensible bets based on the pot odds and a solid strategy, the average size of the bigger pots will be about $100 in a $1-$2 blind game, about $300 in a $5-$10 blind game, and about $500 or more in a $10-$20 blind game.

General Advice for No-limit Poker

Most general poker advice also applies to no-limit. You should be well-rested, in a good mood, free of distractions, not drinking alcohol, and not playing with money you can't afford to lose. You should know the game and the rules, understand poker theory, and know your opponents and their playing styles.

There's an additional factor to consider when calling a bet in no-limit that's not a huge factor in limit poker. And that is, when a player bets into you, you will always have to take into consideration how much money he has in front of him.

For example, a player who bets 85% of his stack might be running a bluff or trying to win immediately with a mediocre *or* a big hand. If you're in the pot against him, you have to decide if you should give up the pot or risk lots of chips—perhaps all your chips—to see if he's got the goods or is on a bluff. This is a problem you don't have to think about when playing in a limit game because players cannot vary the size of their bets. When a player bets $6 in a $3-$6 hold'em game, you don't know if he'd really rather bet $2, $24 or $300 at you. In a no-limit game, you'll often know the answer to that question.

You should avoid pure drawing hands unless you can get in the pot cheaply because the more astute players will know enough to bet an amount that will protect their hands and give you the wrong odds to draw to the straight or the flush. You want to have other value to your hands, such as overcards to the flop.

It is important that you know how much money is in the pot at all times. You need this information because it helps you to determine how much you should bet. It also helps you calculate the odds for drawing hands so you can bet an appropriate amount.

If you are the player who is trying to make the straight or flush draw, you don't always need the right amount of money in the pot at the time of the draw. If you make your hand you can always bet enough on later rounds to make up for the shortage on the earlier rounds.

SAID

Question: When two players have the same hand, who wins?

Answer: The more aggressive player.

"In every battle there comes a time when both sides consider themselves beaten, then he who continues the attack wins."

— **Ulysses S. Grant**

Just as there are players who will play only high cards and make other low-risk decisions, there are no-limit players who specialize in playing in late position only and thereby take advantage of strategic moves like stealing the blinds, catching bluffs and pulling off bluffs themselves. When you're last to act and everyone has checked to you, a big bet will win the pot often enough to show a huge profit in the long run.

World Series of Poker champion Doyle Brunson said that he could be a big winner at hold'em without looking at his cards if he had the button on each hand—as long as no one realized that he didn't look. He's right. Position is that important and powerful in no-limit.

Overly large bets and raises designed solely to steal the blinds are usually not a good idea in no-limit. When you bet an inordinately large amount to win $3, you are risking a lot to win a little. If you bet $60 to win $3, you will have to win twenty times to be $60 ahead. If you are called and lose just one of those twenty hands, you will be a big loser overall.

The fact that all the other players folded to you means that they likely did not have high cards and this increases the likelihood that one of the two blinds has the cards needed to call a raise.

On the other hand, you should usually forget about defending your blinds against large raises because you can afford to let that $1 or $2 go. The reason you can afford it is that you won't lose too many before you randomly get a good calling or raising hand in the blind. If you lost $20 in blinds $2 at a time, you only need to win one hand to get that and more money back.

Chopping

You should let the players on your immediate left and right know how you feel about chopping because it affects how you play the blinds. I think it is usually a good idea to go ahead and chop (take back your blinds) if no one has called and the action is on the small blind. It speeds up the game and saves you from having a pot raked.

Main Characteristics of No-limit Poker

You cannot play a no-limit game like a limit game. If you're an experienced limit player and you've never played no-limit, there are some important differences between the two games that you're going to have to know about in advance. Here they are:

1. The average number of players who will see the flop or initially enter the pot will be much less. Most no-limit hands usually start out with only two or three players electing to call the initial bet. And then, one of them usually drops out quickly, making it a two-player contest.

2. Kickers are much more important. You just can't casually play every ace and then call all the way to the river like a lot of players do in limit hold'em. That's because having a

weak kicker can cost you your entire stack while it will only cost you a few big bets in limit poker.

3. A higher percentage of the hands do not go to the river.

4. Bluffing is much more common. Any time you can bet ten times or one hundred times what is in the pot, you've made it difficult for better hands to call you, unless an opponent holds a monster.

5. You can knock out straight and flush draws when you have a hand worth protecting. These draws need roughly 2 to 1 pot odds on the flop to make it correct to call and you will almost always be able to bet enough to make it incorrect for them to do so. For this reason, you should know in advance not to play purely drawing hands, unless you can get in cheaply. And if you do play them, it won't be nearly as often as you would in a limit game.

When you make a bet big enough to eliminate the drawing hands, what usually remains will be the other hands like pocket pairs or high cards. This makes some opponents' hands easier to read and helps you eliminate some possibilities.

6. More hands are checked all the way to the river after the first bet and call on the flop. Often the first bettor will take a shot at the pot, get called, and then not want to invest any more of his chips in the pot. The caller, not knowing what the bettor has, will also then check along hoping to make a monster hand for free and then either win a small pot or create a bigger one.

7. The ability to read your opponents' hand is much more important than in limit poker. That's because an error in judgment can cost you your entire stack while it costs only one bet at a time in limit poker.

8. You do not have to make the nuts or near-nuts to win the hand. That's because there will usually be only two or three players in the hand—and the fewer the number of opponents, the weaker their hands tend to be. Thus, it's not important that you make the nuts, although that would be great. It's important only that you make a better hand than your opponent, and the fewer of them there are, the easier it is.

9. There is more sandbagging, check-raising, slow playing and trapping than there is in limit hold'em. That's because players will commit a large amount of chips to the pot if you check or appear to have a weak hand, but they won't call a bet from you when they have that same hand.

10. Doubling up is a main objective. Many players like to choose a hand that they know is superior to a particular opponent's hand, and then they try to isolate him by betting and raising and getting him to commit all of his chips.

How Much to Bet Before the Flop

Before you can know how much you should bet before the flop depends on several of the obvious factors. The first thing you have to do is assess the strength of your hand, considering:

1. Your exact hand. Is it AA or 22. Is it AKs or A4?

2. What is your position?

3. How many players have already entered the pot? Did they raise or limp in?

4. How many players are there left to act behind you.

5. How much money do you have compared to the other players?

6. Can you put someone else all-in or can they put you all-in?

7. What is your opponents' style of play? Is he a solid player, a rock, a loose player, unsophisticated or tricky. What hands does he like to play for the position and what hands do you know he won't play in that position?

8. Now, you need to put all of this information together to arrive at a conclusion to determine how strong and vulnerable your hand might be.

9. This, in turn, tells you what your goal is when deciding how much to bet before the flop. Do you want a lot of callers, only one caller, or none?

Keep in mind that you do not have to bet all that you have just because you can. You need to learn how much you *should* bet rather than how much you *can* bet.

When You're First to Enter the Pot

If you are first to enter the pot, you want to come in with a standard raise of about 3 to 4 times the amount of the big blind. In a $1-$2 blind game that would be a raise of $6 or $8 for a total bet of $8 or $10. Most players are accustomed to thinking in terms of round numbers and an extra $2 usually doesn't scare a potential caller off anyway, so I recommend that you always make it $10 to go if you are first to enter the pot. Anybody who was going to call an $8 bet will almost always go ahead and call a $10 bet.

This $10 bet is now your standard bring-in bet. Every time you are first to act and you want to raise, you should always make it $10. Why? Because it prevents the other players from reading your hand and they will never know if you have AA, 22 or KQ suited. I know a player who makes it $25 to go when he has AA, $20 to go when he has KK, $15 for QQ and $10 for AK and JJ. And guess what? He's always the biggest loser in the game because everyone always knows exactly what he does and does not have. No one has yet brought this to his attention because he's so, well...wealthy.

Be aware that different games with the same blinds might have a different standard bring-in preflop raise. It might be $10 at your table and it might be less or more at the table right next to yours. It depends on what the players are collectively used to and how much they want to emulate each other. The particular amount might be a custom, a habit or a lark. The important thing to know is that you should probably adopt that amount as your new standard raise (for that game and time only) because you don't want to get the other players thinking too much when you raise a different amount that they do. You do not want to play against thinking opponents.

There are times when it is correct to bet too much if you understand what you're doing. Chiefly, you need to know your players. If you know a player will call a large bring-in bet and you know you've got him beat before the flop and his call will put him all-in, then you should go for the overbet. An advantage is that it could look like you're bluffing or trying to steal the blinds and he will fall for your trap. Overbetting also sends a signal that you are probably betting a weak hand and you do not want a caller.

When There are Limpers Before You

If one player has **limped in**—just calling the amount of the big blind without raising—on the preflop before it is your turn to act and you're going to raise, you should add his bet to the amount of the big blind and then raise four times that amount. A $2 big blind plus a $2 call times four equals a bring-in bet of $16. I recommend you round it down to $15 and make that your standard bring-in raise in this situation.

If a player has raised in front of you and you want to reraise, you should raise 2 to 3 times what he brought it in for. If he was first and raised to $10, you should reraise to $20 or $30, depending on your exact hand and your goal in the hand. Raise more to drive players out and raise less to possibly let them in to see a flop.

Limping In

A player limping in in a no-limit game has important implications. Here they are:

1. You've got to figure out why he limped in. It's usually for only one of two reasons: he has a hand he wants to play for the least amount of money because it's not good enough to commit more money to it, or he has AA or KK and is waiting for a raise so he can trap with a reraise.

2. Limpers know that limping in makes them a target for a raise. Are they counting on no raise or do they think they're going to be raised.

3. If you have limped in and it's raised, you should know that there's no disgrace in folding before the flop, especially if you think you're beat. You do not have to call a raise.

4. Limping in late position is often a good play because it helps disguise the strength of your hand, it gives you a chance to see a cheap flop and you're in perfect position to reraise, steal, bluff, catch bluffs, or bet for value.

All-in

Because any player can go all in on any one hand, it's going to happen a lot more often in no-limit than it does in limit poker. This fact has certain psychological implications that don't exist in the limit game. The first is, if you bet enough to force another player to go all-in, this gets you some small measure of respect from the rest of the players at the table. This sends a message that you are a force to be reckoned with and that you're not afraid to put it all on the line. This will make the other players think twice before making you call an all-in bet. Players just might underbet when you're in the hand and that's a mistake you want them to make.

There are other advantages if you go all in. The biggest is that you don't have to fold the hand until after all the cards are out. You get to see all five cards on the board. You won't get outplayed or bluffed out of the hand.

Sometimes you will go all-in and lose the hand and be busted out of the game unless you rebuy. I want to tell you that there is no disgrace in going broke on any one hand. It's part of the no-limit experience, it's very common, it happens to everyone, and it shows that you were willing to take a stand with a hand.

How to Play Specific Hands

As your skill increases at no-limit play you might start to get different ideas about how to play some specific hands in different situation and against different opponents. Until then, the following advice will keep you in good stead. The advice I'm about to give you accurately depicts how most of the world's top professionals play their cards. If you were to ask the top ten no-limit players in the world how to play these cards, their advice would all sound roughly the same and would not vary by much.

Hands to Play in Early Position	AA, KK, QQ, AK, AQ
Hands to Play in Middle Position	AJ, KQ, AT, TT, 99, 88 (in addition to the early position list)
Hands to Play in Late Position	77, 66, 55, 44, 33, 22, AJ, AT, QJ (in addition to the early and middle position lists)

AA   Always raise before the flop. You hope to get exactly one caller. This gives you the best chance to win the most money.

Your goal is to get as much money as possible into the pot before the flop so you'll always put in the last raise. You will be at least a 4-1 or better favorite over just one other player before the flop. If you have two callers, you will still be a big favorite but you must be more careful after the flop because there will be a few extra ways that you can be beat.

KK   When you get a pair of kings in the pocket you should pretend that they're aces and play them just like you would play aces before the flop. You have only one thing to worry about before the flop and that is if someone else is holding pocket aces. If you hold KK, it's about 20-1 against anyone else holding AA in a ten-handed game. It's a longshot, but it does happen. In any case, you can't play scared worrying about that rare event.

If it's raised in front of you, you should always reraise in attempt to get the action heads-up with the raiser. Pocket kings is a great starting hand and you want to get lots of chips in the middle.

QQ   Pocket queens is a two-way hand in no-limit. Ideally, you'd like to play them one of two ways: Either raise to get it heads-up with one other player or see the flop with a lot of other players. If you flop a queen in a multiway pot, you're going to win a lot of money. World Series of Poker champion Johnny Chan says that pocket queens is his favorite hand. That's because those times that he flops a set of queens, the flop also often has an ace or a king in it and he traps anyone who made a pair of aces or kings for a lot of money.

When you're faced with a raise or reraise, the most important thing is—and I'll say it again—that you know you're opponents' playing style. Does his raise mean that he has JJ or TT, or does he have AA or KK or AK? The most common heads-up matchup when one player is all-in is AK vs. QQ.

JJ   Pocket jacks is a tough hand to play well. The problem is that even though you might have the best hand before the flop, there are twelve overcards in the deck that can come on the flop. Your goal is to win with a bet on the flop, to flop a set of jacks or get a flop of 8-9-T to make the jack-high straight draw.

And don't forget—there's no rule that says you have to play the hand. If there is raising and reraising before the flop and your opponents are tight, you may be best off tossing the jacks.

Middle Pairs:
TT, 99, 88, 77   See the flop for as little money as possible with these middle pairs, usually by limping in. Your goal is to flop a set because you usually can't afford to call a big bet without that kind of strength. Be willing to fold after the flop most of the time. That's just the nature of these middle pairs. If you do flop a set, you should make the other players holding overcards pay dearly to make their hands.

If another player holds AK or AQ and the flop is A83 when you hold 88, the other player is virtually drawing dead. You now have options. You should play the hand in such a way that gets the most money from your opponent in the pot. You should consider making small bets, checking, check-raising and overbetting… whatever it takes to get more money in the pot.

Small Pairs:
66, 55, 44, 33, 22   All of the advice that applies to the middle pairs also applies to the small pairs —you want to se the flop as cheaply as possible. You will have to throw these hands away after the flop about 80% of the time. If it is raised behind you before the flop, you should usually throw the hand away. But, if you do want to call, make sure that your call will close out the betting. You don't want to call a raise and then have the player on your left raise it again.

AK   AK is a very good no-limit hand. That's because you will usually be able to raise pre-flop to get it heads-up and after that you'll often get to see all five cards on the board. This doesn't happen as often in limit poker.

You should usually play AK just like you would pocket aces before the flop. Bring it in for your standard raise. In the minds of your opponents' you could have AA. They don't know that you have AK. You can take advantage of that perception by the way you play the hand after the flop. If you raised before the flop, you should usually go ahead and make the continuation bet on the flop, unless it would be obvious suicide to do so.

AQ   This is a good-looking hand and it is a good hand in limit hold'em. But in no-limit, it's a horrible hand to call a preflop raise with and you should only play it in late position for the minimum amount of money. The problem with raising with it is that you will often only be called by players who can beat AQ and you will win only the blinds if no one calls. In 2005, this hand picked up the nickname 'Anna Kornikova' after the Russian female tennis pro: looks good but can't win.

AJ, KQ and medium suited connectors: 87s, 76s, 65s   These are hands that you can limp in with in late position but the problem with them is that you can't stand a raise. There is almost no legitimate raising hand that doesn't beat AJ and KQ before the flop. These are the cards that you want the other players to call with when you have a raising hand.

The problem with suited connectors is that you will almost always be left with a drawing hand after the flop. You usually won't have the right odds to draw and those rare times that you do make the draw, you will sometimes lose to a similar, but higher, drawing hand.

Common Beginner Mistakes

If you've read and understand the above advice about how much to bet and which cards to play, you won't be making these mistakes yourself. Because low buy-in no-limit games are so new and popular, the majority of players in these games aren't yet aware of how to play properly. Here's a short list of mistakes that you'll see beginners and weak players make all the time:

1. **Underbetting the pot.** Most players in these game are either totally new to poker and Texas hold'em or they are converts from the limit games. They will often be too timid to bet the large amounts of money that proper bet size calls for. You can often bet this type of player off a hand. These small bets also make it correct for drawing hands to call, which is a disaster for a high pair.

2. **Overbetting the pot.** Beginners don't understand that they are risking a lot to win a little and the move often backfires on them. If you bet a large amount of money into a small pot and you get called…guess what? You're probably beat.

3. **Not making progressively bigger and bigger bets on the flop, turn and river.** You will usually have to bet the size of the pot, or a big percentage of the pot at each stage. That might be $40 on the flop, $120 on the turn and $360 on the river. The player who bets $40 on the flop, turn and river is asking everyone to come in cheap to draw out on him.

4. **Playing drawing hands against big bets or raises as part of their normal strategy.** These players are converts from the limit game who just haven't learned yet. Drawing hands for too many chips are death in no-limit.

5. **Calling on the flop with less than an overpair or top pair with top kicker.** Every other hand is just too expensive to play for a lot of money.

No-limit Poker's Golden Rule

There is one bit of poker advice that applies to no-limit more than any other game, and that is:

You should scrupulously and painstakingly avoid hands where you are either only a very slight favorite or a big underdog to win the hand.

This means you should avoid hands where you are slightly better than 50-50 to win the hand or you are dominated and are therefore a 4-1 underdog.

Of course, the key to being able to follow the above advice is knowing what your opponent's cards are compared to yours when he raises on the first betting round. Since that's just not possible, you're going to have to be aware of some common situations that will get you in trouble. The main thing you need to know is that it does not pay to play dominated hands heads-up for all of your money unless you're going to go all in anyway, or you have to because of tournament conditions.

This means you cannot play:

1. A queen or an ace with a worse kicker when you suspect that your opponent has ace-king.

2. A pocket pair you suspect may be lower than your opponent's pocket pair.

3. Two unpaired cards that may be lower than your opponent's two unpaired cards.

In all of these three instances you will be about a 4-1 underdog to win the hand and you will be getting pot odds of only 1-1 if there's just the two of you.

Starting Hand Matchups

Here's a list of no-limit starting hand matchups that are common when two players are heads-up:

Higher pocket pair vs. lower pocket pair: The higher pair is always roughly a 4-1 favorite. If your opponent has AA, it doesn't matter if you hold KK or 22. You still have to improve to win.

AK Versus AQ The AK is a 70-30 favorite. Against AK, you have roughly the same odds against you with AQ down through A2.

AK Versus QQ The AK is a 57-43 favorite.

Pocket Pair Versus Two Overcards 66 vs. AQ. The pocket pair is a slight 55-45 favorite.

Pocket Pair Versus One Overcard

77 vs. A3. The pocket pair is now a 70-30 favorite.

Overcards Versus Undercards

AK vs. 83. The AK is a 68-32 favorite.

There is one bit of advice that sums up the above statistics: When an opponent has made a large bet for all of your chips, take all of the time you need to make a decision. The players in a no-limit game will patiently wait while you contemplate this important bet—they understand that a bet for all of your chips is a very difficult decision.

You should train yourself to quit making automatic, non-thinking, knee-jerk reaction calls in a no-limit game. You are also going to have to learn to muck a lot of hands before the flop that you would automatically call with in a limit game. There's more money at stake with each bet and every decision deserves your full attention.

Bluffing

Bluff attempts are more successful in no-limit poker than in limit. The reason is obvious. If there is $100 in the pot, it is mathematically correct to call a possible $8 bluff with any weak hand. But if you have to call $100 with that same weak hand, you're not getting the right price and you'll usually have to fold the hand—even if you had the best hand.

If you're the one doing the bluffing, you should make your standard bet when you have a hand in that situation. You want your opponents to be saying to themselves, "I can't tell when he's bluffing or when he has a hand because he always bets the same amount every time." It pays to have a standard bet.

If you're going to bluff on the flop or turn, don't bet without having some outs. This dramatically increases the number of hands and amount of money you win in the long run. If you make a big bet bluff on the turn and you get called, which of the following two statements would you rather be making to yourself?

1. Darn it, I can't win now, or

2. Darn it, I can't win now but at least I have fifteen outs on the river.

Cinderella Poker

What's that? You don't have the $5,000 or $10,000 you need to play a big game of no-limit poker? Sure you do; all you have to do is create the money by playing what's called "Cinderella Poker." It makes for a great home game and it's easy to do. I'll tell you how we do it in my home game.

The first thing we have to do is to decide on how much money each player is willing to buy-in with in a poker game. It might be only $20 or $100 or as much as $500. The only thing that matters is that everyone agrees on the amount because that now becomes the buy-in for all the players.

I'll use a $100 minimum amount in this example, since this is a common amount of money actually used in a lot of these games. One hundred dollars is also 10,000 pennies. Do you see where I'm going with this? Each penny now represents one dollar. You can give each player $10,000 in poker chips and you can now play no-limit.

The game has the look and feel of a real no-limit game, it's a little more fun because you're not really risking losing $10,000 and it's fun to say, "I bet $1,000," when it's really only equal to $10. Of course you can make the minimum buy-in any amount you like and you can make the chips worth any amount you like as long as you can keep the conversion math straight when it comes time to cash out. It's a great game, it's fun, it's a safe, inexpensive way to get some good no-limit experience, and I guarantee you'll like it.

A No-limit Poker Question

No-limit really is different from limit poker. You have a lot to think about every time you have to make a decision and a bad decision can cost you a lot of money in one hand. Here's an example of how involved the decision making process can be in no-limit.

Question: You're playing Texas hold'em and after seeing the river card, you think you have the winning hand. So....how much do you bet?

Take all the time you need to think about it before reading any further. Notice that I did not give you any information about pot size, position, the previous action, how much money you each have, etc. That's because this question is designed to test your understanding of no-limit theory without being specific to any one hand. There are two answers to this question.

Good Answer: You should bet as much as you think he will call, and no more.

Very Good Answer: You should check or bet as much as you think will cause him to reraise you—if he's that type of player—because the size of your bet made him think you have a weaker hand than his or you're bluffing and trying to steal the pot.

Just something to think about.

CHAPTER 9

OMAHA

It seems that 90% of Omaha is luck.
But that is only an illusion.

Omaha poker is the action game of the 21st century. It is dealt and played just like Texas hold'em, with two exceptions: Each player is dealt four hole cards instead of just two and each player must use exactly two of those cards to make his hand at the showdown. This means that each player can make six different hands with his four cards.

For example:

A player holding

can make these six hands:

Since Omaha is just a slightly different version of Texas hold'em, everyone who plays Omaha starts out as a hold'em player. For the student who is learning how to play Omaha, everything about the game is always framed by the question, "How does this differ from hold'em?" The jumping off point for getting into Omaha is to learn how the addition of those two extra hole cards affects the game.

> ## FACT!
>
> Ten players who each have six different hands have a total of sixty hands in the game, which makes for a lot of action.

You might not think that it's much of a difference to have four hole cards instead of two. I have identified fifty-six ways in which Omaha is significantly different from hold'em. These are the things you should know if you're going to be a winner at Omaha.

56 Ways Omaha Differs from Hold'em

1. **Omaha is played for higher limits.**

   That's because it is usually played high-low split and players will often win one-half of the pot. The limits are usually doubled so that half a pot in Omaha is equal to a whole pot in hold'em.

2. **Your bankroll requirements are higher.**

   Since the limits are higher, it costs more to buy into the game. You are compensated for this because you will often win one-half of the pot in Omaha when you would win none of the pot in hold'em.

3. **Kill games are much more common.**

   A kill game is where the betting limits are increased (usually doubled) for the next hand only. These are more common in Omaha because players can play at a lower limit while occasionally playing higher limit.

4. **The betting structure is sometimes different.**

   In hold'em the betting is 1:1:2:2. This doesn't work in Omaha as well because the pots get so big. Omaha often has a betting structure of 1:2:3:4 or 1:2:4:4. This keeps the bad players from playing too loose. A 1:2:3:4 betting structure means that in a

$3-$6 game the progression of the bets will be $3-$6-$9-$12 before the flop, on the flop, on the turn and on the river. A 1:2:4:4 betting structure means that those same bets will be $3-$6-$12-$12.

5. **Omaha high-low has the lowest fluctuation of any poker game for the expert player.**

An expert Omaha player will have fewer and smaller negative swings in his bankroll because of the nature of the game and the skills needed to be a good player.

6. **Omaha is better for you when you are playing against bad players.**

Omaha gives bad players many opportunities to put money in the pot with losing hands.

7. **Omaha is more profitable.**

More hands, more bad players, bigger pots and higher limits all add up to more profit for the good player.

8. **Omaha hand values are different.**

The average winning Omaha hand is always going to be the best possible hand or very near it. Hand values have to be dramatically adjusted upward.

9. **Superior players are handicapped.**

Many of the skills that are required to be an expert at stud or hold'em don't apply to Omaha. This makes the difference between the best and worst Omaha players less pronounced.

10. **Omaha is more fun to play.**

It is correct to play more hands, see more flops, call more often, chase your draws and build big pots. And that's fun.

11. **Omaha hands have more outs.**

In Omaha, you can have a straight, a flush, a full house and a low draw all at the same time. Many times half the cards in the deck will complete your hand and that just can't happen in hold'em.

12. Pot odds are better.

That's because more players correctly see the flop and then make playable hands. This makes for much bigger pots.

13. Implied odds are better.

You will always have enough money in the pot at the end of the hand to have justified your draw attempt, even if that money wasn't there when you started the draw.

14. The small blind almost always plays.

With six hands, a partial bet already called, lots of callers, a big pot and great implied odds, it's usually wrong for the small blind to fold.

15. Seat selection is less important.

Omaha requires you to play in a more straightforward manner than most other poker games. This makes the characteristics of other players and where they're seated in relation to you less important.

16. Incorrect early position play is more costly.

That's because you will usually be calling more bets and playing the hand to the river more often than you would with a similar-quality hand in hold'em.

17. Dominated hands are less costly.

A dominated hand is a 4-1 underdog in hold'em but only a 3-2 loser in Omaha.

18. Drawing dead is more common.

You can usually call in hold'em with the nuts (the best hand) or near-nuts and still be a big winner, but not in Omaha.

19. Omaha jackpots are easier to hit.

It's about four times easier to hit a jackpot in Omaha than in hold'em. That's because everyone can make six times as many poker hands.

20. Raising is less effective.

The goals you accomplish by raising in hold'em just don't apply as much in Omaha. The two best reasons to raise in Omaha are to eliminate players before the flop and to raise for value when you have a winning hand.

21. Bluffing is not a big part of the game in Omaha.

There's almost no such thing as everyone missing their draw or no one having a hand on the river in Omaha, as there is in hold'em. Someone will always have a hand with which to beat you with on the river in Omaha.

22. Check-raising is less effective.

With so many possible hands against you and with such a big pot, you should usually bet for value rather than try to get fancy.

23. Slow-playing is usually incorrect.

It's better to get the money in the pot now than try to trick everybody on a later round.

24. There's less guessing in Omaha.

Someone will always have the current nuts and someone will always be trying to make a better hand than that.

25. It's necessary to fold good hands.

Hands that are good just because they're the best probable hand in hold'em are usually no good in Omaha. That's because in Omaha you need the best possible, not probable, hand to win.

26. Doubt is good in Omaha.

If a player bets and you don't know what to do, it's because your hand is not that good. That's a good enough reason to automatically fold in Omaha where you might have to call in that same spot in hold'em.

27. Hand selection is the key to Omaha skill.

Once you master the art of choosing which hands to play, the rest of the game is a lot easier.

28. Patience is the key attribute.

If you're going to be selective and play only the best starting hands, you'll be folding and sitting out a lot. If you are a patient person, this will pay off in Omaha.

29. Suited aces are very valuable.

You can play and win with A X unsuited in hold'em but not in Omaha. Having a suited card to go with your ace makes your hand about four times more profitable.

30. There are more protected pots in Omaha.

A protected pot is one that's so big that someone will call on the river just because of the size of the pot, regardless of any poker hand strength he may or may not have.

31. Ace-low is worth a lot more.

An ace with a 2, 3, 4 or 5 is not a good hand in hold'em but it's a great hand in Omaha. That's because you can make a good low hand or a wheel with these cards. A **wheel**, also known as a **bicycle**, is a 5-high straight: 5 4 3 2 A.

32. Middle range cards are more costly.

SAID

"Play big cards or little cards."

— Max Shapiro

In Omaha high-low split, it's the very highest and very lowest cards that get the money. That money comes from the players playing the cards in the middle.

33. Beware of A A X X.

In hold'em, it's automatic to raise before the flop. Not so in Omaha. Pocket aces are not a strong hand in Omaha until you see the flop. If the board is A♥ J♣ 5♠ 9♦ 5♥, don't be surprised if a player who never raised at any time shows you pocket aces to make the full house.

34. Kickers are very important.

A kicker is the highest card in your hand that does not help make a straight, flush, full house, or a pair. When all the players have four cards in their hands, it's very easy for someone to have the best possible kicker.

35. Late position is worth less.

Most of the benefits of being in late position don't apply as much to Omaha.

36. High cards are worth less.

That's because players who are trying to make low hands will sometimes back into a high hand and beat you if you're going high. This can't happen at hold'em because it's not played high-low split.

37. Bicycles are more likely.

With players trying to make low hands, a wheel will be more likely any time the board cards make it possible.

38. Your poker hand goal is different.

A top pair with a good kicker or two pair are both good hands at hold'em, but they are nothing at Omaha. In Omaha, you're always trying to make the nuts, and that's usually a straight, flush, or a full house.

39. Small sets are more dangerous.

That's because players are four times more likely to be holding pocket pairs than in hold'em. Any card on the turn or river could make someone a higher set.

40. Cold calling is more correct.

With the bigger pots and the greater number of outs that you will have to draw to, it's usually correct to go ahead and call two or more bets at once to try to make your hand.

41. Backdoor draws are more common.

If you're trying to make one type of hand in hold'em and the turn and river cards give you a chance to make another type of hand, you won't be able to make that second type of hand because you don't have enough cards to go around. In Omaha, however, someone will have the cards needed to make that hand.

42. Threats are more real.

When the flop is all one suit it's very easy for one or more of eight or nine other players to be holding two cards of that suit. When there's a pair on the flop it's easy for anyone to be holding one of those cards to make trips or even a full house. These flops are dangerous enough in hold'em. The threat is real because almost all of the cards in the deck are in the hands of your opponents.

43. Double flush draws are more likely.

If the flop is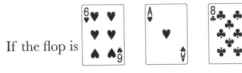

then you are usually looking at a flush draw.

If the turn card is another club then you are also usually looking at two flush draws.

44. Three flush cards means a flush!

Just like a pair on the flop means someone has trips, three cards of the same suit on the flop usually means someone has a flush.

45. Overcards are killers.

In Omaha, every card on the board represents the very real possibility that someone is using that card to make a set. If you have a low set and a card higher than your set is unveiled, then you no longer have the nuts and the chances are pretty good that it matches someone's pocket pair.

46. Free cards are killers.

There's not much difference between a free card and an overcard in Omaha. One is free and the other costs very little in relation to the size of the final pot. This difference is in knowing that it's bad to give your opponents a free card. Do the correct thing and make them pay for it, even if it's likely that the next card could be an overcard that hurts you.

Free cards are something your opponents are supposed to give you—not something you give them.

47. A full house is not a big hand.

In flop games, the strength of your hand is situational and relative, depending on the cards in your hand. A full house ranks high on the list of poker hands but it must be viewed in light of the other cards on the board, the number of other players in the hand, and whether the game is hold'em or Omaha. Learn to be more alert when you make a full house and slow down if you need to.

48. Freerolling is much more common.

Freerolling is whenever you have the nuts with more cards to come and you draw to an even better hand. As you can see by now, it's just the nature of the game. You shouldn't be trying to make just one hand anyway. (The only acceptable exception is if you have four wheel cards in your hand with no flush possibilities.) With five cards on the board and four more in your hand, you can see how easy it is to make a straight or a flush on your way to making a flush or a full house. Don't forget that players with low hands are freerolling for high and could possibly make a low straight or perhaps a backdoor flush. A backdoor hand is one that you originally weren't drawing to or trying to make.

49. Hand reading skills are less important.

The three main tools that help you read other players' hands position, psychology and statistics—are of less use to you in an Omaha game. Since all players have six possible hands, you can never be exactly sure which one to put him on early in the hand. Your main hand reading tool in Omaha is simply knowing what the current nuts is, which draws are possible and realizing that it usually takes the nuts to win. It's that easy.

50. Tells are of less use.

The nature of Omaha requires that all players who want to win the pot should be trying to make the nuts. A quick reading of the board will always tell you what that is. There will be no need for players to fake strength when they don't have it or to pretend to be weak when they have a strong hand. There won't be much acting going on. That's because no matter how a player acts, he's still stuck with the true strength of his hand at the river, and he and everyone else knows it. In my opinion, the best tell that the other players will provide you in an Omaha game is simply the fact that everyone knows what the nuts and what the draws are and yet they are still calling, betting or raising.

51. It's more difficult to outplay your opponents.

There are hundreds of combinations of strategies, tactics, tells and moves that you can put on a player to make him fold or lose a hand when he had or might have made the best hand. These options aren't available to you at Omaha because your opponents will usually be getting the right odds to call to the river because of the pot size and the number of outs they have. Most of the time, you must have the best hand at the river to win the hand.

52. Misreading your hand is more common.

Hold'em players have only one hand made of two cards that they can use in any way with the board to make their hand.

SAID

"Omaha high-low was invented by a sadist and is played by masochists."

— Shane Smith

That's pretty easy to do. Omaha players have four cards with which to make six possible hands and that's further complicated by the fact that they must use exactly two cards from their hand and they can be playing for both high and low at the same time. That's complicated. It's easy to misread your hand and even veteran players do it from time to time.

If you think you have any chance of winning any part of the pot in Omaha, you should always turn all of your cards face-up at the showdown. Other players and the dealer will help figure out what you have and this will help ensure that you don't lose any pots that you were rightfully entitled to. The dealer is required by poker room rules to read your hand before he mucks it, or throws it into the discard pile. You usually don't want to show everyone what you were playing at the end of a hold'em hand because you give too much information to the enemy, but that's not the case in Omaha.

53. "If it's possible, it's probable."

This is an often heard quote used to describe Omaha. It's true, as you can see by now. It's less true in hold'em.

54. "You never know what you have 'til the river."

This is another popular quote about Omaha. With so many cards with which to make so many draws you need to see how every hand turns out. That often takes all of the cards that you can get.

55. Ace-deuce is a good hand.

A wheel is the best low hand and the two best cards in the wheel to have in your hand are the ace-deuce. If there are three other low cards on the board and you don't get counterfeited, you have the nuts. It's like making a royal flush for high. Ace-deuce is a big trap hand in hold'em because it's much harder to make a high hand that will win.

56. You can lose money with the nuts.

It's called "getting quartered." This happens when you make the nut low hand and you have to split the low half of the pot with one or two other players.

Summary

It's amazing how adding just two more cards to a hold'em hand affects every aspect of the game. This is the attraction of Omaha. It appears to be a simple game to play but the expert knows better. Every hand looks like it could be a winner and that's what creates the action. If you're a good hold'em player then you'll also be a good Omaha player as long as you understand how Omaha differs from hold'em, as explained in this chapter.

I just explained how Omaha differs from hold'em in fifty-six different ways. Don't forget, that if you could arrange them into order of importance, skill at hand selection is #1.

Omaha Hand Selection Tips and Guidelines

Being able to correctly decide which hands to play in Omaha is the most important skill neccessary to be a winner. That's because you'll always have to be drawing to the nuts and you'll have to make the best possible hand on the river. Once you have to show your hand to claim either the high or the low end of the pot (or both) the most important thing you'll have going for you is the care you exercised in selecting that hand to begin with.

If you can't be good at the art of hand selection, then ultimately it won't matter how good you might be at other aspects of the game. This is what you need to keep in mind when deciding which hands to play:

1. **Your main objective is to play hands that can scoop the pot.**

   When you play Omaha High-Low, someone usually wins high or low. Keep in mind that you can win the whole pot, both high and low.

2. **You should always draw to the nuts.**

   It does not pay to try to make second- or third-best straights or flushes that might be good at hold'em.

3. **Do not routinely play hands that are too weak for your position.**

   Position is less important in Omaha, but there's still a price for ignoring it's importance.

4. **Only about 15% of hands are playable and profitable.**

   If you play more than that, you're playing too loose.

5. **All four of your cards must work together.**

   All six combinations have to interrelate well. Having one bad card reduces your possible good combinations from six to three.

6. **Ask yourself if every card in your hand has a purpose.**

   This will help you be more thorough and objective when evaluating a hand.

7. **Avoid danglers.**

   A dangler is a card that doesn't fit in at all with the other three cards. If you do have to play a dangler, make sure that your other cards enable you to draw to the nuts.

8. **You can play a half-dangler.**

   A half-dangler is the one card in your hand that you wish could be a little better but it does add a little something to you hand.

9. **Be aware of stopping yourself.**

   You can stop yourself by having the out cards you need in your hand instead of on the board. If you hold J♠ J♣ J♥ 10♥, you have stopped yourself from flopping another jack. You've stopped yourself if all of your cards are of the same suit.

10. **The six different hands you have should give you more than one draw.**

    A straight and a flush, or a straight and a low, or a flush and a low are examples of multiple draws.

11. **Recognize the value of being suited.**

    Suited cards are four times more valuable than unsuited cards.

12. **You should always be trying to make a straight, a flush or a full house for high.**

    Those are the three target hands. In reality, you won't be happy if all you can make is a pair, two pair, or three-of-a-kind. Those hands are not high enough to win at Omaha; don't be content trying to make them.

13. **Two good hold'em hands do not always make a good Omaha hand.**

    For example, Q♥ Q♦ 8♣ 7♣ is a terrible Omaha hand. Of course, if the above is true, then one good hold'em hand by itself is unquestionably unplayable.

14. **Don't overplay or overrate pocket aces.**

    The strength of this hand depends on the other two cards in your hand and what the flop is.

15. **When playing high-low split, avoid playing pocket pairs of deuces through 8s.**

    That's because the card on the board that gives you a set also gives everyone else a low to draw to.

16. It is good to play pocket 9s and higher because a set made with these pairs does not help the low draws.

When you're playing for low, you have to have five cards of 8 or below. One of the cards on the flop must be 8 or lower. Playing pocket 9s or higher eliminates the possibility of a low hand beating you.

17. Be aware of the requirements to hit the jackpot.

If it is four 7s or 8s, then you should play pocket 7s and 8s and accept the little extra risk of making a hand and then losing with it. The size of the jackpot you win will compensate for it. (See jackpot chapter.)

18. Do not play two small pair unless it is A A 2 2, A A 3 3 or 2 2 3 3.

With all other small pairs, you usually can't win for high or low.

19. If you play a pocket pair, the other two cards in your hand should be close in rank to the pair.

A hand like 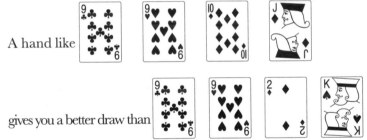 gives you a better draw than

20. In high games, play only the highest cards and make sure you're drawing to the nuts.

Realize that if you get any action, it will only be from other high hands.

21. The worst cards you can have in your hands are the 7s, 8s and 9s.

There are few combinations of winning hands that contain a 7, 8 or 9.

22. If the lowest card in your hand is a 4, 5, 6, 7, 8 or 9, you have a losing hand.

These cards are in the middle range and do not win enough to be profitable at high-low split.

23. Your flush is worth more money to you if you have the ace of your suit but not the king and the queen.

This allows other players to draw dead against you when you have the nut flush and they hold the king or queen.

24. Third-highest flushes are no good unless you back-doored it on the turn and river.

And even then, you have to be very careful.

25. Aces are the key cards in Omaha High-Low split.

You will get one or more 25% of the time and only half of those hands are profitable in the long run.

26. There are only nine Omaha hands that are winners in the long run without having an ace in them:

1. K K Q Q
2. K K J J
3. K K 10 10
4. K K 2 3
5. K K 2 4
6. K K 3 4
7. 2 2 3 4
8. 2 2 3 5
9. 2 2 3 6

FACT!

All of these hands have to be suited at least once to be profitable in the long run; otherwise they are not winners. You need the added equity of being able to make a flush.

27. A 2 X X as your only two low cards is a terrible hand and should not be played.

It's too easy to miss the low draw and/or be counterfeited.

28. The highest cards to hold are A A K K but it is not the best high hand.

The best high hand is a matter of opinion but it is probably A A J 10, double suited.

29. The best high-low split hand is A A 2 3, double suited.

You will win some part of the pot 42% of the time with this hand.

30. A 2 5 6 and A 2 6 7 will enable you to win both high and low when a wheel is possible.

For example, if a 3 4 and 5 come to the board you will have the wheel for low and a 2 3 4 5 6 straight high.

31. A 2 7 8 and A 2 8 X are not good low hands.

You should not play them. The 7 and the 8 are not low enough to be of any practical value.

32. A 2 K Q is popularly believed to be a good hand.

This is because it contains the highest and lowest cards but it is in fact a terrible hand.

33. 2 3 4 5 looks like it should be the near-perfect low hand but it is in fact not very good.

You need exactly one specific card on the flop to help this hand (the ace) and that's not the way to play poker.

34. 3 4 5 6, 4 5 6 7 and 5 6 7 8 are not good low hands.

Don't be seduced by these low cards; they're not low enough. There are too many cards that your opponent can hold that will beat you from the start.

35. One-gap hands like 8 9 J Q have a weakness and that is the fact that your straight draw is a gutshot (an inside straight draw).

This is because you need exactly one specific card to come on the flop—the odds are against it.

36. A 4 X X is not nearly as good as it looks.

In order for you to have the best hand at this point no one else can be holding A 2, A 3 or 2 3. The odds against that are about

500 to 1. The only A 4 X X hands that are profitable are A 4 K K and A 4 Q Q, and they have to be suited.

Hand Selection Summary

It's not necessary to memorize all of the above hand selection criteria. All you need is a general idea and understanding of your main goals. Here they are:

1. Play hands that can scoop the pot by winning both high and low.

2. Be sure that all four of your cards work together.

3. Draw only to the nuts.

4. Realize the importance of being suited.

5. Don't play for low without an ace. Remember that aces are the key cards whether you're playing for high or low.

6. Always have more than one possible draw working.

For a more detailed, in-depth look at Omaha high-low split, you can read my book on the subject, *Winner's Guide to Omaha Poker*.

Omaha Drawing Odds from a Deck of Forty-five Unseen Cards

Note that **outs** are the number of cards available that will improve your hand.

NUMBER OF OUTS	TWO CARDS TO COME	ONE CARD TO COME
30	89.4%	68.2%
29	87.9%	66.0%
28	86.3%	63.6%
27	84.6%	61.4%
26	82.7%	59.1%
25	80.8%	56.8%
24	78.8%	54.5%
23	76.7%	52.3%
22	74.4%	50.0%
21	72.1%	47.7%
20	69.7%	45.5%
19	67.2%	43.2%
18	64.5%	40.1%
17	61.8%	38.6%
16	58.9%	36.7%
15	56.1%	34.1%
14	53.0%	31.8%
13	49.9%	29.6%
12	46.7%	27.3%
11	43.3%	25.0%
10	39.9%	22.7%
9	36.7%	20.5%
8	32.7%	18.2%
7	29.0%	15.6%
6	25.2%	13.6%
5	21.2%	11.4%
4	14.2%	9.1%
3	13.0%	6.8%
2	8.8%	4.5%
1	4.4%	2.3%

Omaha 8 or Better Odds

ODDS OF MAKING A LOW AFTER THE FLOP

YOU HOLD	ODDS OF MAKING 8 OR BETTER
Four different low cards	
Before the flop	49%
Two new low cards on the flop	70%
One new low card on the flop	24%
Three different low cards	
Before the flop	40%
Two new low cards on the flop	72%
One new low card on flop	26%
Two different low cards	
Before the flop	24%
Two new low cards on the flop	59%
One new low card on the flop	16%

Omaha Odds of Interest

- There are 270,725 different four-card combinations that you can be dealt in Omaha. If you ignore specific suits, this is reduced to just 5,277 hands.

> ### FACT!
> If you hold two suited cards, you will end up with the flush 4.02% of the time. If you hold three suited cards, your odds go down to 3.58% (an 11% decrease), and if you hold four suited cards, your odds go down to 3.17% (a 21% decrease from the original).

- 50% of the players will be holding a pocket pair before the flop.

- The odds of being dealt any four-of-a-kind are 20,824 to 1.

- You have a 70% chance of being suited in your first four cards. The odds that you will be double-suited are about 14%.

- If you have a nut flush on the turn, the board will pair on the river 25% of the time. If you have two of the cards on the board in your hand, the board will pair only 20% of the time.

- The odds of one of any three of the thirteen ranks of cards coming on the flop are 46.3%. For example, if you hold A♠ 2♣ 3♥ K♦, and you're hoping not to pair your A, 2, or 3, you will get an ace, deuce or trey on the flop 46.3% of the time.

CHAPTER 10

JACKPOTS

"Bad beats haunt you like bad dreams."

— Alvin Alvarez

Since a poker jackpot can only be won in a public card room, and since Texas hold'em is the most popular game spread in public card rooms, I will use Texas hold'em as the game to teach you what you need to know about jackpots.

There are two ways that the average low limit poker player can score a big win in the game. One way is to win or place high in a poker tournament. The other way is to hit a jackpot. You hit a jackpot by making a very good hand, such as A♠ A♣ A♥ J♦ J♣, and then losing with it!

Actually, it will look like this:

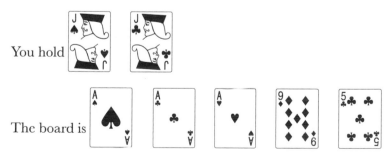

You hold

The board is

Another player holds

You have a full house, aces full of jacks and your opponent has four aces. You should also fulfill six other criteria with this hand:

- You made the minimum high hand required, which is aces full of jacks or better. This would also work if you held pocket queens or kings.

- There were four or more players dealt into the hand.

- There was a minimum of $20 or $30 in the pot, depending on the poker room rules.

- You, as the loser of the hand, are playing both of your hole cards.

- The winner of the hand has made four-of-a-kind, or better, and

- The winner's kicker beats the board.

Before I go any further, I want to make a few comments about jackpots. Any time there is money involved in anything, there is always the possibility of misuse, abuse and plain ole' outright theft of the money. Here are a few things that you should know about jackpots:

1. **The money that goes into a jackpot pool comes from the players.**

   Once a hand reaches a certain threshold one dollar from every hand that is played is taken out of the pot and set aside for the jackpot. It is your money! It does not belong to the casino or the poker room; it is not the property of the poker room manager and casino management cannot touch that money. The money in the jackpot is a side bet between the players, collected $1 at a time.

When the Grand Casino opened in Biloxi and Gulfport, Mississippi, they had a jackpot. They also had a notice on the poker room wall that they were taking a 15% "administrative fee" out of the jackpot money for the costs of administering the jackpot, including the cost of counting, physically protecting the jackpot money and doing the paperwork associated with it.

They took thousands and thousands of dollars from the players over the course of several years before the Mississippi Gaming Commission ruled that they must eliminate the fee. This money probably did help defray the costs of running the poker room, which is what the rake is designed to do. So, those players were getting raked twice.

Another incident happened when the Bayou Caddy Jubilee in Lakeshore, Mississippi closed their poker room while they still had tens of thousands of dollars in the poker jackpot. They took that money from the poker players and used it to enhance the size of some jackpots on selected slot machines. In other words, they took the poker players' money and gave it to the slot players. A group of poker players sued them over this action.

2. **Some poker rooms make the jackpot exceedingly difficult to hit by requiring that four-of-a-kind or better be beaten by a higher four-of-a-kind or better.**

The odds against this happening, especially if both players have to use both of their hole cards, are astronomical. So, why do they do it?

It's because they're greedy. The requirements to hit the jackpot are so ridiculously out of sight that it takes years for the jackpot to get hit. And that's exactly what happens. The jackpot grows steadily and the poker room management uses the size of the jackpot as advertising to attract poker players. This ensures that they have plenty of games to rake and that in turn ensures that the poker room makes a profit for management. It makes the poker room manager look good to his bosses and he is using your money to do it. Also, when a jackpot takes several years to go over $100,000, who do you think is collecting the bank interest on that money? I promise you it's not you.

3. **Some poker rooms have a rule that they can take the $1 jackpot drop when the pot reaches $20 but the players are not eligible to hit the jackpot until the pot reaches $30.**

This means that if there is between $20 and $29 in the pot, you cannot win the jackpot if it is hit even though you've already paid the $1.

Why do they do this? I have asked around and no one will give me a good answer. So, logic tells me that this rule is a device that the poker room management uses to keep a jackpot from being hit as often. It probably works because at the lower limits a big portion of the pots are going to be between $20 and $29. It keeps the jackpot amount big so they can use it to attract players. I believe it is probably an illegal rule because it requires you to pay for something that you can't get. Imagine playing a slot machine with a progressive jackpot, playing the maximum number of coins so you qualify for the jackpot and then when you hit it, management tells you that you can't have the jackpot because it's not big enough yet!

> ### FACT!
> The jackpot money belongs to the players and not to the poker room or casino management.

4. **Some poker rooms require that a minimum number of players, usually four, must be dealt in the hand in order to qualify for the jackpot.**

Why can't two or three players play for the jackpot? This is a rule based on management's ignorance of the jackpot odds. It's an arbitrary rule that is not based on any facts.

5. **Some poker rooms make it a rule that the winner's hole cards must both play.**

That means that in the case of four aces, the winner's kicker must be higher than any other card on the board. This is a bad rule that probably cannot withstand a Gaming Commission challenge because it requires you to play six cards to make up your poker hand. Why does the rule exist? To make it harder to hit the jackpot and therefore to keep the jackpot big, which the poker room then uses to attract more players to play in games that they can rake.

6. **Some poker rooms insist that if the game is a little short-handed and the players want a reduced rake, they cannot play for the jackpot.**

In other words, the poker room manager will say, "Yes, you can play with a reduced rake [usually just $1 maximum], but this makes you ineligible for the jackpot."

Of all the rules that are related to jackpots, this one is the worst because, in my opinion, it is nothing but a scam that the poker room knowingly perpetrates upon the players. Why? Because there is absolutely no relationship between the amount of money that the house rakes to meet their expenses and the side bet that the players make among themselves to put into a jackpot pool. The jackpot money belongs to the players, it comes from the players, it is held in trust by the poker room for the players and only a player can win any of that money. It is not related to anything else that goes on in the poker room.

So why does the poker room management tell you that the rake and the jackpot are connected? Again, it's because they're greedy. They know that most players will want to play for a jackpot if there is one. Most players, when told that they can't play for that jackpot if the rake is reduced, will change their mind and say, "Go ahead and leave the rake where it is because we don't want to hit the jackpot and not win it just because we're a little short handed."

Jackpot Odds

There is no such thing as knowing the exact odds of hitting a jackpot. Have you ever been in a game where someone said after the hand was over, "We would have hit the jackpot if I hadn't thrown my hand away before the flop"? That's why you can never know the exact odds of hitting a jackpot. You cannot account for the actions of all the players with a mathematical certainty. All you can know for sure is that the more players there are in the game who see every flop, especially when they're holding an ace, the more likely it is you can eventually hit a jackpot. On the other hand, it's going to take a very long time to hit a jackpot if you're in a very tight game where hardly anyone ever sees the flop and most hands don't go past it.

The only way you can know the approximate odds of hitting a jackpot is to use hindsight, and that's what I have done. The poker room managers of three different casinos have given me access to their hold'em jackpot histories. This is not privileged, classified or secret information. This information is available to anyone who cares to keep an eye on the jackpot and record how much each jackpot was when it was hit. Then, knowing how each jackpot dollar is distributed (75%-15%-10% or 67%-33%) you can calculate how many hands were dealt, on average, between jackpot hands.

I have ten years' of statistics from three poker rooms for a total of thirty years of hold'em records. It turns out that the magic number is 12,500. That's about how many hands it takes, on average, to hit a jackpot. This takes into account loose play, tight play, players who play every ace, players who only selectively play aces, the play of small pocket pairs and all the other variables that can't be calculated in advance.

Knowing that it takes 12,500 hands to hit a jackpot is not really the whole story. Assuming a full game, every time a hand is dealt there will be forty-five individual hand matchups. In a ten-handed game, all of the players at the table can matchup all of their hands a total of forty-five different ways. So you can see this more clearly, this is how each hand can matchup with the others:

1. The player in the first seat can matchup his hand with the players in seats 2, 3, 4, 5, 6, 7, 8, 9, and 10 for a total of nine matchups. TOTAL: 9

2. The player in the second seat can matchup his hand with the players in seats 3, 4, 5, 6, 7, 8, 9 and 10 for a total of eight matchups. TOTAL: 9+8=17

3. The player in the third seat can matchup his hand with the players in seats 4, 5, 6, 7, 8, 9, and 10 for a total of seven matchups. TOTAL: 9+8+7=24

4. The player in the fourth seat can matchup his hand with the players in seats 5, 6, 7, 8, 9, and 10 for a total of six matchups. TOTAL: 9+8+7+6=30

5. The player in the fifth seat can matchup his hand with the players in seats 6, 7, 8, 9, and 10 for a total of five matchups. TOTAL: 9+8+7+6+5=35

6. The player in the sixth seat can matchup his hand with the players in seats 7, 8, 9, and 10 for a total of four matchups. TOTAL: 9+8+7+6+5+4=39

7. The player in the seventh seat can matchup his hand with the players in seats 8, 9, and 10 for a total of three matchups. TOTAL: 9+8+7+6+5+4+3=42

8. The player in the eighth seat can matchup his hand with the players in seats 9 and 10 for a total of two matchups. TOTAL: 9+8+7+6+5+4+3+2=44

9. The player in the ninth seat can matchup his hand with the player in the tenth seat for only one matchup. Total: 9+8+7+6+5+4+3+2+1=45

This means that for every hand dealt, there are forty-five hand matchups. If it takes 12,500 hands to hit a jackpot, then there are a total of 562,500 hand matchups (12,500 x 45 = 562,500). That is for a full, ten-handed game. If the games were all nine-handed, then there would only be thirty-six matchups per hand and you would have to divide 562,500 by thirty-six to get the number of hands that it would take to hit the jackpot. That comes out to be 15,625 hands (562,500/36 = 15,625).

You can see that having just one player missing from a full table increases the odds against hitting the jackpot by exactly 25% (12,500 + 25% = 15,625) instead of 10% as you might expect. That's because the number of possible matchups decreases geometrically rather than arithmetically as each player leaves the game. Using the above math as a foundation, here's a table that will tell you the odds against hitting a jackpot with various numbers of players in the game.

Odds Against Hitting a Jackpot (Texas Hold'em)

# OF PLAYERS	562,500	DIVIDED BY # OF MATCHUPS	# OF HANDS NEEDED TO HIT JACKPOT
10	562,500	45	12,500
9	562,500	36	15,625
8	562,500	28	20,089
7	562,500	21	26,785
6	562,500	15	37,500
5	562,500	10	56,250
4	562,500	6	93,750
3	562,500	3	187,500
2	562,500	1	562,500

Notice that if the game is only half-full, then the odds against hitting the jackpot more than quadruple rather than just double. This table also shows why, if the game is very short-handed, you should not play for the jackpot if it is very small. That's because with the game already being short-handed, the pots will be much smaller than usual and the $1 that's taken out for the jackpot will be a much larger percentage of the pot than usual. You will make more money in the long run if you leave that dollar in the pot where you can win it now.

Do not try to get a share of that jackpot in the next few hours by making a bet that you can beat the 56,000+ to 1 odds. If your game is five-handed and you're playing thirty-five hands per hour for the next three hours, then you will have played 105 hands. 56,250 divided by 105 comes to 535.7. Your odds of hitting the jackpot in the next three hours are 534.7 to 1. Would you rather have the extra $30 or so that you will win today by not playing for the jackpot or would you rather give up that money in exchange for the long odds of hitting the jackpot? That $30 saved 535 times equals $16,071. Would your share of any jackpot be that big if you hit it? Usually not.

There's one other thing about jackpots that you should know and it concerns the Omaha jackpot, if there is one. My research has revealed that an Omaha jackpot is about four times easier to hit than a hold'em jackpot. Why? It's because there are more hand matchups in Omaha than there are in hold'em.

An Omaha player who is dealt A♣ J♣ 9♥ 7♥ doesn't have just one hand; he has six of them. They are: 1. A♣ J♣, 2. A♣ 9♥, 3. A♣ 7♥, 4. J♣ 9♣, 5. J♣ 7♥, and 6. 9♥ 7♥. Just two Omaha players can matchup their hands thirty-six different ways! It takes nine hold'em players to do that. How many times have you been in a hold'em game and one of the players had the minimum losing hand to hit the jackpot and no one beat him?

In an Omaha game every player in the hand will have six times as many hands as he would in a hold'em game and, because of that, someone will beat him about four times as often as he would in the hold'em game. Why four times and not six times as often? Two reasons:

1. It's impossible for 2s, 3s and 4s to make a qualifying hand under most circumstances.

2. Some Omaha games require that the losing hand be four-of-a-kind rather than just aces full.

What does this mean to you and how do you take advantage of this information? Assuming you're going to let the jackpots be the deciding factor in your game selection, here is some advice:

1. **When you enter the poker room and are deciding which games to play, look at the hold'em and Omaha jackpots.**

If the hold'em jackpot is more than four times as large as the Omaha jackpot, then you should play hold'em. Alternatively, if the Omaha jackpot is less than one-fourth as big as the hold'em jackpot, then you should still play hold'em. Multiply the Omaha jackpot by four and then compare that number to the hold'em jackpot. Play in the game with the larger number.

2. **Learn to play Omaha if you don't already know how.**

Assuming you are going to be a poker player in the larger sense of the word, and not just a hold'em player, you should know how to play more than one poker game. As you can see, it's worth money to you.

3. **Next, you have to determine how many tables there are of each game, because the jackpot can only be hit at one table.**

For example, if the hold'em jackpot is $8,000 and the Omaha jackpot is $2,000, then it's a mathematical toss-up whether to play hold'em or Omaha. But, if there are two hold'em games going, and only one Omaha game going, then that cuts the odds in half that you'll be at the right table when the hold'em jackpot is hit and it clearly makes Omaha the better game.

4. **If you are new to Omaha or you play but not that well, but you think that the jackpot is worth playing for, ask the card room manager to start an Omaha game with the lowest limits that will still qualify for the jackpot.**

You can probably get a $2 to $4 game going, especially if you let the other players in the room know what you're doing and why.

FACT!

Some poker players are almost exclusively "jackpot chasers" that is, they move from poker room to poker room and from game to game in an effort to play in the one game in town that has the biggest jackpot with the best odds of being hit. This type of play can significantly add to your hourly rate.

Don't forget that the money in the jackpot belongs to the players and that you're the customer.

If you are successful at getting this game started, then the most important thing is that you make sure it is for high only, and not high-low split. That's because high-low split is a game that requires a great deal of skill to play well and those games are usually populated by experts.

CHAPTER 11

PINEAPPLE HOLD'EM

"I know of nothing so pleasant to the mind,
as the discovery of anything which is at
once new and valuable."

— Abraham Lincoln

Pineapple hold'em is played just like Texas hold'em but with one important variation. That is, players are dealt three cards face down to start, instead of just two, and they have to discard one of those cards before the flop. There is a deal, a round of betting, and then a discard before the flop.

This has several different effects on the game, as compared to hold'em. The major differences are:

- The quality of the starting hands is better.
- More hands will be suited.
- There will be more pocket pairs.
- Players will flop a set more often.
- More straight and flush draws will be made.
- A full house will be more likely when the board pairs.

All of these differences combined mean that the final winning hands will be a little better than they would be in hold'em.

Since the biggest difference in the game requires that you have some skill at carding, here are some general guidelines:

1. That round of betting before the flop is very important. It tells you how strong your hand must be to win the hand. Based on the pre-flop action, you have to decide if it will take a straight, a flush or a full house to win the hand.

2. If there are fewer players and the betting is not heavy, then one of the weaker, easier to make hands might win for you.

3. If the pre-flop action is heavy, with everyone playing and raising, then it's going to take a very good hand to win.

4. If you have a choice between a pocket pair or two suited cards, you should usually choose the pair. That's because, statistically, it's almost equally likely to flop a set as a four-flush. You also have the added assurance of not having to worry about making the flush or not after flopping the draw.

5. If you have big slick—A K hole cards—and a nut flush draw, such as A♦ K♥ 8♦, you should usually play the flush draw. That's because big slick is a very vulnerable hand in Pineapple. It's too easy for another player to be holding A A or K K.

6. If you have a big pair with a big kicker, such as A K K, A Q Q, A J J or A 10 10, you should usually draw to the pair. The exception is if you think, based on the preflop betting, that your pocket pair is already beat before the flop. In that case, your best bet is to draw to the straight.

7. Do not draw to your own discards. J Q K is a bad starting hand because no matter which card you get rid of, you'll need it to make the straight.

8. Discarding an ace always adds value to your hand. This is especially true if you also hold a high pocket pair because you know that anyone holding A♣ A♠ now has exactly half his usual chance of flopping a set.

9. A pair of pocket aces is a vulnerable hand in Pineapple. Any time you can bet and raise before and on the flop to elimi-

nate players will greatly improve your chances of winning the hand.

10. Drawing to the low end of a straight or to a small flush is dangerous and expensive in Pineapple. To a lesser extent, the same it true about trying to make a small full house.

This is a short chapter and that might lead you to believe that Pineapple hold'em is a very easy game to play and there's not much too it. If that's what you're thinking, you're wrong! Everything that was said in the Texas hold'em chapter still applies to Pineapple.

CHAPTER 12

LIAR'S POKER

> *"Lying is good. It's the only way we ever*
> *get at the truth."*
>
> — **Fyodor Dostoevsky**

Liar's poker is usually played with good ol' United States currency, such as $1, $2, $5 or $10 bills, instead of a deck of cards. Even though you don't use cards to play this game, it still qualifies as a poker game. Liar's poker meets the minimum requirements to qualify as a poker game because it contains the following essential elements of poker:

- You are playing for or risking something of value. In this case, it's the actual bills that you're using to play the game.

- There are rounds of betting, raising, reraising, folding and calling.

- There is an element of deception and opportunities to deceive by bluffing and lying during the game.

- Someone wins and loses and money changes hands at the end of each game.

- There is the appropriate ratio of skill and luck in the play of the game. Bad players can get lucky and win and good players will not win every time. But, just like in a traditional poker game, the good players will eventually beat the bad players in the long run.

How to Play Liar's Poker

Liar's poker can be played with as few as two players or as many as can fit around a table or into a room. As a practical matter, it's best played with six to eight players as the maximum.

The only other ingredient essential to the game is a large supply of U.S. currency, in any denomination. It does not have to be the same denomination for the entire playing session, as long as every player uses the same denomination for each game.

It is important that you have enough bills so that each player will have a big enough supply to play with that no one particular bill can be picked out of the supply. There are two common ways to meet this need. The first is to have all the players bring twenty or more bills with him to the game. The other option is to get a pack or two of one-hundred $1 bills from the bank.

The entire game revolves around the serial numbers on the bills. For that reason the bills should be used, well-circulated, and completely random. A pack of freshly-printed, cut and packaged bills directly from the mint is the exact opposite of what you want for this game, because the serial numbers would be sequential and there would be very little difference between the bills. Once you know what numbers are on one bill, you pretty much know what the numbers of the other bills are. And so does everyone else. It would be like playing poker with only the spades in the deck—everyone would make a flush every time.

Players can purchase their bills from the pack that came from the bank. If the players brought their own bills to the game, then each player contributes an equal number of bills to a pot. The pot is mixed, scrambled and shuffled and then each player draws one bill from the pot. The idea is that no one should be able to see the serial number of his or any other bill before he gets it.

This one bill constitutes your entire private hand—do not show it to another player. It is customary to fold the bill in fourths so that you are looking at the serial number and no one else can see it. Each serial number contains eight digits with a letter before and after it. A typical serial number looks like this:

B 4 4 5 5 8 4 7 0 G

or

D 4 8 9 3 4 6 3 2 *

The letters are ignored and are totally irrelevant to the play of the game. The * (asterisk) is used to indicate that it is a replacement bill that was printed to replace an original bill that was somehow defective or imperfect when it was printed. It is also irrelevant to the play of the game.

It is considered unethical and contrary to the spirit of the game for any player to try to memorize the serial numbers of any bills he brings to the game. Although the chance is very small that he will know the location of the bill during the game (either in the pot or in a player's hand), he has a big advantage if he knows it's in play. It is also improper to bring "ringer" bills to the game. The serial number of a ringer bill might look like this:

C 3 3 5 1 1 1 1 D

or this:

F 2 4 0 0 0 0 0 2 L

A ringer bill is one that has four or more of the same numbers in the serial number.

The odds of having four of one number on a bill is less than one in twenty-three and the odds of having five of the same number on a bill are about one in 200. Knowing that a ringer bill is in play is definitely cheating.

On the other hand, the advantage gained from this knowledge is not that great and good for only the game currently being played. Since it's obviously easy to cheat at this game if you wanted to, Liar's Poker is usually played for low limits among close, trustworthy friends. Since, as they say, "It's the thought that counts," don't lose sight of the fact that anyone who tries to cheat only just a little bit is still a thief trying to steal your money.

The Object of the Game

The object of the game is to win the other player's bills, of course! You do that by trying to guess, estimate, deduce or calculate the total quantity of a particular number among all the bills in play, including your own. There are ten numbers, from lowest to highest: 2, 3, 4, 5, 6, 7, 8, 9, 0 and 1. The 0 represents a 10 and the 1 is an ace. The poker hands you can make in this game are pairs, trips, four-of-a-kind, five-of-a-kind, and on up the scale. There are no straights, flushes or full- houses.

If there are five of you in the game then you have a total of forty numbers in play (5 x 8 digits in each serial number = 40). The object of the game is to guess the exact total—or come as close as you can without going over—of a certain number contained in all of the bills. That certain number is determined by the players and their bids, as you will see.

Play of the Game

To start the game, each player draws a bill at random from the pot. One player starts the game by announcing a bid. He may look at his bill, see three 4s, and bid, "Three 4s." The next player may have a 4 in his bill and he will bid four 4s. Remember, they are trying to guess how many 4s there are combined in all the bills.

As an extremely simple and obvious example, I will continue with the 4s to show you how the game works. Each player, in turn, must either make a bid higher than the previous bid or he may pass without making any bid at all. Bidding escalates until someone says something like, "Nine 4s," and no one in the game wants to bid anything higher that that. In other words, everyone passes until the bid comes back around to the player who bid the nine 4s.

You may bid a lower quantity if it is of a higher number than the number currently being bid on. For example, you may bid on any number higher than 4s, such as five 5s, but you may not bid on the 2s or 3s. You may also skip to any other number higher than 4s if you like. They do not have to be bid on in numerical succession.

Whoever made the last bid without getting raised is the player in the hot seat. All of the players then show their bills to each other and they then add up the total of the bid number, in this case, 4s. If there are indeed nine or more 4s among all the bills, then the bidder is the winner and he collects one bill from each of the players.

If there are fewer than nine 4s among all of the bills, then he has overbid and lost the game. In some games, there is a bonus provision. If a player's bid is exactly on the mark, then he is paid double, but it is an optional rule that must be agreed upon by all the players before the game starts.

Tips for Playing Liar's Poker

1. **You should probably have a rule against thinking out loud or verbalizing your mental analysis during the game.**

   Poker, even Liar's Poker, is a game of concealed information and it's not a good idea to educate the opposition while the game is in progress. If you have to recount the previous action and bids, do it silently.

2. **When bidding on 8s and aces, be sure that the players speak clearly.**

   Aces and 8s can sound alike and that can lead to a lot of confusion and disagreement. It helps if you can substitute another word for aces, like bullets.

3. **Do not criticize another player's ability or strategy.**

   Beside being a rude thing to do, it encourages them to play better against you—something you don't want.

4. **Do not overuse your right to call in all the bills for inspection when you lose a hand.**

   This can lead to hard feelings and ruin the friendliness of the game.

HOME POKER GAMES

"The more wild cards and crazy rules, the greater the expert's advantage."

— John R. Crawford

For the first one hundred years that poker was played in America, most games took place in bars, saloons, riverboats, gambling houses, or on the dusty trail. The enforcement of Prohibition in the 1920s closed public poker rooms. This led to the explosion of private games held at the players' homes.

Home poker games are now an American tradition. If you're going to host a game or play at someone's house, there are a few details that must be worked out in advance and there are some questions that have to be answered. You know why you're playing poker, and you know how to play poker. So, the remaining questions will have to answer the who, what, when and where.

> ## FACT!
> It was the state of Nevada that was the 36th, and final state needed, to ratify the Prohibition amendment to the Constitution.

Here's a list of things to consider when having a home game:

1. Who's house are you going to play at?

2. Who are you going to invite to the game? Who are you not going to invite?

3. When does the game begin and end? Is it okay to leave early? Is it okay to play later than originally planned? How do you handle players who habitually show up late?

4. Who has the final word in deciding disputes or irregularities?

SAID

"The better part of one's life consists of his friendships."

— Abraham Lincoln

5. What food or drinks will be provided? How will they be paid for?

6. Will there be a rake or a time charge for playing?

7. Will alcohol be served?

8. Will there be a written set of rules? Can you all agree on the rules in advance?

9. Will you play with chips instead of cash?

10. Who will be the banker?

11. Will borrowing money during the game be allowed?

12. Can you agree on the ranks of hands? This is especially important if you're using wild cards. Five-of-a-kind outranks all other hands.

13. What is the best low hand? Are you using the California Lowball scale where a A 2 3 4 5 wheel is the lowest hand? Or, are you using the Kansas City scale where the lowest hand is 2 3 4 5 7, with straights and flushes not being allowed in low hands?

14. What kind of cards are you using? Are the decks new and unmarked? Do you have plenty of replacement decks?

15. Are you playing table stakes or is playing on credit allowed? What is an acceptable maximum amount for an IOU?

16. Are the losers expected to pay up at the end of the game or at the beginning of the next game?

17. What constitutes a misdeal and what are the misdeal procedures?

18. Will there be a limit on the dealer's choice games?

19. Will asking to see what the next card would have been after the hand is over, otherwise known as rabbit hunting, be allowed? I don't think that it should be allowed because it's pointless, slows up the game, and sometimes leads to arguments.

20. What happens when a player runs out of money in the middle of the hand? How are you going to handle the all-in question? Are you going to allow a player to draw light from the pot?

21. How many raises are allowed? Three, four or five? Some home games allow every active player a chance to raise, regardless of how many raises have occurred in front of him.

22. Will check-raising be allowed? I recommend that it is not allowed in low limit games but it should be allowed in higher limit games. That's because novice recreational home players have a preconceived notion that check-raising is a dirty trick. It is only as they gain more experience and skill, and perhaps read some poker books, that players come to see check-raising as a regular part of the game.

23. Can a player's spouse or friend sit in for him and play his hands while he's taking a break?

24. Will you allow straddles? Will you allow players to play the overs? Are you going to play with the kill rule in effect?

25. Can the dealer ante for everyone?

26. How are you going to declare in High-Low games? There are three common methods:

> **A.** Cards speak is when the best hand is determined by a show of hands. All casino games are played cards speak, and if you turn your hand face up at the end of the hand, the dealer will read the hand for you. This is done in turn beginning with the last bettor.

SAID

"Poker among friends and colleagues should not drive anyone to the poorhouse but should be expensive enough to test skill and make it interesting."

— Harry S Truman

B. Chip declare is when you use poker chips to announce which pot you are going for. One chip is for low, two is for high and three is for swing.

C. To Swing is to declare for both high and low in a high-low split game.

27. How are you going to handle a swinger who loses in one direction? Does he still win in the other direction or must he win outright both ways to get any part of the pot?

28. Who gets the odd chip when dividing the pot?

Here are some additional tips to insure that you have a smooth home game.

1. Always cut the cards. Every dealer should offer the deck to the player on his right for a cut.

SAID

"Trust everybody, but cut the cards."

— Peter Finley Dunne

2. Some home players allow the deck to be cut again during the play of the game if the player who wants the cut donates $1 to the pot.

3. Do not criticize another player's actions or quality of play.

4. Be a good winner and a good loser. Nobody wins or loses all the time. Be friendly and don't hurt another player's feelings over his loses.

5. Do not needlessly delay when it is your turn to act. It is rude to deliberately waste everyone's time when you know what you're going to do anyway.

SAID

"Courtesy is as much a mark of a gentleman as courage."

— Theodore Roosevelt

6. Keep all of your cards in plain view of everyone all the time. This helps reduce the number of misdeals and players acting out of turn.

7. Do not deliberately act out of turn.

8. Do not help another player with advice about what to do or not do in the middle of the hand. The rule is: One player per hand.

9. Do not allow spectators or kibitzers to hang around the poker table.

10. Do not take chips off the table during the game.

I think the best overall advice is to always remember that it is a home game and not a public poker room or casino game. Everyone should conduct themselves in a relaxed, friendly manner and decisions and disputes should be settled in a way that keeps the personal relationships intact. To do otherwise usually leads to the game breaking up and you don't want that to happen.

Popular Home Games

Most of the dealer's choice games are already covered in the draw, stud and hold'em chapters of this book. However, there are two more games that are extremely popular home games, Anaconda and Seven Twenty-Seven.

Anaconda   This is a high-low split game with many betting rounds and a lot of action.

Each player is dealt seven cards face down. There is a round of betting. The player chooses his best four cards to make either a high or a low hand. He then passes the other three cards to the player on his left, while receiving three cards from the player on his right. He selects his best five-card hand, while mucking the two extra cards. Then he arranges the order of the cards to roll face up one at a time. There is a round of betting. Each player turns up one card. There is a round of betting. The next three cards are then turned face up with a round of betting between each card.

When only one card remains face down, each player declares for high or low. Some games allow for an additional round of betting at this point, now that everyone knows who their competition is. The last card is revealed and the winners are determined.

Your best strategy for this game is to try to make a wheel, or a 6 4 for low, or a full house of aces-full or better for high. Most other hands are losers.

You should remember which cards you passed because if you don't see one of them face up in your neighbor's hand, then you will always know what his hole card is. Conversely, make sure that you always expose one of the cards that you received.

Seven Twenty-Seven

This is a game where the hands are determined by the point values of the cards. The object of the game is to have your cards total as close as you can to either seven or twenty-seven. The perfect swing hand is A A 5. That's because $1 + 1 + 5 = 7$ and $11 + 11 + 5 = 27$. Face cards count as one-half point.

Each player is dealt one down card and one up card. There is a round of betting. Each player then has the option of asking for another card to increase the point total of his hand. A player does not have to take a card if he does not want one. There is a round of betting after each player has had the option of taking a card or not. This continues until everyone passes. At this point the dealer then asks everyone again if he wants a card. If everyone passes a second time, the game is over. There is another round of betting and then everyone declares for high, low, or swing. There is a round of betting after declaring and then there is a showdown. High hand splits the pot with the low hand.

This game is also played as two twenty-two, three thirty-three and four forty-four. The higher the number, the more betting rounds there will be and the bigger the pots will be.

If you are a dedicated traditional poker player and you have not yet tried one of these two games, I heartily recommend that you do. You'll be pleasantly surprised to discover what fun they are to play.

"People's hobbies are more their measure than their jobs. Never mind what they are forced to do, like fight wars or make a living or embrace the kings's religion. What do they choose to do in their spare time, if they have any?"

— Robert Byrne

CHAPTER 14

POT ODDS

*"Don't let adverse facts stand in the
way of a good decision."*

— General Colin Powell

The concept of pot odds is easy to understand. It is simply the relationship, expressed as a ratio, between the size of the bet you are making or calling in comparison to the number of those bets in the pot. For example, if there is $12 in the pot and you have to call a $3 bet, then you are getting pot odds of 4 to 1, expressed as 4:1. The "4" in the equation is the number of bets in the pot (not the amount of money) and the "1" in the equation represents your bet. If you have to call $6 with that same $12 in the pot, then you are getting pot odds of 2:1. If you have to call $8 with a $12 pot, then you are getting pots odds of 1½:1.

Sometimes, oddsmakers will factor out any fractions to make the odds easier to understand and they do this by multiplying the odds by two or three. Odds of 1½:1 then becomes odds of 3:2 and odds of 3½:1 becomes 7:2. It's exactly the same thing; it's just easier to read and understand.

TIP

When you are in a hand, and you have a hand that you know you're going to be playing, you should always be aware of what the pot odds are.

When you are in a hand, and you have a hand that you know you're going to be playing, you should always be aware of what the pot odds are. This is a relatively easy thing to do once you get into the habit. Knowing the pot odds will have a positive effect on your hourly rate, which is what it's all about. When the action starts at the beginning of the hand, count the number of bets that go into the pot. Do not get sidetracked, as so many players do, with the actual amount of money in the pot.

Since Texas hold'em is the most popular poker game and it's the easiest to understand, I will use examples from hold'em to teach you about pot odds.

If you are in the dealer's position, you are last to act throughout each betting round of the game. This is called being **on the button**. Assume you're on the button with K♥ 10♥. The big blind is already in the hand so you start counting, "one, two, three," and so on for each bet that goes into the pot. If there are six callers by the time the action gets to you, and you call, then you are getting pot odds of 6:1 with the small blind left to act. If he calls, then you are getting odds of 7:1.

What if someone raises? If everyone calls then there will be fourteen bets in the pot, not counting the two bets that you called with. This is a ratio of 14:2, which is the same as 7:1. What if it's re-raised? If everyone calls then there will be twenty-one bets in the pot, not counting the three bets you called with. This is a ratio of 21:3, which is still a ratio of 7:1. Listen to the dealer when all the action is completed before the flop. He will announce, "eight players." This will help you keep the count straight. Continue counting the number of bets that go into the pot on the flop.

At this point, you should recall the total number of bets in the pot, subtract one, and then divide that number by two after the action on the flop is complete. Why? Say there are twenty-eight bets in the pot. These are small bets, if you're playing in a $3-$6 or otherwise structured game. The rake, the jackpot drop and the dealer's tip all come out of the pot, if you win it. Subtract one bet to account for this loss. If you want to play it safe, then subtract two bets. If you're playing in a $2-$4 game and the maximum rake is 10% up to $4, then you should subtract two or even three bets from the preflop count. A $4 rake, a $1 jackpot drop and a 50¢ to $1 dealer tip is a lot to take out of a pot. It pays for you to be the one player in the game who knows to take this into account ahead of time.

So, twenty-eight bets minus one bet equals twenty-seven bets in the pot after the action on the flop is complete. The reason you now divide that number by two is that it represents the number of small bets and since the bet doubles from this point on, you need to convert the count to big bets. Dividing twenty-seven by two gives you thirteen big bets. I recommend you drop any fractions because this gives you a very slight cushion in your favor. Now there are thirteen bets in the pot and all you have to do is add one for each additional bet that goes in the pot. Your ultimate goal is to know how many bets are in the pot when it's your turn to act on the river.

After your decision to call with a hand to see the flop, the next most important decision you will make during the play of the hand will be whether or not to bet, or to call a bet on the river. That's because decisions regarding betting for value and bluffing require that you know exactly how many bets are in the pot at that point. When there are no more cards to come, when you know exactly what the nuts are, when you know how close your hand is to the nuts and you have an idea of what your opponents' hand might be, you also need to know how many bets there are in the pot. That's because all mistakes are not created equal. A mistake on the flop might cost you one bet but a mistake on the river will cost you the entire pot.

How do the pot odds affect how you play a hand? The answer lies in the fact that you somehow have to connect your pot odds to the value of your hand. Let me start with a few simple examples that will work toward answering that question.

You and I are going to flip a coin and bet on the outcome. Every time it comes up heads, you win, and I will pay you $1. Every time it comes up tails, I win, and you will pay me $1. How much money do you think you would be winning after 20, 100 or 500 trials? The fact is, we would be about even, especially as the number of trials gets larger and larger. That's because this is a situation where the pot odds exactly equal the odds of winning the bet. Both of those odds are 1:1.

There's nothing I can do to improve my chances of winning the bet. So, how can I make money from this bet? The answer is that I have to change the odds that I'm being paid when I win a bet. If you now pay me $2 every time I win the bet, and I pay you $1, I will be a winner in the long run. After 500 trials, we will each win 250 times. I will pay you $250 but you will pay me $500. I will be a net $250 ahead. That's because I was getting pot odds of 2:1 when my chances of winning the hand were 1:1. Obviously, the only thing that changed was the pot odds.

Suppose we're betting on the roll of a single die (singular for dice) where the outcome has to be a 1, 2, 3, 4, 5 or a 6. We're betting that the roll will come up a 6. If we bet $1 on each roll of the die, with no odds, then I will lose the bet five times for every one time I win. The odds against me are 5:1. If I could get you to pay me $5 every time I win, I would break even in the long run. Obviously I need the odds to pay better than the actual odds of winning the bet in order to get ahead.

How does this relate to poker odds? Suppose you have two hearts and you get two more on the flop. You know that the odds of making the flush are about one out of three, or 2:1. For your flush draw to be profitable, the pot must pay you odds of better than 2:1. This assumes that making the flush is the only way you can win. In real life, you will often win without making the flush, either by pairing one of your hole cards, by making a backdoor straight, by just having the highest card at the end of the hand, or by betting as a bluff and not getting called.

SAID

"For the true gambler, money is never an end in itself. It's a tool, like language or thought."

— Lancey, in "The Cincinnatti Kid"

If you flop a four-flush, you have nine outs and your exact chances of making the hand are 35%, which is slightly better than 2:1 against. If you flop an open-end straight draw, you have eight outs and your chances of making the straight are 31.5%, slightly worse than 2:1 against. I tell you this because as a practical matter, you can look at both of these draws as having the same odds, which is 2:1 against. That's because you have to do some rounding off in the game. If your opponent bets $6 and you're going to call, you have to call $6, not the $5.82 or the $6.13 that your hand might theoretically be worth. I can tell you, that in most instances, "close enough" is good enough if you know that that's the situation you're in.

Recall the chapter on Texas hold'em where I discuss dominated hands. Most dominated hands are 4:1 underdogs. That is, their chances of winning against the other hand were only between 18% and 21%. I'll bet that fact left you with the impression that you should never play one of these hands, yet I deliberately did not make any recommendations about playing the hands. I want to tell you that, under the right conditions, most of those dominated hands are great hands to play! When I say "the right conditions" I mean you have to have the right pot odds to play the hand.

If you're playing a hand that's a 4:1 underdog, then you need pot odds of at least 4:1 just to break even in the long run. That's because on average you'll call a bet and lose four times and then you'll win those bets back on the fifth time, when you win the hand. But playing to break even in the long run is not exactly the way to play winning poker. You always want more than the bare minimum number of necessary bets in the pot in order to play a hand. Excess bets equal better pot odds. Better pot odds is called an **overlay**.

As a poker player, you're always looking for a spot to put your money in play where you have an overlay. If you stick to playing good, high cards for your position and you play in a game where you can consistently get five or more players to play most pots, you are practically guaranteed to have a positive hourly rate and be a winner in the long run.

It's okay to play hands that have big odds against them as long as the pot is offering even bigger odds. If you hold a small pocket pair, then your odds of flopping another one to make a set are about one in eight. That's 7:1 against. If you add in the fact that you can win the hand a few other ways without flopping the set, then you will win the hand about one out of three times. The odds are 2:1. This means you need two other players in the hand to get the right odds to play the hand and break even in the long run. If you have three other players in the hand, then you have a slight overlay, but it may not be enough to overcome the effect of the rake, the jackpot drop and your relative inexperience at the game. In other words, if you play the hand, you risk being outplayed by and losing to a better player when you might have won the hand against weaker players.

This is why I strongly recommend that you don't play small pocket pairs unless you're getting pot odds of at least 5:1. This will save you a lot of losing hands, a lot of fluctuation in your bankroll, and it will keep you out of trouble. And when you do win the hand, it will be a good-sized pot because you made sure of that before you called the first bet. Don't forget that when you flop a set, or any other good hand, there's one more thing that you have to do to get the pot—and that's win the hand.

Not only do you need the right odds to play a hand, you need to cushion those odds to allow for the fact that you'll sometimes make the hand and then lose with it. It's very expensive to be holding A♦ K♦, get two more diamonds on the flop, get the fifth diamond on the turn, make the nuts, and then lose the hand when the board pairs on the river. I don't worry about or give too much thought to **padding the odds** (requiring grossly excess odds) when I hold two big cards, but I am a stickler about that when I play smaller cards. I like to play hands like 8♥ 7♥ or especially 6♠ 5♠ (now named for me because I won two tournaments with that hand), but I only play them in late position and when there are a lot of players in the hand. If there are seven or more players in the hand, I will usually raise before the flop to build a big pot in case I hit my hand.

This is a profitable move for me because I'm getting great pot odds and I, unlike a lot of other players, can throw the hand away on the flop if I miss. Since I was going to play the hand for one bet anyway, the move actually only cost me one bet, and I know I'll get that bet back in the same situation in the long run.

SAID

"Poker is about getting players to take bad odds. Most of the errors that bad players make involve taking too many cards off when the pot is not offering them the right odds to hit their hand."

— Ed Hill

If you've played in a few hold'em games, you've undoubtedly noticed that it's not pocket aces or kings that win every hand. Usually, it's a hand that you might not bet on every time, like K♥ 9♣, Q♣ 3♣ or 5♠ 5♦. No hand is totally worthless, it's just that some are obviously worth more than others. Given the right circumstances, almost any hand can be an underdog. Even pocket aces are not a favorite if there's more than six players in the hand. The secret—the thing that makes it alright to play an apparently bad hand— is pot odds.

This book is intended for beginners, so I did not develop a graduate course in odds for you to memorize. Mainly, I just want you to see that you can profitably play hands that are obvious underdogs if you know in advance that you'll be adequately compensated for it. This chapter is intended to serve as a simple introductory lesson and begin your education on pot odds.

TOURNAMENTS

*In a tournament you have all the weapons in
the world available to you, except time.*

Other than hitting a jackpot, one way that the average low limit player can score a big win and increase his hourly rate is to win or place high in a poker tournament. Sometimes you can win more than $1,000 for about three hours of play. Learning tournament strategy could be very valuable to you because it speeds up your learning process and helps you play in your regular ring game. A **ring** is a poker game that is played for cash, but is not a tournament.

There is a big difference between tournament and ring game strategy. So much so that a player who is a good player in his regular ring game will almost never win a tournament if that's the way he plays throughout the tournament. There are so many differences that the subject of tournament strategy is more properly addressed as the subject of its own book.

Here are some of the more important points you should know if you're thinking about playing in a tournament.

Top 41 Tournament Tips

1. Should you play in a poker tournament?

I play tournaments and the criteria that I use to answer that questions is:

A. I have to believe that I have a reasonable chance to make the final table, or,

B. I must think that the tournament practice and experience I will get by entering will be worth the entry fee. There are many, good tournaments with $5 to $20 entry fees that are worth the experience.

2. **Before you play any tournament, make sure you know all of the rules and conditions. Questions that need to be answered are:**

A. How much is the initial buy-in?

B. How much are rebuys?

C. When can you rebuy? In some tournaments you can't rebuy unless you're below your initial buy-in.

D. How much is the add-on and when can you make it?

E. How many players will be at each table?

F. How many tables will there be?

G. What is the estimated total payout and how is the payout ladder structured?

H. Are the players allowed to make a deal at the final table?

I. Will there be pictures taken or an award ceremony after the tournament?

3. **You must determine if the tournament is designed to be fast or slow or somewhere in between.**

The three factors you look at to determine this are:

A. The amount of chips you start with

B. The initial betting limit

C. The time length of each round.

First, determine the ratio of total chips to the size of the big bet. Ideally, you'd like this number of be fifteen or more. Some tournaments start with $200 in chips with a $10 to $20 betting limit, for a ratio of 10:1. It is possible to lose all of your chips in the first hand. As you can see, a low ratio equates to a fast tournament. If the length of each betting stage is fifteen or twenty minutes, then that also makes for a fast tournament. A ratio of fifteen or more with stages of more than twenty minutes makes for a slower tournament.

How does knowing this help you? The main purpose of a tournament is to get poker players into the poker room on that room's slower days. The idea is for players to bust out of the tournament and then take seats in ring games that can be raked. This obviously creates business for the room when there might not otherwise be a game there that day.

Knowing if the tournament is designed to be fast or slow tells you what the mix of luck and skill will be and what the chances are that you'll make the final table. Good players will beat bad players in the long run. Bad and lucky players, however, can and do beat good players in the short run. The best weapon that good players have to use against bad players is time. The longer each stage of the tournament is, the better the odds are for the good players. A tournament with a small betting ratio and short time limits is almost like a crap shoot. Anyone can win. If you're a good player, you should look for the slower tournaments.

SAID

"Skill is important in tournaments. If you're three times as good as other opponents, you might expect to win one tournament out of a hundred."

— Mike Caro

4. **The number one difference between a ring game and a tournament is that a tournament is all about survival.**

In a ring game, you can consistently play inferior hands because you can lose five hands in a row and then make it all back on the sixth hand. And if you run out of poker chips before you win that sixth hand, you can always buy more. You can't do that in a tournament one or two could take all of your chips.

5. **Any game or tournament will always have a mix of good and bad players; however, the skill level of the**

players in tournaments is almost always much higher than in a typical ring game.

This is a double-edged sword. It's more difficult to beat better players, yet in a tournament they are easier to read and more predictable than the bad players.

6. **If you're playing in a tournament that allows rebuys and add-ons, then you should be prepared to make the maximum number of rebuys and add-ons.**

   Tournaments like this are as much a contest to see who can buy the most chips as they are a contest to win those chips. You need to be able to keep up with the competition just to have a chance to make the final table. You can play a little faster earlier because of the rebuys and add-ons.

7. **If you're going to make a rebuy and/or an add-on, there are two questions you must answer before doing it:**

   A. Why did I lose all of my chips? If you were unlucky or just failed to make routine draws then you should go ahead and make the rebuy. If you lost because you were outplayed and you're facing superior-quality competition, then you should consider not making the rebuy.

   B. Who has most of the chips at my table? If it's the good players you should realize that your chances of making the final table just got worse and you should consider not making the rebuy.

8. **If you're free to make the rebuy and add-on at any time, you should consider waiting as long as possible to do it. A short-term run of bad luck can wipe out your stack before your skill has a chance to kick in and take effect. It's better to go all-in with what you have and lose, and then make the rebuy. Going all-in will cut your losses when you lose the hand and you will still have the rebuy option available to you.**

   Some players like to have as many chips in front of them as possible so that, "When I make my hand I want to be able to play it all the way and get maximum value from it." That's a good ring game strategy but it's a bad tournament strategy. It's a very bad idea to push small, statistical advantages and edges in a tournament. It's a high standard deviation strategy and you can have negative swings big enough to knock yourself out of the tournament. If anything, save your rebuy and add-on so you can lose it later rather than earlier. And since only one player can win the tournament, this is what will happen anyway unless you're the winner.

9. **During the first hour of the tournament you should be watching all of your opponents closely to determine their skill level, playing style, level of patience, playing patterns, personality and availability of tells.**

   If you don't want to do all of this, or you don't see the value in it, you should at least pay attention to the cards that the players turn up at the end of the hand. With that information you can make a judgment about their skill, knowledge of position, and hand selection. I guarantee you that the players who will make the final table are already doing this to you.

10. **Each player's stack size is of paramount importance in a tournament.**

    You should not ordinarily attack a bigger stack than yours because you could be eliminated from the tournament if you lose the hand, while your opponents will only lose some chips to you and will remain in the tournament if you win.

11. **If it is a rebuy event, you can and should play a little more liberally during the rebuy period.**

    You can afford to take chances in an effort to get ahead and losing won't bust you out of the tournament.

12. **Alternatively, you might already be a great tournament player and you want your image to be that of a tight, aggressive player. You should play super tight and "by the book." This will discourage other players from playing when you're in the pot which will in turn increase your chance of winning the hands you do play. You won't be bluffed as often. You will be able to check down more hands and you might be able to bluff**

a little more often because of your image. Checking down is a common tournament strategy to avoid getting busted out of the tournament. It involves staying in check after the flop to conserve chips.

However, the major reason for playing tight is not listed above. The number one reason you want to have a super tight image is so that you can change gears in the later stages of the tournament, when the limits are higher and mistakes your opponents make are more deadly for them. No one will know what happened until they lose a big pot to you because they misread your hand. I promise you that the winner of the next tournament you play in will do this to you, so you might as well learn how to do it also.

13. Decide ahead of time exactly which hands you will play and under what circumstances.

Decide which hands you will call preflop raises with.

14. Be aware of your position relative to the button.

This will help you decide if another player is making a move based more on his position than his cards.

15. Be aware of the other players' stack sizes, especially before the play of the hand.

Players with small stacks are usually more reluctant to call your bets and raises if you act before they do on the hand.

16. If you are short-stacked, the time to make a move is before you are reduced down to about four times the combined amount of the blinds.

Most players wait too long to do this because they are just trying to survive. If the blinds are $50 to $100 then you should not let your stack get below $600 ($50 + $100 x 4) before taking a stand with a hand. This gives you the freedom to play the hand correctly and get maximum value without taking extra risks.

> ☞ **TIP**
>
> Poker chips won in a tournament should be held onto like you inherited them.

17. Always be aware of how much time is left in the current stage of the tournament.

Certain strategies become more effective near the end of each stage.

18. Always have an idea of how much the blinds and the antes will cost you to play each round.

Use this to determine how many hands you have before you will be blinded out if you don't win a hand or make a move.

SAID

"They've got us surrounded again, the poor bastards."

— General Creighton Abrams

19. Pay attention to the cost of calling the rest of the small blind.

Most of the time the correct play is to fold. Do not overdefend your big blind. No amount of pot odds can turn a losing hand into a winning hand.

20. When an opponent plays a hand, and he is not in one of the blinds, you need to determine why he is playing that hand.

Sometimes the reason will be obvious. He might be a bad player, he might be short-stacked or he might be in good position. Whatever it is, you need to know why playing that hand makes sense to him. This will help you read his hand and avoid mistakes when playing against him. Both of these factors contribute to your overall goal, which is not to lose any chips

21. The same thing applies when you play a hand when not in the blind.

You better know exactly why you're playing the hand because if you haven't given it any thought, someone playing against you already has.

22. Keep in mind that you cannot win a tournament before the half-time break, but you can lose it.

Your job in the first half is mainly just to survive and put yourself in good position to begin the second half.

23. Tighten up considerably after the rebuy period ends.

You're playing for keeps now. You cannot replace the chips you lose except by winning them back from the other players.

24. Never miss an opportunity to put a player all-in.

If your opponent bets ten of his eleven chips, and you have forty-five chips, you should always raise one more to get him all-in. You may have heard the saying that all a player needs to beat you is a chip and a chair. It's true. Try to deprive him of both.

25. Learn to gang up on all-in players, especially at the final table.

If one player is all-in and is called by another player, you should also call with any reasonable hand if you don't fear a raise. All of the players with chips should then check the hand all the way to the river in an effort to increase the odds that one of them will beat—and therefore knock out of the tournament—the all-in player. You should bet only if you have the nuts on the river. This helps all of you because the objective in a tournament is not to win pots, but to move up the payout ladder.

26. Do not underestimate the value of a single chip.

Do not play too loose, wild or reckless in the beginning of the tournament just because you have a lot of chips and the limits are small. This is one of the more common mistakes that beginning players make. Do not confuse this with playing fast, which is often correct. Playing fast is betting and raising at every reasonable opportunity rather than playing a little more conservatively.

27. Be aware of how many total chips are in play in the tournament and how many players are left.

With this information you'll be able to determine what the average number of chips is for each player.

28. If you have a small stack late in the tournament, you must realize that you will probably not win the tournament. Your goal therefore is to move up the payout ladder as best you can.

Look at the other players' stacks and give those players every chance to bust each other out before you get blinded out.

29. Throwing away A♣ A♥ or K♦ K♠ before the flop can be profitable, especially at the final table.

As an example, consider this scenario:

There are five of you left and the payouts are:

1st–$4,000   **2nd**–$2,000   **3rd**–$1,000   **4th**–$500   **5th**–$300

The chips are distributed as follows:

Beth–$30,000   **Jim**–$2,000   **Neil**–$2,000   **Dora**–$2,000   **You**–$500

At least you made the final table and you're getting $300 in prize money. You get your hand and Dora raises to $2,000 all-in, Neil calls all-in, Jim calls all-in and Beth calls leaving her with $28,000 in chips. You look at your hand and you have A♣ A♥! What do you do?

If you call and win the hand, you will have $2,500 in chips. If you lose the hand, you'll be busted out and receive $300. If you fold, you're guaranteed to move up the pay ladder no matter what happens after that. In the very unlikely event of a tie, two of the players with only $2,000 in chips will be eliminated and quite possibly, all three will lose to Beth. This means you move up two or even three places by not playing the hand.

If Beth wins the hand your payout goes from $300 to a guaranteed minimum of $2,000. If she does not win the hand, then she will have $28,000 in chips and the winner of the hand will have $6,000 in chips. Then this line of logic starts all over again. If you can stay out of the way while she knocks off the other player, you then get second place for sure.

FACT!

If you understand the fundamentals of tournament strategy and recognize how tournaments differ from regular ring games, you will do well in any tournament.

This example is extreme and unlikely but I made it that way to illustrate the point. You'll often be in a spot where you'll tell yourself, "I'm not going to play this (usually playable) great hand because all I need to do is sit back and wait for one player to bust out another player," or "I don't need to play this hand knowing that I could bust someone out because I can already see that another player is going to do that for me."

30. If you're short stacked, try to survive your big and small blind by not calling in the small blind or playing after the flop.

This might give you as many as eight more hands to look at before you get blinded out.

31. The IRS requires casinos to issue a WG-2 form to anyone in the tournament who receives $600 or more.

If you're making a deal at the final table and you don't want a WG-2, you can ask for $599 or less and avoid the IRS paperwork.

32. Players who are eager to make a deal at the last table will probably play more conservatively than usual if their offer to make a deal is refused.

After all, they did just tell you that they don't want to put any more money at risk.

33. It is never too late to make a deal.

As soon as you realize you're in chip trouble or you're facing elimination, you should try to make a deal. You have a lot to gain and nothing to lose.

34. Traditionally, tournament players are not allowed to select their table or seat at that table. However, there are a few poker rooms that allow it, even though it may not be well known.

Ask if you can choose your own seat and table. If you can, get a seat at what you know will be the final table. That way, you will be one of the few players in the tournament who will not be forcibly moved from table to table, possibly avoiding paying double blinds and being in bad position.

35. **If you can choose your own seat at the table, you should choose the three or the eight seat, because all of the players will be in your field of vision at the same time.**

This helps you pick up tells and gather all the information you need to make your decisions. If the three or eight seat is not available, then the seats on either side of them will serve equally well.

36. **Watch the best tournament player at your table, especially early in the tournament.**

Stay out of his way unless you have great cards.

37. **If you bust out of the tournament before making the final table, you should stay around to watch the play at the final table.**

Not only will the winner of the tournament be unwittingly giving you lessons, you'll know who the good tournament players are. Do this often enough and you'll be able to recognize these players at the beginning of future tournaments.

38. **Find out how long it takes to play a tournament down to the final table and then compute how much each place is worth.**

Use this information to calculate how much each tournament is worth to you per hour (assuming you get in the money) and convert that number to the number of big bets per hour, using the size of the big bet in the game you usually play. You can then use this information to compare the potential worth of various tournaments and ring games.

The tournament advice you just read is designed for and applies to almost any poker tournament, especially Texas hold'em. If you understand the fundamentals of tournament strategy and recognize how tournaments differ from regular ring games, you will do well in any tournament.

Here are a few more points that apply only to Omaha hi/lo split:

39. Consider limping in with big hands like A A 2 3, A A 2 4 or A A K K.

You should occasionally not mind trying to win more than the blinds.

40. High hands gain value later in the tournament because the low hands don't want to draw to their lows. It's the same as playing a straight or flush draw.

You're going to miss two out of three times and that's too much to give away in the late stages of a tournament.

41. Don't play for low when it's two- or three-handed. You will miss too often and you will win very little when you do make the hand. Winning one-half of the pot one-third of the time is a sure-fire way to give your money away.

I have one final thought about tournaments. If you are new to poker and you've decided that you're going to do what it takes to be a better player, then you've probably decided to set aside a certain amount of time and money to accomplish this goal. You've decided that you're willing to make an investment in the game, knowing that it will pay dividends for you in the future.

I want you to know that in this situation, dollar for dollar, the experience you will get from tournaments will be more valuable to you than the same amount of time and money spent playing in a ring game. If you have, for example, $100 to invest in learning the game, you will get the most for your dollar if you can play in several small buy-in tournaments rather than taking a seat in a poker game with that $100. If anything, you'll see that you pay closer attention and learn a lot faster if you're faced with the possibility of being busted out of the game if you lose.

CHAPTER 16

BLUFFING

> "Owing largely to the bluff, poker has influenced our thinking on life, love, business and war. In fact, mathematical theory of games... was given a high security classification by the armed forces during World War II."
>
> — A.D. Livingston

Bluffing is betting with a hand that you know cannot win if your bet is called. Often, if you do attempt to bluff, you will be in the position of having a good flush or straight draw that didn't quite develop and you'll be trying to win the pot by making the other player fold what you believe is a better hand than yours.

Knowing when to attempt a bluff is often just a simple matter of knowing the pot odds on the river and having an idea of what your opponent's hand is. The mathematical rule of thumb for attempting a bluff is this: The pot odds must be greater than the odds of successfully pulling off the bluff. For example, if you estimate that you have a one in five chance of bluffing, then there must be more than five bets in the pot when you attempt the bluff.

Here's an example of how you would break even in the long run when bluffing:

Assume there are five bets in the pot and you bet on the river as a bluff because you know you can't win any other way. If your opponent calls and beats you, then you are losing one bet in attempted bluff situations. If you do this four more times, and lose all four of those times, then you will be losing five bets in attempted bluff situations. If you try it a sixth time, and this time you win the pot, you get back those five bets, as well as the bet you made the sixth bluff with.

If there are ten bets in the pot, you can attempt to bluff ten times, and lose all ten of those times as long as you win the pot on the eleventh try, on average. It's the same thing as unsuccessfully bluffing twenty times and then winning the next two times you bluff. You will break even in the long run as long as the pot odds are the same as your chances of successfully bluffing.

The way to make a profit from bluffing is to have the pot odds be greater than your chances of winning the hand. In the first example, where you had a one in five chance of bluffing, what if there were ten bets in the pot instead of five? Then you would invest, and lose, five bets and then win ten bets when you won the hand. You would lose four out of five times but you'd be ahead five bets in bluffing situations overall. That's what pot odds will do for you.

"I have found that when one is embarrassed, usually the shortest way to get through it is to quit talking about it or thinking about it and go at something else."

— Abraham Lincoln

On the other hand, what if there were only two bets in the pot when you attempted a bluff? You would invest five bets on losing bluffing attempts and then win only two of those bets back when your bluff succeeded. Clearly, you should not attempt a bluff when the pot is not offering you the right odds. That's because you are still losing even though you might win one particular hand.

Now that you know that the pot has to be offering you the right odds to attempt a bluff, that raises the question: How do you know what your odds of successfully bluffing are? How do you know if you only have a 5% chance of bluffing and you therefore need twenty or more bets in the pot? Or how do you know that you have a 33% chance of bluffing and therefore you need only two or more bets in the pot? This is a difficult question to answer precisely because it depends on your experience, your skill at reading your opponent's hands, your estimation of what all of the action up to that point means and who the other players are.

You cannot bluff bad players because they are not astute enough to recognize the fact that you could be betting a good hand for value. They will often call, expecting to lose the hand anyway, just because they play too loose and it's worth the extra bet on the end to them just to see your hand. That's what makes them bad players.

It's hard to bluff good players because they recognize bluffing opportunities and they factor in the fact that you could be bluffing when deciding to call. And you cannot bluff a player who has a good hand but you've misread him for a busted straight or flush draw. All of the conditions have to be right, and all of the planets must be in their correct orbits to pull off a bluff, especially when you're trying to run it through more than one opponent.

There's a little bit more math to bluffing that you need to understand and it has to do with how many potential callers you have when you attempt to bluff. To see this point, assume that it's equally likely (50-50) that each player will call when you attempt to bluff in the end. If you're first and there's just one other player, then the odds that you'll be successful are 50-50, or $\frac{1}{2}$. That's odds of 1:1. If there are two players, then you have odds of one out of four ($\frac{1}{2}$ x $\frac{1}{2}$). That's odds of 3:1. Three players ($\frac{1}{2}$ x $\frac{1}{2}$ x $\frac{1}{2}$) is one out of eight, which is 7:1. Four players is 15:1 against. Five players is 31:1 against. You can see how these odds increase geometrically rather than arithmetically. They get out of hand pretty quick. This is exactly why bluff attempts work best against only one or two players.

There's another factor that works against you when you're trying to bluff, especially when you're bluffing against more than two players. Some beginning and low limit players feel that they are honor bound to call you with anything, especially if they are the last player in the hand who could keep you from winning the pot. The last player will often call your attempted bluff just because he's the last player, and not because he's considering pot odds or his poker hand. So, it pays to realize, in advance, who that last player is if you're thinking about bluffing.

Medium-sized pots are the most difficult to steal. There's a reason they got to be medium-sized. It's usually because an average number of players got average cards, made average strength poker hands and then created an average sized pot. If you try to bluff into one of these pots, you'll get called by—guess what—an average hand.

Very small pots are the easiest to steal because there are usually a very small number of players in the hand and they will fold slightly better than average hands when you bluff at the pot because they often correctly realize that they are not getting the right pot odds to call you.

Often, they will have only one small bet invested in the pot and they don't want to call a big bet on the river because there's so little to win by risking so much. If you're interested in bluffing at a small pot, it helps if you keep the pot small by not betting on the flop whenever you think it's safe to do so. You generally don't want to give free cards but, in those instances when it's correct to do so, one of the benefits is that it may help you successfully bluff on the river.

It can be very profitable to bluff large pots. The difference is, you may go a long time between winning bluffs, and when you do win one, the pot odds will more than compensate you for the times you lost. In summary, unless you have very good, specific reasons for bluffing at medium-sized pots, you should try to make most of your bluffing attempts at very small or very large pots.

Favorable Times to Bluff

I've identified ten instances in the game when you might be thinking about bluffing. You should occasionally review this list to help keep these points in mind. I will use examples from Texas hold'em as the common point of reference since hold'em is currently the most popular game in the country.

1. **When you have ace-king suited**

   If you raised before the flop and you played the hand strongly from the beginning, then your opponents will give you credit for a good hand. In addition to ace-king suited, they might give you credit for having A♣ A♥, K♦ K♥ or whatever two cards it takes to make a completed hand. A bluff attempt on the river will often work because they won't think you're actually bluffing.

2. **When you have excellent pot odds**

   If you missed your draw on the river, and the pot is huge, you should at least think about bluffing before checking and folding. Sometimes the pot is so big it's worth a try.

3. **Against good players**

   An experienced player is capable of figuring out what you might be holding and giving you credit for it. He will then make a mathematical calculation and, if he doesn't have the right pot odds to call, he will fold. Bad players don't do this; they just call anyway.

4. **When you have hidden strength**

   If you're in the blind with unusual cards and you get a flop to match them, or if you've varied your play and gotten a good flop, you have hidden strength. Your opponents will not often realize that a check from you means you have a strong hand.

5. **In higher stakes games**

   These games have better players who are capable of folding one pair or two pair when they think they're beat.

6. **When the flop didn't hit anyone**

   If you read everyone in the hand for holding high cards and the flop is all low cards, then you might be able to bluff at the pot.

7. **When the board pairs on the turn**

   If the flop is K♦ 8♥ 3♣ and there is no bet, then you can often steal the pot when another king comes on the turn. You know this because top pair is almost always bet on the flop. In this case, you can be sure that no one has three kings and they will fold, giving you credit for the three kings. Even if they think you might not have three kings, you've got them playing a guessing game and they will often fold.

8. **Against just one opponent**

If I had to bluff at a pot, I know that I'd like to be facing only one opponent. It doesn't get any better than that. Well, actually, it does. Sometimes, when the river card comes and it's just you and your sole opponent, he will sometimes fold and concede the pot out of turn if he completely missed his draw. But it doesn't get any better than that!

9. **Faking a rush**

If your seat is hot and you've just won five of the last seven hands, you can sometimes act very confident when betting in the hopes that your opponents will think you're still on the rush.

10. **From the blind, you could have anything**

Most players recognize the fact that you could have anything in the blind. Rather than play a guessing game, especially with a small pot, they will fold unless they have a better than average hand.

Unfavorable Times to Bluff

Take another look at the above list of favorable times to bluff and then look at it from the other player's point of view. For everything you can figure out about the other players, they can also figure out about you. And you're outnumbered; there's only one of you to keep an eye on them but there's nine of them to watch you. That's why it's so hard to get away with a bluff.

SAID

"When I am getting ready to reason with a man, I spend one-third of my time thinking about myself and what I'm going to say, and two-thirds thinking about him and what he's going to say."

— Abraham Lincoln

Here are a few more points to be aware of when thinking about a possible bluff.

1. **Any flop with an ace**

These flops are hard to bluff because players just seem to play every time they get an ace. If one comes on the flop it's very likely to have made someone a pair of aces and you'll certainly get called.

2. **Any flop with a jack or a 10**

   These two cards are what all good straight draws are made of and good players will usually have cards that would go well with these cards. You can practically forget about bluffing when there's both a jack and a 10 on the board.

3. **If there was a preflop raise**

   This indicates that there are some premium hands out there. You can't be sure that one of them is not A♥ A♦ or K♣ K♠ and you'll get called when you bluff on the river. Sometimes, a player will raise before the flop with 4♣ 4♥ just for fun and then call with it on the river... just for fun.

Your Opponent Might Be Bluffing if...

1. **The flop had two cards of the same suit and another one did not come on the turn or the river or there was an obvious straight draw that did not get there.**

   In a case like that, his only option might be to try a bluff.

2. **It's just the two of you.**

   If he's first to bet or if you're first and you check to him, he could be bluffing. He won't always be bluffing just because there's only the two of you, but it's something you should keep in mind.

3. **It only cost him one bet to steal the pot.**

   If your opponent can induce you to make a mistake that will cost you the pot, and it will only cost him one bet, you should be aware of that.

4. **The pot is huge.**

   I'd say that any pot with more than fifteen big bets qualifies in most players' minds as a huge pot and is worthy of a steal attempt.

5. **The river card did not help the flush draws that came on the flop.**

6. **The player betting on the river, and is therefore possibly bluffing, raised preflop and no aces, kings or queens are on the board.**

7. **Everyone checked on any round of the hand.**

   This usually means that no one flopped anything worth protecting.

8. **Of course, whenever there are a combination of two or more of the above reasons to believe your opponent might be bluffing, it is more likely that he is bluffing.**

   The way to make money on your bluffing attempts is to always have the pot offering you greater odds than the odds of successfully pulling off the bluff attempt. If the pot odds and the odds of successfully bluffing are the same, then you will not make any money in the long run. In those instances, I think it's best that you don't try to bluff.

FACT!

In the long run, you don't lose or gain anything in these even money situations so it doesn't matter if you bluff or not. These even money situations, however, can cause you to go through large negative swings in your bankroll before they eventually even out. Because of that, I always make sure I'm getting the right odds to bluff.

CHAPTER 17

TELLS

> "Players are either acting or they aren't.
> If they are acting, decide what they want
> you to do and disappoint them."

> — Mike Caro's Greatest Law of Tells

A tell is a clue that a player provides about his poker hand by the way he acts. The tell can be either verbal or nonverbal, it can be made unconsciously or knowingly, and it can be either genuine or part of a deliberate act.

General Advice

Before I get into specific tells, there are a few guidelines that apply whenever you see a tell and you're trying to analyze it. They are:

1. **At the lower limit games, where most of the players aren't very sophisticated, it is popularly believed that the best way to fool the other players is to act weak when it's strong and act like it's strong when it's weak.**

   It's very common to see players who have a full house act like they can't even beat ace-high and vice versa.

   This is why I am going to advise you that, if you're going to act at all, act like your hand is strong when it is strong and act like it's weak when it's weak. All too many of your opponents will think you're acting, because that's what they would do, and they will often misread your hand.

2. **Don't make figuring out a tell harder than it has to be.**

   If you suspect that the other player does not know he just gave you a tell, then you can go with what it usually means. If you think he's acting and he gave you that tell on purpose to manipulate your response, then you can proceed based on that conclusion.

3. **If you spot a tell and you honestly can't decide what it means, you have several options.**

   You can stop the action, think about it until you arrive at a conclusion, and then make your play. Or, you can ignore it completely and rely on the other information you have to help you evaluate the hand.

   Chances are, if you can't decide what a tell means after reading this chapter, it's probably not that valuable to you. The best you can do is to remember the tell, remember the cards the player had when you spotted the tell, make a note of it, and think about it after the game.

SAID

"If you know poker, you know people; and if you know people, you got the whole dang world lined up in your sights."

— James Garner, as Bret Maverick

4. **A player's general demeanor during the play of a hand is a big clue as to the strength of his hand.**

   If he appears to be happy, enthusiastic and not worried, then he probably has a good hand. If he appears to be unhappy, acts disgusted with his hand or makes negative remarks, then he probably has a bad hand. This won't tell you exactly what his hand is but it is one more bit of information that you can consider when making your decisions.

Specific Tells

What follows is a list of tells that you might see during the course of a hold'em game. All of these tells are covered in more depth in my first book, *Winner's Guide to Texas Hold'em Poker*, and in Mike Caro's fantastic book, *Caro's Book of Poker Tells* and the companion video, *Caro's Pro Poker Tells*.

Here's a list of those tells with a brief explanation of each one. To help you develop a sense of the relative value of each one, I've rated each tell for you using the following scale:

★ You won't see it often, has little value

★ ★ Occurs often enough to help your hourly rate

★ ★ ★ Common tell, well worth knowing, good value

★ ★ ★ ★ High frequency, very reliable, high value

1. Players in wheelchairs and walkers. ★ ★

Players who are wheelchair-bound or otherwise have trouble physically getting around like to stay put once they get in the game. They usually play conservatively but not great. They are often tight/passive players.

2. Neat and conservative players. ★ ★ ⸗

A person's style of doing one thing is usually his style of doing most other things also. A player who dresses and acts conservatively usually also plays conservatively.

3. Impatient players. ★ ★

If a player is in a hurry to play his hand, that usually signifies that he has a decent hand. It won't be a great hand because a player holding A♦ A♥ or K♥ K♣ will usually wait until it's his turn to act to let anything be known about his hand.

4. Mannerism changes. ★ ★

Players who suddenly sit up in their chairs, put out their cigarettes, quickly finish their drinks, abruptly end conversations, or summarily dismiss any spectators usually have very good hands. You don't have to do any of these things if you intend to fold when it's your turn.

5. Players showing their hands to spectators. ★ ★

A player who shows his hand to a non-player at the beginning of the hand usually has a good starting hand. A player who shows his hand to a non-player at the end of a hand, particularly when all of the cards are out and he is awaiting a call from a lone opponent, usually has a bad hand. Showing it is an effort to convince the other player that he has a hand that he is proud of. When you see this tell, the bettor is usually betting as a stone cold bluff.

6. When a good player plays his first hand. ★ ★ ★

Good players like to win the first hand they voluntarily enter the pot with so they can then play with "your" money instead of theirs. Keep an eye on the player who usually doesn't play when he's in the small blind. If he calls in the small blind then he has a very good hand.

7. Players who stare at the flop. ★ ★ ★ ★

Players who continue to stare at the flop after the dealer turns it up usually did not flop anything. There's nothing there for them and it takes a few more seconds to double check it and make sure.

8. Players who see the flop and then quickly look away. ★ ★ ★ ★

the flop is easy to read even if you still have to take an extra second or two to make sure.

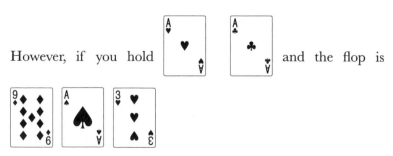

It will look like this to you:

When you see this you'll instantly know you're going to bet, you'll quickly glance at your chips to make sure they're still there and then you will look away from the table, feigning total disinterest in the hand.

9. **Players who cover their mouth.** ★ ★

A player who covers his mouth after betting is usually bluffing. What you're seeing is a conflict between the external physical action of betting and the internal knowledge of knowing you're lying.

10. **Players who bet in a flamboyant style.** ★ ★

A player who throws his chips into the pot in a forceful or obviously exaggerated manner is usually bluffing. Or, at the very least, he's trying to intimidate you into checking into him on the next round.

11. **Players who make directed bets.** ★ ★ ★

A player who calls a bet by throwing his chips in the specific direction of a particular player (usually the bettor) is trying to intimidate the bettor into checking on the next round.

12. **Players who stare at their opponents.** ★ ★ ★

This tell occurs most often after the river card comes and a player has missed a big draw. He will often noticeably raise his head from looking down at the flop, turn his head to the left or right to squarely face his sole opponent and then stare right at him. In poker language, this means, "I just missed my flush draw, I'm entitled to win this hand but I can't call a bet. Don't you dare bet into me."

13. **A player who immediately calls your bet.** ★ ★ ★

A player who calls your bet and has his chips in the pot almost before you do has a weak calling hand. He'd rather you not bet, but since you did, he wants his apparently quick and easy call to make you have second thoughts about betting into him on the next round.

14. Players who reach for their chips to call your bet before you can make the bet. ★ ★ ★

In poker language, this means, "Of course I'm going to call your bet! It's such an easy decision for me that I don't even have to wait to think about it. If you were betting to eliminate me, you can save that bet since you can see that I'm going to call."

15. A player who delays in calling your bet. ★ ★⤴

A player who genuinely couldn't decide between folding and calling when you bet on the flop is more likely to fold if he does call and you bet again on the turn. He will usually have been looking for a miracle card, took one shot at it and is willing to fold on the turn if he misses, which will happen most of the time.

16. Players who flash one of their hole cards. ★ ★⤴

A player who makes sure you "accidentally" see one of his hole cards is bluffing. He almost never has exactly what you're supposed to think he has.

17. Tells on fabulous-looking flops. ★ ★

Whenever the flop contains a high pair or three straight flush cards, or even three-of-a-kind, you should pause for a second to observe the other players' reactions before acting on your hand. Often, a player who threw away a hand which contained a card that would fit well with the flop will let it be known. He might swear, moan, pound the table, slap his forehead, elbow his neighbor or actually announce out loud what card he folded before the flop. The secret is, you have to wait to give him a second to do one of these things. This is a very reliable tell since a player not in the hand has no reason to influence the play or outcome of a hand that he's not in.

18. Players who unnecessarily show the nuts at the end. ★⤴

He might just be bragging but sometimes it's because he intends to bluff you in the near future and he wants you to remember that he only plays the nuts.

19. Players who coax along an opponent's end decision. ★

If a player bets into you as a bluff, and it's blatant that you are reluctantly about to fold, your opponent will often say or do something to help you confirm that you're about to make the "right" decision. He wants you to hurry up and fold before you take a second to rethink what you're doing.

20. Players who show visible disappointment. ★ ★ ★ ★

If the pot is very big and a player is on a draw to the nuts, and misses on the end, he will often let you know about it. Again, the secret is that you have to wait a second for him to do it. He might exhale deeply, slump down in his chair, curse, look sad, turn his cards face up as a gesture of folding, throw his cards into the muck out of turn, hit the table or tell you what hand he missed.

21. Players who rabbit hunt. ★ ★ ★

Rabbit hunting is the term for, "Can I see the next card, please?" after the hand is over. It seems that bad players like to do that and good players don't.

The above tells were specific to flop games like Texas hold'em and Omaha. The following tells apply to seven-card stud and five-card draw.

22. Players who shuffle their cards. ★ ★ ★ ★

A player who draws one card and then slowly shuffles all of the cards one at a time is drawing to a straight, a flush, a full house or a nut low hand. They have an all-or-nothing hand and they usually wait until the last minute to see if they made it.

23. Players who double-check their cards. ★ ★ ★ ★

A player who receives an up card and then immediately double-checks his hole cards usually has a card that fits with the new up card. If he has two ♣s showing and double-checks his hand when he gets the third ♣, it means he has one more ♣ in the hole.

24. Draw players who rap pat out-of-turn. ★ ★ ★

A rap pat means to check by rapping one's hand on the table to signify a pat hand. A player who does this is trying to make you think he has a pat hand when in fact he intends to draw. It's a short-sighted strategy because this is such a reliable tell and of course you're going to see him draw anyway.

25. Players who start to show their hands and/or start to take the pot while awaiting a call. ★ ★ ★

This is a move made by weak, inexperienced players who think that this sign of obvious strength will encourage a fold.

How to Be Tell-Less

Get Into a Routine

Make sure you are very familiar with all of the tells mentioned in this chapter. Think about how you look to the other players. Try to do the same thing every time you bet. In advance, think about the physical actions that you go through when you bet or check. Knowledge is power. Do your best.

Be Prepared

Often your opponent will actually ask you what your hand is or what your hole cards are. My reply is always the same, with a smile: "I don't remember." Or you can deflect the question with a question of your own: "What do you think I have?"

Use Time to your Advantage

When you get your cards, wait until it's your turn to look at them. When the flop comes, spend that time observing the other players' reaction to the flop, especially if there was a preflop raiser.

Watch your Table Talk

Don't talk about the hands you've played, the hands you've folded and why you did or didn't play a hand a certain way. And don't show your hands if you're not called.

Back in 1985, when my son Neil was six years old, he and I were playing heads-up no-limit hold'em at the kitchen table. During one hand he made a pot-sized bet and I folded. After I threw my cards in the muck I asked him, "What do you have?" He had a stack of chips in front of him that was so high I could barely see him sitting behind them. He raised himself up so that I could see his eyes peering out from behind that stack, he shook his head from side to side and said, "Oh, no. You got to pay to see 'em."

MONEY MANAGEMENT

No style, type or form of money management will work if you play a game of skill without the skill.

Money management is a term that includes just about every aspect of poker playing. Everything you think and do when playing poker can somehow be connected to some principle of managing your money. That's because there would be no poker playing without money. So it follows that your relationship with money is very important if you want to be a poker player.

Money management can be broken down into these three categories:

1. Understanding basic money management theory and principles.

2. Understanding money management theory, principles and facts in a casino.

3. Understanding money management as it applies to playing poker.

If you're going to war, to work, to play poker, or just about anywhere else, there are some things you had better understand before you even leave the house. It's best to start by looking at the big picture and then narrowing it down from there once you begin to make specific choices.

The Top 10 Money Management Principles

1. **Do not spend your poker-playing bankroll!**

   Your bankroll is the tool you need to get the job done at the poker table, assuming you're a winning player. It's all too easy to mix your poker money with the household money and not keep track of it. If you spend it all, you'll have to get replacement money from the household funds and sometimes this is just not possible.

   Think of your bankroll as a set of tools that you need to work with, much like a carpenter or a craftsman. You don't see them selling, losing or giving away their tools, do you? You should be just like that.

2. **Learn to perform an honest self-evaluation.**

   If you're going to play a game of skill, that usually means that you're going to pit your decision-making abilities against those of your opponents. Are you in the right mood to play? Are you awake and alert? Are you able to concentrate, not feeling rushed or in a hurry? Does everything about your decision to play poker feel right?

3. **Think about the conditions that offer you the best opportunity for success.**

   Are you able to go by yourself to the game with your own transportation? Do you have an open-ended time limit for your play? Do you have an adequate bankroll for this playing session? Are you going to the poker room that offers you the best opportunity to have a positive hourly rate?

4. **Are you impatient to play or to be in action?**

   We all have other commitments from time to time. Family, work, friends and other hobbies take up our time. You might rather be playing poker than taking care of some of these obligations. You should realize that time away from the poker table actually helps your game. It gives you time to rest, reevaluate your play, plan future strategies

SAID

"Eat your betting money, but don't bet your eating money."

— Horse Racing Wisdom

and think about your next game. You know, things you can't do at the poker table.

Whenever I get impatient to play, I just tell myself that not playing is the same thing as playing and staying even. If I happen to get to the poker game two hours later than I wanted, I just pretend that I've been playing for those two hours and that by still having all of my original buy-in, I'm still even in the game. That's better than playing for two hours and being a loser. Works for me.

5. **What is your risk tolerance?**

How much excitement in your poker playing do you need? Would you rather be in a game full of slow, dull, boring, no-action rocks? Or would you rather be in a game where everyone bets and raises every hand and you're effectively playing showdown poker? If you mismatch your preference with the actual game you play in, this will have a negative impact on your hourly rate.

6. **If you're taking a once- or twice-a-year trip to Las Vegas or Atlantic City, you need to protect your bankroll in advance.**

Decide how much money you're going to put at risk and stick with that amount. Leave unnecessary blank checks, credit cards and cash at home. They make it too easy for you to access your money.

"Big egos and big losses go hand in hand."

— John Gollehon

Learn to spend only a certain amount of your bankroll every day. Divide your bankroll up into equal parts and do not spend more than the predetermined amount. That way, you'll be able to stay in action every day that you're there. If you run out of money too soon, you'll be tempted to exceed your allotment, and that can be very expensive.

7. **Of all the games that you can play in a casino, poker is the most time-consuming of all.**

You can achieve satisfactory results (if you're lucky) at all of the other games in a casino faster than you can in a poker game.

Keep this in mind because how you manage your time has an impact on how you manage your money.

8. **When deciding where to play poker, the most important thing to consider is where you have the highest win rate per hour.**

Unless you're going to knowingly and voluntarily give up an edge for the sake of increasing future winnings, you should play where you do the best.

9. **Realize that the casinos and public poker rooms have already addressed this question of money management. It's you against them.**

Their very existence depends on the quality of decisions that they've made. This means that you should take into consideration the cost of playing poker. Think about the rake, travel expenses and the comps that the poker room offers.

10. **Keep your poker playing bankroll separate.**

For the serious poker player who wants to do everything right and give himself the best chance of succeeding, you have to take positive steps to protect your bankroll.

I suggest that you open a separate bank checking account to keep your poker bankroll in. If possible, use a bank different from the one that you use for your household. This has several advantages. Mainly, it adds stability and protection for the household funds. You should use your checks only for withdrawing money for poker playing. You can deposit your winnings in the account. Since the monthly bank statement will be easy to recognize without having to open it, it will be easier to keep it separate.

Money Management in a Casino

When you walk into a casino and you're trying to decide which game to play, you should realize that all of the games have a different house edge, and therefore, a different theoretical long-term payback for you. Given the same beginning bankroll, you will be able to play longer and make more bets at some casino games more than others. The smaller the house edge, the longer you will last without losing all of your money and the better chance you have of scoring a big win.

The Big Advantage of Being a Poker Player

When you play live poker in a poker room, you are not playing against the house. Yes, I know that they make their money by charging an hourly rate for your seat or they drop a certain percentage per hand to cover the costs of providing the game. You do pay for the privilege of playing but you and the other players are not betting against the house—you are betting against each other.

When you are playing a hand, the most important money management concept concerns your pot odds, your drawing odds, and the odds of your hand winning versus the other players' hands. There are times in a poker game where your edge against another player can be as much as 60% or more. In addition to that, you could be getting as much as 40 to 1 or more on your last bet or two in the hand. Just think about how that compares to taking 5% the worst of it on an even money bet against the casino.

> ## SAID
>
> "If you are not a winning player, your bankroll will never be large enough. To completely eliminate the possibilities of ever going broke, losing players need a big enough bankroll to outlast their life expectancy."
>
> — Lou Krieger

Obviously, for the player who is looking for the best place to put his money in action, poker is where it's at. That's why when I go to a casino, I head for the poker room. How would you like to play blackjack knowing that you're going to win 80% of the time and you'll be paid as much as 7 to 1 when you win? That's what it's like to play poker.

Money Management for the Poker Game

Here are some useful principles to be aware of if you're going to be a poker player. If you want to be a winner, you need to know that part of your job is to think about poker away from the game. You need the time and freedom to reflect upon these ideas and to then think about how you're going to implement them, given your own unique personality.

1. **Why do you play poker?**

    Whether it's for the camaraderie, the excitement, as a hobby, as a profession, as an intellectual challenge, for the money or something else, you must realize that your motivation for playing must be compatible with your method.

    You can't win if you don't understand the intricacies of the game. You have to understand a little math and a little psychology and have an ability to put it all together so that you can make quick, intelligent decisions. You have to play smart or you will lose to the players who do.

    On the other hand, some people do not actually play to win. They play because they're gamblers and they have discovered that playing poker is how they can play the longest amount of time on their gambling dollar.

2. **Don't forget that every great poker player once played at the level of expertise that you currently do.**

    Everybody started out as a beginner and then improved from there. If you are losing at poker, take heart because there is room for improvement and you can be a winner.

3. **Always play your best game.**

    This means that you should make the best decisions you can because that represents your current chance of winning. Don't deliberately play bad, sloppy or carelessly just because you feel like it. You give up your edge that way and you will lose even faster.

FACT!

Second-class poker players sometimes beat first-class poker players because, occasionally second-class players play a first-class game.

---

4. **It's a tough world out there.**

    If you are a moderately successful poker player and you'd like to move up in limit, I can probably guess what's holding you back. The biggest problem that an aspiring player has is that he has trouble keeping his poker bankroll separate from his living money and he usually can't play anytime he wants for as long as he wants.

    Once you decide that you want to become a semi-professional poker player you'll realize that it takes a big commitment in time and effort. That usually means that it will interfere with your family life and possibly your job.

5. **It's okay to occasionally take a shot at a higher limit game than what you usually play.**

   Just make sure you do it intelligently. Know who else is in the game, estimate your chances of success and limit your exposure to the better players. Try to learn something from your experience.

6. **You don't have to be the best player in your game to be a winner.**

   Usually, just being a little better than the other players is enough. Also, it helps if there are a couple of bad players in the game. To the left is a joke that makes this point more clear:

   SAID

   Two friends decide to go on safari to Africa. One of them says, "Well, I better go to the sporting goods store to get a good pair of running shoes, in case a tiger spots us." The other fellow says, "That's ridiculous, you can't outrun a tiger," whereupon his friend says, "Ok, I don't have to outrun the tiger; I just have to outrun you!"

7. **Low stakes games can be very wild, with everyone betting, raising and calling every bet all the way to the end.**

   It is, effectively, just showdown poker with very little opportunity to exercise your skill.

   A good player can have very high fluctuations in a game like this and he can often book several consecutive big losses without a win.

   Fortunately, there's an easy solution. That is, to move up in limit. You've heard that old saying, "water seeks its own level." That's what you will be doing when you look for a game where the players are a little better, it takes some skill to be a winner and there is more stability in your wins and losses. You don't have to worry too much about playing above your best limit because, chances are, that's why the other players are in the game also.

8. **Impatient to play once you get in the game?**

   If you play a hand just for the sake of being in action, you are not managing your money very well. You know what kind of player you are. You should decide in advance exactly what your minimum starting hand should be. Don't play unless you get that hand or a better one. This will give you time to relax, settle down and focus on the real goal of the game, which is to make your best decisions.

9. **If you have a choice of more than one poker room to play in, you need to give serious thought to the rake.**

Even though you aren't playing against the house, the rake comes out of the hands you win and this in turn reduces the pot odds you're getting on your money, even if it's a very small percentage. Keep in mind that small percentages add up over time.

10. **Playing tight may not always be the best way to play but it does have some advantages that you don't have when you play too loose.**

Playing tight means that you don't play very many hands and when you do play, you almost always have the best hand to start with. This is good because it limits the number of times you expose your bankroll to the other players, the rake and the dealer's tip, if there is one.

This means that:

A. You will be able to sit in the game for a longer period of time.

B. You'll get to see more hands.

C. You'll still be in the game when game conditions change for the better.

D. You'll still be there when the other players get tired and start making mistakes.

E. You will have given yourself a better chance of being in the game when the jackpot gets hit.

11. **If you are playing $3-$6 or $1-$4-$8-$8 hold'em, then a $100 buy-in is actually too small.**

For years I have advocated a $100 buy-in, but I have come to realize that such a buy-in is inadequate. That's because you need to look at it from the perspective of the number of hands it allows you to play, and not just how much it costs to play.

If it costs $20 to $25 to play a hand to the river, you can afford to lose only four or five hands before your buy-in is gone. That's not enough. I now think that a $200 buy-in is necessary to give you the best chance of winning. There are times where you might lose $100 and have to quit the game, but if you had an additional $100 in front of you, you'd be able to eventually win a hand and begin to recoup your first $100 loss. Don't deprive yourself of this winning opportunity by buying in for just $100 any more. Buy in for $200. Be kind to yourself.

12. If you are a winning poker player, then that means the long term odds are in your favor.

In this situation, your goal is to protect your bankroll from short term losses or losing streaks so that you can still be in the game when your skill kicks in. This means you should play only when the odds clearly favor doing so, and avoid those very close decisions to play or not to play.

13. On the other hand, it is okay to risk a small bankroll if that is what you want to do.

There have been many times when I have bought in for $100, won the first hand I played and went on to be a big winner from there. In a case like that, it would not have mattered if I had bought in for $500 because I never needed it.

Money Management While You're Playing

Good players have a lot to think about when playing poker. Cards, position, pot odds, tells, reading hands, computing outs and putting it all together takes up a huge portion of your mental energy. There's another part of the game that you have to think about and it concerns looking at the big picture.

This is what you should also be thinking about while the game is in progress:

1. **What is your table image?**

    This is a function of money management because how the other players look at your style of play affects your winnings—and your losses. Most players will try to act like they are tight, aggressive, passive, or loose. This doesn't work when playing against experienced players because once they know what image you are locked into, they know how to take advantage of it.

    Don't try to project any one image until you're in the game for a while and you've seen quite a few hands. If you get a long run of unplayable hands when you first sit down, then you will look like a tight player to the others. You should then deliberately play tight in order to confirm your opponents' suspicions about you. Then you can change gears to take advantage of their misconception.

    If you sit down in the game and you get a run of great, playable hands, you will look like a loose player to everyone else. At that point, you should play as loose as you can without playing badly. After you've established your loose image, you can start playing tight. When you play a hand after that, you will get called a lot more with losing hands because it takes a long time to change an initial impression.

    SAID

    "At gambling, the deadly sin is to mistake bad play for bad luck."

    — Ian Fleming

    Let the cards you get determine your image and then you can take advantage of that.

2. **Small, statistical advantages can cause big swings in your bankroll.**

    If you are a 4-1 favorite you don't have to repeat that situation too many times before those big odds overcome the times you lose. However, if you're a 4/10ths of one percent favorite, you will be a winner in the long run, but the long run might take tens of thousands of hands. In the meantime, you can lose an astronomical amount of money pushing that small advantage.

3. **If you are a losing poker player how can you tell if it's due to your lack of skill or to a very long run of bad luck?**

    All of us can go through long periods of missing our straight and flush draws and then finally make a hand only to come in second place. That's very expensive.

> "If you can't quit when you're winning and won't quit when you're losing, that leaves only one logical time to stop—when you're broke."
>
> — Tex Sheahan

    There is one very reliable indicator that will answer this skill/luck question. And that is, are you losing more than 300 big bets in the game you're playing? Are you losing more than $1,800 at $3-$6 hold'em or $2,400 at $4-$8 hold'em or $1,500 at $1 to $5 seven-card stud? If so, then there's a better than 99% chance that it's because of your lack of skill and not bad luck.

4. **There are only a few genuinely legitimate and relevant reasons to quit a poker game. Here they are:**

    A. Game conditions have changed for the worse. Perhaps bad players have been replaced by good players. Maybe the game is short-handed and you don't like that.

    B. You become ill, distracted or too tired to play.

    C. You unexpectedly loose too much money for the game you're playing and you can't emotionally handle it.

    D. You can move to an even better game.

    E. There is a better use of your time right now. Perhaps you have an appointment to keep.

    F. You are worried about being cheated. This is not a concern in a casino poker room; however, if you are playing in a home game it might be on your mind. It is not necessary that you are actually the victim of cheating for it to be correct for you to leave the game. If you suspect cheating and it's consuming your mental energy and affecting your game and concentration, then you should leave the game. Rule E then applies. There is a better use of your time right now. Namely, you can use that time to look for a better game.

5. **It is wrong to quit just because you are losing.**

It is the reason that you're losing that is important. If you are being outplayed and you're in over your head, talent-wise, then you should quit because you're also losing. Do not quit if you're a favorite in the game and you just happen to be temporarily down. If you've missed a few expensive draws or had a bad beat or two, don't quit if you're still one of the best players in the game.

6. **Leaving when you're winning can also be a bad move.**

Again, you need to know why you're winning. If you are clearly not one of the best players in the game and you are lucky enough to win some big pots early on, then you might want to think about leaving because you're winning. The longer you stay in the game, the chances are greater that the better players will win back that big stack you have in front of you.

SAID

"If you are a favorite, you should continue to play even if it means using toothpicks to prop up your eyelids."

— David Sklansky

7. **The truth about all low limit poker games is that the players tend to play looser the longer the game is in session.**

Your job is to wait for that to happen and then take advantage of it. Usually, the best way to do that is to loosen up a little bit yourself, but not too much.

8. **Do not be concerned with how much money another player is winning.**

Too many players mistakenly think that this is important. We all have lucky streaks and there's not much you can do about it. Do not make the mistake of thinking that you have to get even with that player or you have to immediately match his winnings. Your job is to play your best game, make your best decisions and, as they say, let the chips fall where they may.

9. **Only change decks if the people you are playing with believe that it affects your luck.**

I have been playing poker for more than twenty years and I have never, not once ever, asked for a deck change. Until recently. The cards do not know you, they don't know how to play poker or how to rank hands, they don't know or care if you're winning or losing and they certainly don't have a memory. It is superstitious and a waste of time to change the deck just because you're losing.

However, there is a good reason to get a deck change, which is that the other players may believe it affects your luck. If you're losing and you ask for a deck change, the other players will treat you as if you just changed your luck on demand. They will treat you differently and you will have new-found respect when you play your next hand.

10. Be friendly and cordial to the dealers.

Besides the fact that it's the right thing to do anyway, remember that it's the dealers who describe problems and irregularities to the floorman. If a dealer wants to he can sway a decision against you.

11. Older, tight players could profit by continuing to play when the game gets looser.

This note is for my older poker playing friends. Guys, your tight, conservative style of play can be very profitable when the games get a little looser. Instead of going home at 5 p.m. why don't you hang around a little longer in the evening and on weekends and take advantage of the bad players? Yes, you'll have some ups and downs but your style of play will keep you focused and you'll win bigger pots and make more money.

12. Can you drink alcohol and play poker?

The answer is a resounding yes! But, that's if, and only if, you're already the worst player in the game. You are the only one who has nothing more to lose. In fact, you might misread someone's hand or your own hand and win a pot that you might have folded if you were completely sober. They say that in an imperfect world, imperfection works best. You never know.

Summary

Managing your money is what you're doing. The decisions you make while playing the game is how you're doing it. The two are inseparable and the player who just thinks about playing poker without being aware of the money management aspect of the game cannot be a winner.

RATE YOUR POKER ROOM

I am lucky enough to have played poker in almost every major poker room in the United States of America. About seven years ago my wife got sick and I needed better health insurance than what I had at the time. I looked into it and learned that the over-the-road truck driving industry offered some of the best insurance in the business that was not too hard on preexisting conditions. So, I took a job as an eighteen-wheeler truck driver.

It turned out to be one of the best moves I've ever made in my life. I got paid for traveling all over the country. I couldn't believe how much I liked the job and how well it paid, once I got past the training period. The best part was that I was always able to park at and play in poker rooms from Connecticut to California and from Seattle to Florida. Many times my job required me to spend the weekend in Las Vegas, Reno, Phoenix or Biloxi.

The company I worked for knew that I was a poker player and writer and they would usually try to get me a load that delivered somewhere near a poker room. It worked for me because my company's headquarters was in Phoenix and that city has some of the nicest, best managed poker rooms in the nation. Actually, I think I ended up as a poker player who was using a trucking company as a means to get around to all the poker rooms in the country. As long as I picked up and delivered my loads on time, my free time was my own.

FACT!

Not all poker rooms are the same quality and there can be quite a difference between them.

As a result, I've been there, seen it and done that many times. I've learned that not all poker rooms are the same quality and there can be quite a difference between them. When I go to play poker, I have a wide range of factors in mind that I use to evaluate that room. Here's a list of some of the things I think about:

Accessibility

1. Do they have adequate parking?

2. Do they have covered parking or a garage you can use in case of bad weather?

3. How far is it to walk from the parking lot to the building?

4. Do they have shuttle transportation?

5. Once inside the building, how close is the poker room? Is it on the main floor or is it way back in the far corner of the top floor?

The Poker Room

1. Is the poker room closed in or are there a thousand slot machines being played all around you?

2. Where is the poker room cage? Is it always open when there are games in progress?

3. Do they have coat racks, shelves, or lockers for personal belongings?

4. Do they have chip runners that you can buy your poker chips from?

Customer Service

1. Can you sign up for a game by phone?

2. Is the list for the games publicly posted or is it a secret list kept behind the podium?

3. Can you get a beeper so you can leave the room while you're waiting for your game?

4. Do they announce games and call players over the public address system?

5. Do they try to interest you in other games they might be trying to get going?

6. Do they have enough dealers to start a game when there are enough players? Or are there twenty names on the list at noon and they say, "Sorry, we don't have a dealer scheduled to come until 2 p.m."

7. Are the floor persons friendly and communicative? Or do they look the other way when they know you're approaching them to ask a question?

8. Do they have copies of *Card Player* magazine or other such material?

Food and Drink Service

1. Are the drinks complimentary, or do you have to pay for them?

2. Do they have a water fountain and an self-serve soda fountain in the poker room?

3. Do they have a poker player's mini-buffet filled with snacks?

4. Do they offer comps for a free meal if you play a certain amount of time?

5. Do they have a half-price player's menu?

6. Can you eat your meal at the table while playing poker?

7. Do they have food service in the poker room?

8. Can you earn money toward meal comps for time played?

9. Do they bring free pizza for the players in the evening or free donuts in the morning?

Promotions

1. Do they have a reduced rake on their slower nights?

2. Can you get $25 for a $20 buy-in or some other deal early on their slow mornings?

3. Do they have double jackpot or $10,000 added to the jackpot on their slow week nights?

4. Do they have special promotions during football and baseball season? Is the jackpot bigger during Monday Night Football? Do they have a baseball pool for the poker players?

5. Do they have seat drawings for cash?

6. Do they have splash pots? That means adding chips to a pot in progress.

7. Do they have giveaways on special holidays? One poker room I played in gave away televisions, VCRs and DVD players last Easter.

8. Do they have special hotel room rates for poker players?

Riverboat Casino Poker Rooms

If you play at one of the poker rooms in Indiana, Illinois, Iowa, or Missouri, there are a few other things you might want to know about. These states have what they call riverboat gambling. All of these casinos have to be built on boats that can be floated on major waterways like the Mississippi, Missouri and Ohio Rivers.

These states have a limit on how much a player may lose in any one two-hour period, and that limit is $500. This is mandated by state law, and means that the riverboat you play on has to have some way to keep track of how much money you buy-in for. To accomplish this, everyone who enters a riverboat casino is issued a card by the casino that serves to identify players and keep track of spending, wins and losses. It has a magnetic strip on the back just like a credit card and a player cannot buy chips or slot tokens without it.

This has some implications for the poker game that you don't see in places like Las Vegas, Reno or Phoenix. This is what it's like to play poker on a riverboat:

1. You have to present your card at the casino entrance where it is swiped and read by a computer. This activates your card

and allows you to buy up to $500 in chips or tokens until the beginning of the next even-numbered hour.

2. The clerk who swiped your card will look at his computer screen, your card and then at you. He will then wish you luck while calling you by name.

3. These riverboat casinos do not have a cashier's cage in the poker room. If you want to play poker, you have to go sign up in the poker room and when you get your seat, you cannot buy your chips from the floor man or the dealer. You have to make your way back into the casino and stand in line to buy your chips from the casino cashier, along with all the slot machine players.

4. When you buy your chips, the cashier will swipe your card and tell you how much of your $500 limit is left, while again calling you by name.

5. You are not allowed to give or loan any of your chips to another player and you cannot cash in any chips for another player. It is actually a violation of the state law.

6. If you run low or run out of chips while playing poker, you cannot buy any chips from the dealer or play with cash, even large bills. You must get out of your seat, make your way back to the casino cashier and buy more chips. Again, you have to do this yourself. No one else may do it for you and there is no such thing as a chip runner.

7. This loss-limit requirement has a negative impact on the types and limits of poker games offered in these riverboat casino poker rooms. Because of the $500 limit, there are no game limits higher than $15-$30 hold'em or a $2-$5 ante/$200 buy-in pot-limit hold'em game. The casino has to play games that give most players a chance to have their $500 last at least two hours. Cash games are strictly against the law.

8. There is one legal way to play a higher limit and that is to have a particular game start at noon, 2 p.m., 4 p.m. or some other even-numbered hour. This allows the players to buy in for $500 right before the game starts and then they can buy

another $500 a few minutes later right after the big hand passes twelve. This way, all of the players can get $1,000 on the table to start the game.

9. The fill procedures are so cumbersome that the dealers ask the players if they can buy their white or red chips as needed rather than ask for a fill. The fill has to be made by security and the chips have to come from the main casino cashier's cage. There was one instance where I asked the dealer to break a $100 chip for me and she curtly told me, "Get it from another player," even though she had the chips in the tray in front of her.

This is not to say that playing poker on a riverboat casino is all bad. It's just that there are some big differences and it seems that they are all negative from the player's point of view.

CHEATING AT POKER

If you can't be an honest poker player, then you should just be honest without being a poker player.

From the early 1800s until about 1910 poker was known by it's more common and popular name, "That Cheating Game." It seems that almost everyone who played the game cheated in some way, that cheating was almost expected of players, and that good cheats could make a comfortable living at the game.

Cheating was so pervasive that one story will give you an idea of what it was like to play poker in the 1880s. There was a regular high stakes game in Cincinnati, Ohio that was frequented by men from the highest levels of society. Regulars in the game were the city's movers and shakers and most prominent citizens. The players were bank presidents, owners of corporations, elected politicians and the like.

On one Saturday night, one of the regulars was caught using a holdout device. A holdout device is a mechanical contraption that is strapped to the body from the thighs up to the chest with a smooth-operating, retractable arm that goes down the inside of the shirt sleeve and emerges at the cheater's palm.

Using a combination of thigh contractions and special arm movements, the retractable arm can be made to barely come down past the shirt sleeve where the cheater can place a certain card (or cards) in the clip and then have it retract back up his arm, out of sight. He can then holdout those cards until he needs them for a certain poker hand.

Well, as I said, he got caught. There was almost one hundred thousand dollars in play in the game. What do you think the other players did when they caught him? Banned him from the game? Took his money? Had him "taken care of" by hit men? Exposed him publicly? Getting caught wearing a holdout device under your clothes during a poker game is positive proof that you're cheating. You can't explain that away or try to convince anyone otherwise.

You would have thought that he would have been found floating down the Ohio River the next day. But he got lucky. He was caught by a group of players who turned out to be just as dishonest and greedy as he was. They forced him to acquire a holdout machine for each one of them and teach them how to use it!

If there's any attempt at all to cheat at poker in a public card room, it's almost always done by a dishonest player or by two players in collusion with each other. The card room manger has the right to look at player's cards whenever he detects suspicious betting patterns that are the telltale signs of player collusion. You won't see that very often. I've seen it only one time in twenty-two years of playing.

If you're ever in a poker game where there's some cheating going on, you can be sure that it's going to be in a home game, a dormitory or office, or at a "Las Vegas night' charity event. It will be at a time or place where the safeguards mentioned above are not in place.

SAID

"When I told Canada Bill that the game he was playing in was crooked, he said, 'I know it is, but it's the only game in town.'"

— George Devol

There are dozens of easy ways to cheat in a poker game. Most of the cheating moves are simple to learn, easy to execute and have a very high probability of success. So, if you think that by time you finish reading this chapter you will be an expert on how to cheat at poker and, by cheating, you will be a big winner at the game without having to learn how to play the game the right way, you're wrong!

I'm not going to teach you how to cheat at poker. The purpose of this chapter is to alert you to most of the ways that you could be cheated yourself, especially if you're playing in a home-style game. A simple, basic knowledge of the different methods of cheating is all you need to know to protect yourself from most home game cheats.

Most home game poker cheats are young, clumsy at the cheating moves, inept, beginners, poor poker players and, surprisingly, losers even when they're able to successfully cheat at the game. All you need to do is be aware of some of their tricks because they're usually easy to spot by knowledgeable players.

Cheating at poker can be broken down into six major categories:

Kill game: A game where the betting limits are increased—usually doubled—for the next hand only.

1. Passive Cheating

2. Pot Work

3. Marked Cards

4. Manipulating the Cards

5. Collusion

6. Professional Cheating

Let's look at each one of these categories individually.

1. Passive Cheating

Passive cheating is a form of cheating that does not require any advance effort or plans, is more of a mental activity than a physical activity and is almost always accomplished as a result of a certain situation presenting itself randomly during the game. These activities include:

A. Being seated next to a player who accidentally exposes his hole cards to you during the play of a hand without his being aware of it.

This gives you an unfair advantage over the other players. Without having done anything to cheat at the game yourself, another player has unknowingly put you in a position where you have an opportunity to do the unethical thing without anyone knowing about it.

The correct move is to immediately and very politely bring this to the attention of all the players at the table. Usually, that's all it takes to remedy the situation.

B. Sitting across the table from a dealer who deals the cards so high that you can quickly see the colors, suits or actual rank of the card as it flies toward the player being dealt to.

Some dealers hold the deck in such a way that all of the players to his left or to his right can catch a glimpse of the cards being dealt to all of the players in that direction.

The correct thing to do is to immediately tell the dealer that he needs to keep the cards lower to the table when he's dealing. A dealer who deals like this is probably not aware of it and will appreciate you bringing it to his attention.

C. Peeking at the bottom card.

Often the dealer will keep the deck in his hand for the entire time that the hand of poker is being played. During the course of dealing the game and playing his own hand he will often turn the bottom of the deck up high enough for a player at the table to see it.

It's usually unintentional, but the damage is done anyway. All it takes is a polite word to the dealer and the situation is remedied.

D. Recognizing an innocently marked card.

Many home poker games use the same deck of cards month after month. During this time a card may be accidentally marked by having some drink or food spilled on the back of it, it may be bent in a distinctive way, it may be actually torn or cut or cracked or have some other distinguishing mark on it. This happens to paper cards when they're used past their intended life.

The correct thing to do is make sure that all of the players know exactly what the marked card is and then immediately put a new deck of cards into play. If possible, it is worth it to buy the more expensive plastic cards. They last fifty times longer than the paper cards and they can be washed with soap and water when they get dirty.

2. Pot Work

Pot work refers to the ways a cheater can increase his winnings by handling the chips in the pot, instead of handling the cards. Different methods of pot work are:

A. Shorting the Pot

By far, this is the most common and easiest form of pot work to get away with. When it's your turn to call, and you have to call an $8 bet, all you have to do is throw $6 into the pot and you've made an instant $2. This is called splashing the pot.

The correct thing to do is to place your bet in a neat stack directly in front of you so that everyone can see the chips. Then slowly push them toward the pot without mixing them in with the chips already in the pot.

B. Splitting the Pot

Many home games are played high-low split, meaning the highest hand gets half of the pot and the lowest hand gets the other half of the pot. Splitting the pot after the hand is over is tedious and a lot of work for a player who is otherwise trying to enjoy the game.

Keep a close eye on the player who eagerly volunteers to split every pot. It's a chore and most players don't like to do it any more than they have to. The player who likes to do it all the time might be cheating. He cheats by

SAID

"Be more concerned with your character than with your reputation. Your character is what you really are, while your reputation is merely what others think you are."

— John Wooden, Basketball Coach

purposefully dividing the pot so that one stack has more chips in it than the other. He will then offer you your choice of which stack you want and if you pick the short stack he will quickly take the big stack. If you choose the big stack he will quickly discover his "mistake" and make the count right before giving you your stack.

Some cheats take this move to the next level to further reduce their chances of getting caught. At the beginning of the game the cheat will split the pot fairly and ask you which stack you want. He will then do this several more times while all the time offering you fair, honestly and correctly counted stacks. Before you read further, can you figure out why?

It's because it is true that we are all creatures of habit. Chances are, you will choose the stack on your right-hand side every time or you might choose the stack closest to you every time. Once the cheat learns which stack you will probably choose, that will be the short stack in the future. Sneaky.

C. Palming the Split

Some cheats will split the pot but will palm a chip or two while offering an otherwise fair split. And if they're going to do that, you can be sure that the chip in the palm isn't going to be the lowest denomination chip in the pot.

3. Marked Cards

Playing with marked cards makes it very easy for the cheat to be a winner in a poker game, if he's the only one to know that marked cards are in play. Poker is an easy game when you know for certain what the other players are holding, what card is coming next off the top of the deck, or which cards are in the discard pile. Playing with marked cards also has a few drawbacks, though. The biggest problem with them is that, if caught, they are proof that cheating is going on. Is there any other reason that marked cards would be used in a poker game? From there, it's just a simple matter of determining who's responsible for putting the cards in play.

The other drawback of using marked cards is that it causes the cheat to bet, raise and fold in odd and unnatural patterns. He will often fold a big hand that would have lost to an even bigger hand when it's obvious that all of the other players would not have folded. To draw an analogy from blackjack, what player would take another card when he's holding 17, 18 or 19? Answer: The player who knows the next card to come is a 2, 3, or 4 and he needs it to beat the dealer's 20.

Here's a list of the most common ways that cards can be marked for use in a home game:

A. Thumb Nail

When the President Casino opened their poker room in Biloxi, Mississippi in the summer of 1992, I played there almost every day for a month. It was the first public poker room to open within hundreds of miles and every home game player in the area came by to play in the new poker room. During that time the casino was forced to use dozens of new decks of cards because the cards put in play always ended up with thumb nail marks put there by the former home game players. A deck of brand new playing cards right out of the factory packaging would always have numerous thumb nail marks in the deck within thirty minutes. The marks would usually be on the aces and kings and no other cards.

Thumb nail marks are easy to make, can't be traced to the cheater and usually go unnoticed if they aren't made too obvious. The best solution is to insist on using plastic cards for your poker games. If you detect thumb nail marks on the cards, you can be sure they were made for the purpose of cheating, even though they may look small, innocent and incidental to normal use of the cards.

B. Creasing

The card can be bent in a way that looks natural and innocent but has a specific meaning to the cheater who did it.

C. Corner Work

The corners of the cards are usually the first part of the card to show natural wear and tear when they are used for a long time.

A cheater can take advantage of this knowledge by bending, tearing or cutting the corner in a way that looks natural.

D. Waving

To put a subtle curve in the card without making a full bend. You do this by gently bending the card about your finger until it is misshapen.

E. Pegging

To make a sharp, pointed indentation in the card by use of a nail, needle or thumbtack. The mark is made into the face of the card so that it can barely be felt or seen on the back of the card. If made in the right spot, the dealer will know the value of the card as he deals it off the top of the deck.

F. Shading or Daubing

This is also called art work. It is to paint the backs of the cards with a gold or silver oily substance that can be seen only with the use of special glasses or contact lenses.

For this type of cheating to work, the cheater must wear glasses or lenses tinted the same color as the daub. If you're playing with red cards and someone is wearing red tinted glasses, then you should be suspicious. You could ask to borrow his glasses so you can look at the cards yourself, but you run the risk of directly accusing him of cheating this way.

What I would do is casually stand behind him and look down through the side of his glasses at the table to see if you can see any marked cards. Even a clumsy attempt to do this would tip him off that he's a suspect and that might be all you need to stop the cheating.

G. Sunning

This is simply the practice of putting the chosen cards out in the direct sunlight until they have faded enough that only the cheater knows to look for the slight fading and lack of bright color and luster.

H. Shaving

This is the practice of slicing 1/64th of an inch off the sides of the cards so that they aren't as wide as the rest of the deck, but only so much so that the cheater alone will notice it. Some novelty supply houses carry a specially-made paper cutter that is specifically designed to shave playing cards.

I. Dotting

This is art work that is done to the backs of playing cards that have busy artful designs on them. It's easy to add a dot or two in the right spot to help identify a specific card.

J. Line Work

As an alternative to dotting, certain lines in the design on the back of the card can be thickened. With just a little awareness and practice, it makes reading the card from the back very easy.

K. Sanding

All you need is an emery board or some very fine sandpaper to gently rub off the protective coating on the back of a desired card. This can be both seen and felt by the cheater.

L. Shadowing

The poker table used in home games will often have a sheet or blanket over it to help with picking up the cards off the table, absorbing noise made by the chips, and keeping the table clean. If you use a very white sheet and you have very bright lights you can determine which cards are the court cards as they are being dealt to the players. It takes practice and you have to be quick, but, believe it or not, the court cards cast a darker shadow over the sheet while they are in the air to the players. This knowledge is most valuable to the cheater if you're playing lowball.

> **FACT!**
> Poker is not a team sport.

M. Waxing

This is the practice of applying wax to the back of a specific card, usually an ace. This is so that when cards are placed on top of the ace, and the deck is then tapped, the cards on top of the ace will slide enough to allow the cheater to cut the deck at that point, thus putting the ace on the top of the deck after the cut. This is usually done to only one card in the deck, otherwise the entire deck will be sliding off all the time.

N. Sorts

I saved the best way of using marked cards for last. There are many manufacturers of playing cards who make cards with designs on the backs that extend all the way out to the border of the cards. The Bee brand of playing cards is the most popular. The design covers the entire back of the card. It does not have a white border around the card.

The secret to cheating with these cards lies in the fact that it is impossible for every one of the millions of cards that come off the press to have the design in the exact same place on the card. If you look at the corners of the cards you will see that the design, usually diagonally crossed lines, varies in its position on the card by the smallest of margins. Each card is randomly different in the way that the design is off by that small fraction of a millimeter.

The way to cheat is to buy dozens of packs of these cards and then to sort through them to find enough cards that are off in exactly the same way. Once you memorize the positions of the patterns you can then put together an entire deck to suit your needs. The advantage of this type of cheating is that no cards are actually marked by anyone. You're using real cards that don't have any of the marks or art work mentioned above. The problem is that it is common knowledge that borderless cards are prone to being used in this way.

4. Manipulating the Cards

The purpose of shuffling, boxing and cutting the cards is to randomize their order in the deck and to make the exact location of any one specific card impossible to know. A dealer who handles the cards in such a way so as to circumvent this purpose is manipulating the cards for the purpose of cheating. There are many ways this can be done:

A. Stacking the Deck

This is the practice of picking up the discards in a certain order so that the cheater knows which cards are placed together in the deck. This is so that when he sees one of the cards in play, he will know that the other cards he has memorized are either right after that card or were dealt immediately before that card. This is also called running up a hand.

B. False Shuffle

If you're going to stack the deck you have to then employ the false shuffle. The cheater usually does this by pretending to be very awkward at shuffling and therefore unable to adequately mix the cards together. He will always make sure that the cards he has placed on top are the last cards to be shuffled, and they will always be on top when the shuffle is completed.

C. False Cut

The easiest way to perform a false cut is to have the player to your right cut the top of the deck and place it on the table for you to complete the cut. All you have to do is put the top of the deck right back on top of the bottom of the deck where it came from. The secret is that you have to pause to allow for a distraction after the other player cuts the deck. Often, in a home game, everyone will be distracted enough so that they will not notice what happened.

D. Close Dealing

Dealers who deal everyone's cards directly in front of themselves and then push the cards to the players could be examining the backs of the cards for marks. This is a slow and unnatural way to deal and is often, but not necessarily always, a tip-off that some cheating is going on.

E. Muck Work

Players who discard in turn and then go back into the muck to 'verify' which cards they threw away are often switching cards with the discard pile. It happens quickly before you fully realize what's going on and it takes some daring and some practice, but a lot of players are good at this. Unless you can replay a video tape of the action, there's almost no way to prove they were cheating. The best move is to have a strict policy of not touching the discards during the hand.

F. Double Discard

This is used during draw poker games. A player will discard, say, three cards and then put those three cards face down on the table in front of him. He will then pick up and look at his three new cards. Then he will quickly—while the action is on the next or subsequent players—discard again and pick up the cards he needs from his original discards. It's like getting to draw twice while the other players draw only once.

5. Collusion

This is the term for two or more players acting in concert for the purpose of cheating. Instead of having one player in the game who is cheating, there will be two and their efforts will be coordinated and they will be in step with each other. This also means that there is one less honest player at the table to help detect this cheating. The most common types of collusion are:

A. Dealer-Player

This means that the dealer, who can control the cards, will give his confederate the cards he needs to win. A player who cheats when he has the deal will win an inordinate number of hands and draw unwanted attention to himself. To get around this, he will deal the winning hands to his partner, which does not cause any suspicion. The dealer will often ensure that he only breaks even at the end of the game or is only a small winner or small loser while his partner is the big winner. Later, away from the game and unseen to everyone else, they will split the winnings.

B. Signaling

This is a way of communicating between cheaters. If the game is high-low then the way a player turns his cards will indicate the direction he is going, so his partner can go the other way. If a cheater needs a specific card, he can insert a specific word into the conversation. If he needs to give his partner information about his hand, he can place his chips on his cards in a certain manner. There is no limit to the number and types of signals that cheaters can agree upon before a poker game.

C. Whipsawing

This is the term for trapping an unsuspecting player between two players who are cheating by raising each other for the purpose of getting the player in the middle to put more money in the pot. After all the raising is done, one of the players will fold his bad hand and let his partner win the big pot from the victim.

D. The Ultimate Collusion

You will probably never see this unless you are very rich, but it has happened. This happens when you're playing in a full poker game and every other player in the game, including the butler, is in collusion against you.

SAID

"At the card game, one of the boys looked across the table and said, 'Now Reuben, play the cards fair. I know what I dealt you.'"

— President Lyndon B. Johnson

You should realize that if you're going to be cheated by partners in a poker game, the partners will probably arrive at the game in separate vehicles at different times; they may appear to not even know each other that well; they may leave the game at different times and they might even take the trouble to publicly dislike each other. There's no substitute for knowing the people you're playing poker with.

6. Professional Cheating

This type of cheating is characterized by older, more experienced players who cheat to acquire a substantial part of their income, to make a living from cheating and who are willing to go to extraordinary lengths to accomplish their goals. They are willing to work long and hard at being good at cheating. Here's a list of some of the things a professional cheat will do to steal your money:

A. Invest Money for Cheating Purposes

The things that a professional cheat will buy as an investment are:

1. Professionally marked playing cards:

   Card manufacturers do not mark their cards. Their cards are bought by gambling supply houses who hire experienced artisans to mark the cards. The cards are then professionally repackaged using the original stamp and wrapping. You first see them when your host throws a pack of new, unopened playing cards on the table and somebody else opens them for the first time.

2. A holdout table:

   This is a card table that is built specifically for card cheats. It has a small, thin, hidden slit under the table where the cheater sits. That slit is exactly the width, length and thinness necessary to slide an entire playing card into. And there it stays until another card is pushed into it to force the first card forward and out of the slit so that the second card can take its place.

   It is impossible to be a winner if you're playing at a holdout table. The best possible defenses are to periodically count the cards and to thoroughly inspect any card table that looks too good to be true.

B. Invest Time for Cheating Purposes

Many professional cheats are mechanics. No, I don't mean they work on cars; they work on cards. They are experts at manipulating the cards. It takes hundreds of hours to be even remotely competent at false shuffles, dealing seconds, dealing off the bottom, cutting to a specific card, dealing exact cards to a confederate and performing what genuinely looks like magic. Like Jack Benny said about playing the violin, "You have to practice just to be bad."

C. Invest More Time for Cheating Purposes

SAID

"Don't compromise yourself. You are all you've got."

—Janis Joplin

A cheat who makes a living from cheating has a full-time job. He has to ensure that there are enough regular players to keep the game going. Because this involves personal relationships, this takes a lot of time, especially if he's using a relationship as a cover for cheating. He just can't call you Friday afternoon and say, "Hey, make sure you're at the game at my house tonight because I need to cheat you out of your money." He will be much more subtle than that, and that takes a lot of time.

If your poker game host contacts you repeatedly and keeps the pressure on for you to show up at the game, that's a good sign that he's interested in more than just your friendship. But that doesn't always mean that you're being cheated. You could just be a bad poker player.

D. Cold Decking

A cold deck is one that's been inserted into the game when everyone is distracted all at once, say, when the butler drops a tray of drinks on the floor. And you thought my earlier comment about the butler cheating you was absurd! The cards in the cold deck have been prearranged so as to give the cheat a powerhouse hand at the same time everyone else makes a fantastic, but second-best, hand. It's called a cold deck because it is literally colder than the deck that's been in play up until now. It hasn't been warmed by human hands and the ambient room temperature.

7. Protection Against Cheating

You've already taken the first step to protect yourself against cheating just by having read this far. Knowledge is power. Just being aware of the possibilities makes the battle half-won. A few more things you can do are:

A. Always know the other players in your home game.

Know their motivations for playing, what their jobs and hobbies are, their education level, marital status, poker skill and anything else you think will help size them up.

B. Always cut the cards.

This is your best and easiest insurance against most kinds of amateur cheating. It's easy to do, doesn't require any special skills or tools, and your insistence on always cutting the cards will help inspire other players to do the same.

C. Always use a cut card.

A cut card is a card that is the exact size and shape of the playing cards except that it is a blank card. It could also be a leather or metal card made specifically for this purpose. This will prevent any problems arising from anyone being able to see the bottom card of the deck.

D. Don't ever be tempted to do anything unethical yourself.

Be the most honest player in your game. Your reputation will pay dividends down the road.

8. Catching Cheaters

My advice is not to directly confront the person you suspect or have seen cheating. You should say something generic to the players like, "I think there's some cheating going on here," without naming anyone. You don't want to risk having a direct accusation turning into a fist fight or a one-sided gunfight. Leave the cheater a way to save face and get out of the situation without feeling trapped. Usually that's all it takes.

"The severest justice may not always be the best policy."

— Abraham Lincoln

THE SMARTEST & DUMBEST THING I'VE EVER SEEN

"Bear in mind that your own resolution to succeed is more important than any other thing."

— Abraham Lincoln

I have two stories to tell you. They both happened during a poker game taking place in a casino poker room. These events are important because they both can serve to show you how people think during the heat of battle. Both times I almost couldn't believe what I was seeing because it was so incredible to me that anyone would even consider doing what they did.

The first remarkable incident happened at the Stardust Casino Poker Room in the summer of 1985. I was an U.S. Air Force air traffic controller at the air force base there just north of the Las Vegas city limits. For a while I worked the night shift and because there is no night flying there at the base, I was often given the rest of the night off after reporting for work at 10 p.m.

I was in the poker room one of these nights waiting to be called for my seat in the $3 to $6 hold'em game. I happened to be watching a pot-limit hold'em game on a nearby table when it looked like everybody in the game got a good hand all at once. The first player raised the pot. So did the second and third players. The fourth player raised all-in, making it $3,000 to call to the fifth player. It looked like the other players were going to call as soon as he did.

The fifth player hesitated. He studied the situation. He computed the odds. He read the other players. He counted his outs. Then he counted all of the chips and cash he had in front of him, which came to exactly $3,000—precisely the amount he needed to call. Then he slowly picked up his cards, looked at them, and held them so that we spectators on the rail could see that he had A♥ A♦. Then he slowly lowered his cards and as he was about to place them on the table in front of his chips, he quickly threw them into the muck!

Well, you already know that I think that this was either the smartest or dumbest thing I've ever seen in a poker game. Before you read any further, what do you think?

The instant I saw what he had done, I thought it was the dumbest thing I had ever seen at a poker table. I mean, pocket aces is the best hand you can get in hold'em and if you're not willing to play them, then what hand are you waiting for? For a long time afterward, I thought it was the dumbest thing I'd ever seen. But I was wrong. Once my understanding of the game improved, I came to realize that it was the smartest thing I've ever seen.

That's because there are a lot more factors to consider than just the fact that he had the best hand going in. This player did the right thing by folding because:

1. Even though he had the best hand at the moment, the hand is not over until the river.

2. Against four players who are willing to put $3,000 in the pot before the flop, you have to assume that they all have very good hands. Even though it's unlikely for five players to get great starting hands all at once, that's what happened here.

3. With pocket aces, he was a 4-1 or better favorite over any one of the other players alone, but he was not a favorite to beat all of them at once. With each of the four other players having an approximately equal chance of winning, his chances with the aces might have given him a 35% chance of winning. The problem is, that means he's going to lose this hand an incredible 65% of the time, even though he's a heavy favorite over each opponent individually.

4. The $3,000 he had on the table was his case money. It was all he had to play poker with at that time. It was early and he was a favorite to be a winner if he didn't get busted out on this hand.

5. He was patient. He knew that this was not the best spot to put all of his money in action. He knew that if he waited for other hands later in the game, he would have opportunities to put his money in the pot when he was a 4-1 favorite against just one player.

You can bet that I hung around to see how the hand turned out. One player made a straight on the turn and another player made a flush on the river. The player with the pocket aces would have come in third. At the time, I thought that this actually didn't matter because I believed that if it was right to call, then the right decision is the right decision no matter how the hand turns out. I was wrong because I wasn't aware of all of the factors that I just pointed out to you.

The dumbest thing I've ever seen happened in the spring of 2003 at the Vee Quiva Poker Room in Phoenix, Arizona. By the way, the Vee Quiva is one of the nicest, player-friendly, and best managed small poker rooms in the United States of America.

> ## FACT!
> There's a heck of a lot more to poker than just looking at your cards and putting your money in the pot.

I was in the three seat when Fred in the ten seat raised before the flop. Joanna, in the one seat, re-raised. Everyone else folded, Fred re-raised and Joanna called.

The flop was A♣ A♦ 8♥. With the raises and re-raises before the flop and the two aces on the flop, everyone instantly knew that a possible jackpot was brewing here. The jackpot requirements were that the loser had to make aces full of 10s or better and the winner had to make four-of-a-kind or better, and he had to play only one card from his hand.

This means that if Fred held one ace and Joanna had a pocket pair of 10s, jacks, queens or kings, we would have a jackpot if another ace came on the turn or river. It won't ruin the story for you if I go ahead and tell you now what they had. Fred was holding A♠ K♠ and Joanna had 10♥ 10♦. If the A♥ came on the turn or river, we would hit the $15,462 hold'em jackpot.

Fred bet on the flop and what happened next was the dumbest thing I've ever seen in a poker game. Joanna showed everyone her cards and said, "Well, Honey-bunny, if you're going to be a jerk and bet it, I quit." And then she threw her hand in the muck.

I am familiar with players who want to draw and play the hand for free whenever a jackpot is possible. They're afraid that if you bet you might force the potential jackpot loser to fold his hand without trying to make the hand and then hit the jackpot. This is because they have not thought the situation all the way through.

Whenever you are in a situation where you need a specific card to come on the turn or river to hit the jackpot, you should pretend that all of the money in the jackpot is actually on the table in the pot. That's because it really is in the pot, even though it's not physically there. If you hit the jackpot, they will bring the money.

Before Joanna folded, she should have realized a few things:

1. Given that they held the cards necessary to hit the jackpot, the odds of getting the A♥ on the turn were 44 to 1. If we missed, the odds are 43 to 1 of getting it on the river. Combined, we are about 22 to 1 to hit the jackpot.

2. If it costs her $3 to call on the flop and $6 to call on the turn, that will be $9 it will cost to possibly hit the jackpot. She gets to see the river card before she has to call any bet, so I count that as a free card at this point.

3. Her share of the jackpot would be $7,731. So, after the flop, she's in a position where she might have to call $9 to win $7,731. That's odds of 858 to 1 on a 22 to 1 draw!

4. The size of the pot had to be only $198 after the turn for it to be mathematically correct for her to play the hand. The size of the pot was, in effect, $7,731. So you can see what a horrible play it was for her to fold. The only way it could have been correct for her to fold was if her share of any jackpot was less than $198. This is the dumbest thing I've ever seen at a poker game.

TIP

Whenever you're in a position to possibly hit the jackpot, you must understand that all of the jackpot money is on the table in the pot for you to win on this hand—even though it's not actually physically there yet. They'll add it to the pot after you hit the jackpot.

INTERNET POKER

"Computers are useless.
They can only give you answers."
— Pablo Picasso

A 2002 survey of 10,000 high school English teachers nationwide revealed that a majority of those teachers thought it was more important that high school students learn how to navigate the internet than it was for them to learn Shakespeare. My, how the world has changed.

Modern poker has only been around for about one hundred and fifty years and while it has evolved and different games have come into existence, certain aspects of the game have always remained the same. To play poker, you've always had to physically travel to get to the game, or the other players have had to come to you. You've traditionally had to have cold, hard cash to play and if you were a winner, you always took your winnings with you when the game was over.

The biggest change in poker today is not in the game itself but rather in how easy it is for you to get to a game.

Due to the development of the internet, there are thousands of internet casinos and hundreds of other sites where you can play poker. The volume of money put into action through on-line gambling is second only to the amount of money involved in internet "adult entertainment" sites. Well, I guess in one way the world hasn't changed that much after all.

If you're a poker player and you want to use your computer to help improve and enjoy the game, there are some things that you need to know about: internet casinos, sites dedicated only to poker, and your computer itself.

Internet Casinos

There are some very good reasons why there are so many internet casinos and why so many people like to gamble over the internet. The most attractive features have universal appeal. All you need to play is a computer, an internet connection and a means of depositing funds in your account.

There are many benefits of internet casinos. Since you can play from home, you have total privacy. You don't have to dress up to leave the house, you can play anytime around the clock, it's very convenient because you don't have transportation issues, you don't have to wait for anyone else, you have an incredible choice of different games and limits and you can quit any time.

On the other hand, you will have to give up some information about yourself. For you privacy advocates, the news is good. The only thing an internet casino will know about you is your e-mail address and the small amount of technical information your internet provider delivers with any e-mail you send. You will be asked to provide a name to go by when you play against other players at a poker table, but it can be any name you choose, real or fictitious.

You can get a list of all of the on-line casinos at www.where-tobet.com and www.internet-commission.com. There are some things you need to know before choosing an internet casino and sending them any of your money.

All internet casinos operate from outside the geographical and legal borders of the United States. Most of them are located in the Caribbean Islands. That's because current federal law prohibits this kind of gambling activity and the use of interstate communications to place and collect on these types of bets. Currently, all internet casinos and the attendant gambling are legal in the United States if the casino originates from offshore.

Because of this, you don't have all of the checks and balances and safeguards that you are accustomed to when doing business with a company or a "brick and mortar" casino within the United States. There is no government body, council, oversight committee or watchdog agency overseeing or monitoring the activities, standards or honesty of any of these internet casinos. That old saying, "Let the buyer beware," certainly applies in this case. However, the news is not all bad.

TIP

Check the site to see how long they've been in business.

Despite the lack of government regulation, most internet casinos offer you quite a good experience and are scrupulously honest. Why? It's because they are in business to make money, and like every other good businessman, they know that a long-term, mutually satisfying relationship with a customer is the best way to make the most money in the long run.

The very best recommendation that an on-line casino can have for itself is simply the fact that they have been in business for a long time. They know that they have a lot of competition and they are in a "word of mouth" driven business. The longer a casino has been around, the more you can be sure that they are honest, they give the player a fair shake and they are customer service oriented.

If you find a casino site that you like, there are a couple of things you should do before playing:

1. Find out if the casino is licensed. Even though most of them aren't, some of them are.

2. Check the site to see how long they've been in business.

3. Ask your friends (you know which ones) about their on-line experiences and what they do or don't recommend. Get on www.rec.gambling.poker.com and make a few inquiries.

4. Look for the 24/7 customer service toll-free phone number and/or the customer service e-mail address. Call the phone

number and see if you can talk to a live person. But before you do that, check with your phone company to make sure you know in advance how much the per-minute charges will be.

5. Find out if they pay for advertising. This is a positive sign that the site is legitimate and that they intend to stay in business for a while.

6. Send an e-mail to them and tell them that they are being tested to see how fast they can answer your e-mail.

7. Look out for the phrase "For personal rather than professional play" or variations thereof. It's a disclaimer in disguise. This is their way of telling you that their odds are so bad that you will never win.

8. Competition among on-line casinos is fierce. Be aware that if you sign on with an internet casino, that you will soon begin receiving unsolicited e-mail advertisements from similar sites. Some people call it junk mail.

Once you decide to actually play at an on-line casino, the next thing you need to know is that almost any computer will do except for the very oldest ones.

To fully enjoy the game, your computer should have the following features:

1. Windows 95 or Higher

Almost all programmers who design poker software use Windows. This means that you are out of luck if you use a Macintosh computer. If you're going to be a serious poker player and you're going to use a computer to help, you're just going to have to switch over to a Windows computer. This is just the way the market is today.

2. A Pentium-class Processor Using Mmx Technology

This will allow you to enjoy the premium-quality graphics and run videos on your computer.

3. 64 Megabytes of Random Access Memory (RAM)

That's because poker playing programs are complicated and they use a lot of RAM. You might even want to have more RAM added now to accommodate future programs and upgrades.

4. A Modem Capable of 33,600 Bits Per Second (Bps) or More

The next higher speed is 56,800 bps. Much faster ways to access and navigate the internet are available, such as DSL (Digital Subscriber Line) or a cable modem.

5. A Sound Card

This will allow you to hear all the sounds that are built into your poker game, like the chips being thrown into the pot, the dealer's comments or the beep that tells you it's your turn to act.

6. A CD-ROM or DVD Drive

This is so you can easily install more poker programs.

7. A Vga Monitor that Can Handle 256 or More Colors

There are three ways to play on-line:

- You can download the entire casino package on to your hard drive. The disadvantage is that it initially takes a long time—up to thirty minutes. After that, everything is an advantage because this provides you with superior animation, graphics and sound. The download is permanent and you can play any time.

- You can use the JAVA format, which runs through your computer's browser. This saves time but sacrifices the quality of the sound and graphics.

- You can use HTML. The biggest advantage is the speed and immediate availability of the games you want to play.

Once you actually get into a casino site, you will see that you will get to play for free with worthless, imaginary money. This is so you can become familiar with the casino and try out the games with no risk. After you lose all of your free stake, or you have played a certain amount of time, you will be asked if you want to deposit real money in an account.

To play for real, you must have real money in an account with the casino. This is decision time. If you decide to go ahead, there are a variety of ways that you can get the money to them:

1. You can send them a personal check; however, you have to wait for the check to clear before the funds will be made available to you.

2. You can send a money order; however, you also have to wait for that to clear.

3. You can send a cashier's check. Some casinos will credit your account immediately and some will wait until it clears.

4. You can use your credit card and the transfer of funds is instantaneous. However, one major credit card company recently took themselves out of the send-cash-to-on-line-casinos business.

Note to the extra cautious: If a site advertises that they use a secure server to transfer funds, the use of a credit card is completely safe. There is no way that anyone else can acquire, use or abuse your credit card information. That's because they use the same type of secure encryption technology (128 byte) that major banking institutions and governments worldwide use to transfer billions and billions of dollars every day.

5. Sending money through Western Union is universally accepted.

6. You can use PayPal or a similar secure method.

Once your money is on deposit with the casino, you will be given an account number and a password to access your account. I recommend that you open your account with a small amount of money, perhaps $50 or $100. You should play at the small limits until you are comfortable and you feel like you know what you are doing. And then you should request that a small amount of the money in your account be returned to you. The purpose of this is to see if you get a refund and how long that process takes.

You should also keep a record or ledger of your on-line gambling, in the event of some sort of system failure or other problem. If there's a dispute, you are more credible if you have a record and you can definitively state which days you've played, how much you won or lost and especially what your current balance is.

I recommend that you get more deeply involved with an internet casino after you've gone through the above suggestions. Shop around. There are a lot of excellent sites to enjoy, and again, word of mouth is the best advertisement.

Internet Poker Rooms

Internet sites that are dedicated exclusively to poker are, on average, safer, better quality and a lot more fun to play at than poker rooms accessed through on-line casinos. You should always exercise judgment and prudence whenever you do business over the internet; however, I can tell you that the dangers and possible problems associated with internet casinos just don't exist when you play at the best internet poker rooms.

They also use very sophisticated computer programs to detect possible cheating and collusion. They are so good at it that, while some cheating is still possible, it's just not worth the effort to the cheaters.

Some of the best features and advantages of playing poker on-line are:

1. You can open an account with as little as $5.00!

2. Many poker rooms will add a 25% bonus to your initial buy-in if you are a first-time customer. Some poker rooms will give you up to $100 (in real money) when you open an account, regardless of your initial buy-in.

3. You can play 10¢-25¢ limit or 25¢-50¢ limit.

4. The quality of the live support and service through e-mail is superior. Many of these poker rooms are endorsed by well-known world-class players. These rooms don't have any problems to speak of because these players' reputations are on the line.

5. The rake is much lower than in a live game in a brick and mortar casino.

6. This is a great place to play tournaments. There are tournaments starting every hour of the day, the entry fees are low, some are freeroll tournaments and you can play any game you want. Some tournaments play up to 50 or even 100 places.

7. There are a lot of satellite tournaments. You can parlay a small buy-in into a poker cruise or a tournament with a $1,000,000 guaranteed prize pool.

> ## FACT!
>
> If a site advertises that they use a secure server to transfer funds, the use of a credit card is completely safe. There is no way that anyone else can acquire, use or abuse your credit card information. That's because they use the same type of secure encryption technology (128 byte) that major banking institutions and governments worldwide use to transfer billions and billions of dollars every day.

8. Many poker rooms have free hourly cash giveaways and other promotions.

9. You have the option to straddle, play the overs or play in kill or half-kill games.

10. You have the option to chop, although that doesn't happen that often. It seems that the games are so loose that it's never just the blinds in the hands.

11. An option that amazes me is the one where you can request a computer-generated profile of the playing habits of your opponents!

12. A couple of these poker rooms also offer you the services of a sports book while you're playing poker.

I think playing poker on-line is the wave of the future. Just like the automobile replaced the horse-and-buggy, the passenger airplane replaced the dirigible and the computer replaced the typewriter, the on-line poker room will replace the brick and mortar poker room. I don't think that B&M poker rooms currently in existence will fold up, never to be seen again, but I do think that fewer poker rooms will be built in the future than would have been, due to the internet. That's just my opinion, I could be wrong.

Poker and Your Computer

You can also play poker on your computer without being on-line. There are several good poker-playing software programs that you can use. The one I recommend is the Turbo Poker software by Wilson Software. There are three good reasons why you should use this software:

1. If you're going to be a serious student of the game, you're going to have to try all of the different software anyway.

2. Most everyone that you will play against in a live game or for money on the internet will have already used this software. They will have practiced and prepared while you haven't.

3. It's the best software of it's kind.

The different software available in the Turbo Poker Series covers all of the major poker games:

1. Seven-card stud

2. Omaha high only

3. Omaha high-low split

4. Texas hold'em

5. Seven-card stud 8-or-better

6. Tournament Texas hold'em

The number-one feature that makes all of these software programs so attractive is the fact that you can change any or all of the parameters of the game to suit your needs. Some of the features of a poker game that you can change, set and control are:

1. The limit

2. The number and amount of the blinds

3. The number of players

4. You can give any card to any player at any time.

5. You can specify which cards will come on the flop, turn or river.

6. You can freeze the button so that the deal does not rotate after every game.

7. You can peek at your opponents' cards.

8. You can record a game and play it over and over.

9. In a tournament, you control the limits, the length of the betting rounds, the number of re-buys (if any) the number of tables and players at each table and the payout structure. The software also saves all of your tournament payout information and history.

10. You can control the speed of play and if you decide to fold right away, you can zip to the end of the hand without having to play it out.

11. You can choose your opponents' playing profile from a list of more than one hundred profiles. Some of these computer opponents are very tough.

12. You can ask for tips and advice on how to play while you're in the middle of the hand. The software has an advisor that you can set and adjust for the skill level you want and your drawing and pot odds can be displayed anytime you wish during the hand.

And there are easily a dozen more options at your fingertips. These options will allow you to practice at home before you risk your money in a live game.

When WSOP Champion Johnny Moss passed away, it was estimated that he had played over two million hands of poker in his lifetime. Nowadays, using a good computer and a Wilson Software program, you can see the results of two million hands of poker in less than one hour.

Would you like to know how one specific poker hand fares against another specific hand over the course of your lifetime? It's easy. All you have to do is set up those two hands on the computer and specify the number of times to play the hand and you'll get your answer in minutes.

Did you play a live game yesterday and lose a hand that's been bothering you? You can perfectly recreate that hand and have it replayed on the computer hundreds, or thousands, or millions of times in just minutes. Then you'll know what the long-term expectation of that situation was.

www.rec.gambling.poker.com (rgp)

www.rec.gambling.poker.com is a site established to unite poker enthusiasts through the internet. You can think of it as a discussion group where you can talk to other poker players and share information about poker.

You can post and read messages, ask and answer poker-related questions, learn about other, new links and possibly meet new friends. And you could very well get a response from a well-known poker player or writer.

CHAPTER 23

POKER AND THE IRS

"The income tax has made more liars out of the
American people than golf has."

— Will Rogers

The average American who plays poker will probably have a poker-generated contact with the IRS sometime during his poker playing career. Millions of Americans regularly play poker in public poker rooms and many of those players will play in a poker tournament. The IRS knows this and they have gotten in on the action by beginning to enforce reporting and tax withholding regulations against poker players.

I want to stress to you that what you are about to read in this chapter cannot and should not be taken as legal advice or looked upon as advice from a tax advisor, a tax attorney, an accountant, or financial advisor. It is each individual taxpayer's responsibility to understand and apply the tax law as it pertains to his or her own personal, unique tax situation. The purpose of this chapter is just to serve as an introduction to the most basic and simple guidelines that you would want to know about as a poker player.

Top 10 Tax Reporting Facts and Guidelines

1. You must report all of your winnings from all forms of gambling even if they have not otherwise been reported to the IRS. Winnings are reportable even if they were not large

enough to trigger the issuance of a W-2G. Some examples of the activities covered, but are not limited to:

- Poker playing in ring games

- Poker tournaments

- Other casino table games such as blackjack (21), Caribbean stud poker, Let it Ride, three-card poker, baccarat, roulette, big 6 wheel

- Slot machines

- Bingo

- Race track (horses and dogs)

- Sports books

- Raffles

- Lotteries

Non-profit churches or civic organizations are usually exempt from the IRS reporting requirements.

2. You may write off your gambling losses up to the amount of your gambling winnings. This is the big one that helps most taxpayers. This means that if you had gambling income reported to the IRS, you can reduce that amount by the amount of gambling losses you also had during that tax year.

For example, assume you won a poker tournament and were issued a W-2G for $1,000 in gambling winnings.

Without any losses to offset this win, the $1,000 is added to your taxable gross income for the year and you would probably have to pay some taxes on that $1,000.

If you had gambling losses for that tax year, you could subtract the amount of your losses from that $1,000 and then be subject

---

FACT!

The rule to report all gambling winnings really does apply to all gambling winnings. This means that money won from illegal gambling must also be reported to the IRS. My attorney has told me that, in a twisted application of justice, the penalty for participating in the illegal gambling activity can sometimes be much less than the penalty for not reporting it to the IRS. Go figure!

---

to a possible tax on the difference. The catch is that you can only subtract up to (in this example) $1,000 in losses because that's the amount of your win.

In other words, if you win $1,000 but have losses of $5,000, you cannot claim the other $4,000 as a loss.

3. Do not assume that you do not have to report gambling winnings just because you know you lost more than you won and you therefore think it is a push. Unbelievably, a win with an equal offsetting loss does not always mean that no additional tax is due. Each individual's tax status is different and the gambling winnings reported to the IRS affect your tax in ways you may not yet understand. That's because the gambling winnings affect certain Social Security income, certain standard deductions and your eligibility for itemized deductions.

    My advice is to always report your winnings since it's required by law and then carefully figure your taxes from there. Don't assume anything.

4. In what is really a convenient break for the taxpayer, all wins and all losses (up to the amount of the wins) from all types of gambling may be lumped together for the purpose of computing totals. This means that you do not have to fill out a separate tax form for each type of gambling activity being reported. Furthermore, a husband and wife filing jointly may then combine all of their totals so that they only have to use one tax form (Form 1040).

5. The cutoff period for determining gambling wins and losses is the tax year of each individual taxpayer. For the typical poker playing taxpayer, this is from January 1st through December 31st of each year. Other individuals may have a tax year that begins with a different day of the year and ends 365 days later.

    The point is that gambling winnings and losses are reportable for the one tax year only and may not be applied retroactively or rolled forward. You cannot offset a win next year with a loss this year and vice versa. You can, however, amend a previous tax return to correct a mistake or omission within three years of filing that return.

6. Your responsibility for being liable for paying federal income taxes is based on a combination of your citizenship, your residence, your source of income and some other factors. Money won gambling is not considered income unless you are a professional gambler. Otherwise, it is considered to be "other income" for tax purposes.

This means that the average American poker player must report all income from gambling on:

- Cruise ships anywhere in the world, regardless of registry or whether or not they are in international or U.S. waters

- Brick and mortar casinos or poker rooms on U.S. soil

- Foreign casinos or poker rooms

- Military installations anywhere in the world

- Internet web sites regardless where the site originates from

7. The amount of money won necessary to trigger the issuance of a W-2G varies by the game being played. Those games and amounts are:

- Keno: $1,500

- Slot machine: $1,200

- Poker: $600

The amounts for keno and slot machines are for net wins only, not gross wins. For example, if a Keno player bought a $1 ticket and won a $1,500 jackpot, his net win would be $1,499 and a W-2G would not be required.

The requirement to issue a W-G2 to poker players who win more than $600 is currently ambiguous. That is to say that in some areas of the country the poker rooms issue the forms and in other areas of the country they don't. That's because the exact law requiring this is extremely difficult to interpret and apply to poker as it is currently written. It's best to check with the poker room staff where you play if you're concerned with it. The practical application here is that if you're playing in a tournament and you're negotiating a deal at the final table, you can ask for $599 or less and avoid the IRS paperwork.

8. A person who is in the business of gambling and attempts to gamble for a living has a different tax status and different burdens than a recreational gambler. The IRS recognizes the job of professional gambler as a bona fide occupation if the gambler can meet three specific criteria:

A. The motive to gamble must be for profit. There must be a demonstrable attempt to make a living at it and it clearly cannot be done as only a hobby.

B. The gambling must be done regularly and the gambler must spend a considerable amount of time participating in gambling activities.

C. All of his activities, taken in their entirety, must show that he is in the business of gambling for a living. The first ironclad requirement is that he maintains an accurate set of books. After that, he should have as many of the trappings and signs of running a legitimate business as possible. This might include business cards, professional stationery, a post office box, a business bank account and a business listing in the phone book.

The professional gambler may then deduct expenses from this income that the average recreational gambler cannot. A sample list of deductions is:

• Professional books, magazines, journals, seminars, conferences

• Organizational dues

• Insurance

• Office supplies

• Transportation and travel expenses

• Meals and entertainment

- Legal expenses, other professional services

- Tax preparation

- Other unspecified gambling related items as applicable.

The professional poker player has to pay a self-employment tax. That tax is 12.4% of the first $65,400 of income and 2.9% of his total net income for Medicare.

9. All poker players who have a W-2G issued to them should take the time to obtain a copy of and become familiar with the requirements of IRS Revenue Procedure 77-29. You can get a copy from your local IRS office or online at www. irs.gov. If you've been issued a poker-generated tax form of any kind, it's to your benefit to understand what's in this law.

    Revenue Procedure 77-29 was written to provide guidance for taxpayers with gambling wins and losses.

    When the IRS audits your tax return and determines whether or not the deductions you're claiming are allowable, they use Revenue Procedure 77-29 as a guide. And if there's a problem, they're going to ask you why you didn't use it also. A word to the wise should be sufficient.

10. All gamblers are required by IRS regulations to maintain an accurate log, diary, journal or some other type of record of their gambling activities. The purpose of this record keeping is to substantiate wins and losses in the event of an audit. These records should include, at a minimum:

Keep these records "highly legible." The law actually states it!

- The type of game played

- Limits and/or size of bets made

- The date

- Where the gambling took place, including the name and address or location of the casino

- Who else was there

- The number of the table or the machine played

- The kind, amount and value of any casino comps

- A declaration of the amount won or lost

There are other incidentals that the gambler should make note of to help authenticate his claim:

- A statement from the casino

- Personal bank records, including canceled checks

- Records of cash advances

- Records of bank withdrawals and deposits

- Credit card records

- Hotel charges and records

- Transportation expenses

When dealing with the IRS, especially during an audit, the more voluntary documentation you provide, the easier it will be for them to allow your deductions.

I recommend that your diary entries be made in ink rather than pencil because you will be required to keep these records for up to seven years.

IRS Publication 529, "Miscellaneous Deductions" has additional guidance on how to substantiate your gambling deductions.

FACT!

The IRS employs the services of professional handwriting analysts when a gambling journal appears to have been "made up" because of an unexpected audit. If the expert determines that your journal was written all at the same time (and yes, they can positively do this), your deductions will be disallowed and you will be subject to fines, penalties and possible criminal prosecution.

SAID

"The wages of sin are death, but by the time taxes are taken out, it's just sort of a tired feeling."

— Comedienne Paula Poundstone

A CARD TRICK

"A Smith & Wesson beats four aces."

— Poker Wisdom

I'm going to teach you how to go through a deck of fifty-one cards one-at-a-time and then know exactly which card is missing from the deck. You do not get to look at all of the cards at once; instead, you are going to look at a card, think about it and then go on to the next card in the deck. You will be looking at only one card at any one time during the trick.

This trick takes a good deal of concentration, attention to detail, above average memory and some math skill. This is not a common, run of the mill, party magician's card trick. Rather, it is an impressive demonstration of above average intelligence suitably appropriate for poker players. If you're wondering if you have what it takes to pull off this trick I can assure you that, yes, you do. The fact that you're reading this book is a good indicator that you'll be able to do this.

You begin the trick by starting with a thoroughly shuffled deck of cards. Make darn sure that all fifty-two cards are there before the shuffle. The trick doesn't work if there's a card missing or if there's somehow an extra card. Make sure the jokers are removed. It's good to have a disinterested spectator shuffle the cards.

After the deck is shuffled, one card is removed at random while the deck is face down to everyone. Set that card aside and place something on top of it so that it cannot be moved or touched while the trick is in progress. You are going to set the deck down in front of you and turn the top card face up, for all to see.

You are going to look at that card, pause while you perform a mental exercise and then set that card aside. You then draw the next card off the top of the deck and do the same thing. You keep going until you've gone through the entire deck and after looking at the 51st and last card you announce which card is missing from the deck. You then turn up the card that was taken out of the deck at the beginning and you will all see that you have correctly named the missing card. See how easy that is?

This is how you do it. A deck of cards has a certain value. The ranks of the cards have a value that you're probably already familiar with. Each card is worth it's face value as follows

Card Value

A:	1
2:	2
3:	3
4:	4
5:	5
6:	6
7:	7
8:	8
9:	9
10:	10
Jack:	11
Queen:	12
King:	13

The ace is worth only one point, not one or eleven as it usually is. You could make it worth eleven points but that makes the math unnecessarily complicated.

Since there are thirteen cards of each suit, each suit is then worth ninety-one points $(1+2+3+4+5+6+7+8+9+10+11+12+13=91)$. All four suits then make the deck worth 364 points $(91 \times 4=364)$.

The deck also has a second point value and that is for the suits. Each suit is worth:

Suit Value

♠:	1
♥:	2
♣:	3
♦:	4

Notice that the point value of each suit was chosen because the number physically resembles the suit it represents. A spade has one big point at the top of it like a Christmas tree, so it is worth one point. A heart has two sides to it and has a rounded point on the top of each side so it is worth two points. A club has three leaflets so it is worth three points. A diamond has four points like the four bases of a baseball diamond so it is worth four points.

There are thirteen spades worth one point apiece, so this makes the spades worth thirteen points. There are thirteen hearts worth two points apiece, so this makes the hearts worth twenty-six points. There are thirteen clubs worth three points apiece, so this makes the clubs worth thirty-nine points. There are thirteen diamonds worth four points apiece, so this makes the diamonds worth fifty-two points. This makes the suits in the deck worth 130 points $(13+26+39+52=130)$.

Your starting point for performing the trick is knowing that you're going to start with two separate running counts. There are two ways to do this. One way is to start at 0/0 and work up by adding as you look at each card and the other way is to start at 364/130 and work down by subtracting as you look at each card. I prefer to start at 0/0 and work up because it's just a lot easier. But suit yourself.

Starting with the first card you look at, you mentally add to each of your running counts until you have added up the entire fifty-one card deck. The hard part about this trick is that you must add correctly, be accurate and always remember what the count was when you are looking at your new card.

Sometimes when you are performing this trick, there will be someone present who doesn't want you to succeed. Your best defense is to already know that ahead of time. You are in charge, you control the pace of the card count and you only proceed to the next card when you are ready. If you get distracted or have to stop the trick for any reason, be sure you have the current count firmly stored in your mind before you turn your attention to anything else. Be sure to take as long as you like and as long as you need to be certain that you're adding correctly.

After you add the last card to your count, you will have a minimum count of 351/126. This allows for the fifty-second card to be the K♦, which is the highest point count card that could be remaining. Alternatively, if you've started at 364/130 and are subtracting, the count should be 13/4 or lower after you've gone through fifty-one cards. If you haven't reached these numbers then you've miscounted or done something wrong.

Obviously, the numbers that you're left with are the value of the card that's missing. Just so that we're all clear on this, here's the value of the cards:

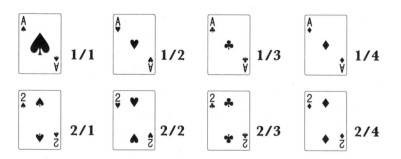

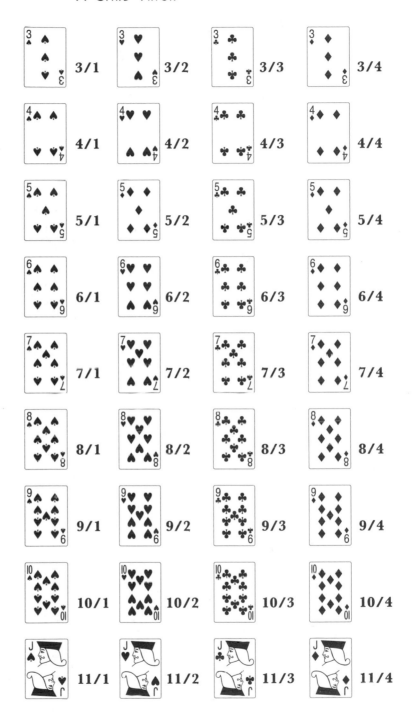

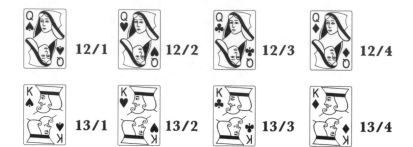

12/1	12/2	12/3	12/4
13/1	13/2	13/3	13/4

I've been doing this trick for twenty years and yes, I've won a few bets with it. The only time I've ever had a problem was when one of the spectators deliberately removed more than one card from the deck without my knowledge. The main benefit you'll get from knowing this trick is that it will add immeasurably to the respect you'll get as a serious player who can obviously keep track of the cards in a poker game. Enjoy!

SAID

"In an otherwise even contest, the man with the best concentration will almost always win."

— Johnny Moss

MOST IMPORTANT SKILLS

CHAPTER 25

If you want to be a professional poker player,
there is no elevator to the top.
You have to take the stairs.

There are dozens, if not hundreds of different poker games and variations of those games. No one can be an expert at all of those games, especially if he's never even played some of those game before. It's not possible to instantly know how to play every game perfectly from the very first hand. So, what do you do when you're confronted with a game you've never played before, and possibly have never even heard of before?

There is an answer, and that is to take a look at the big, overall picture. All poker games have certain elements in common. It doesn't matter if you're playing with wild cards, you're passing cards, you're playing high-low split or you can exchange cards at the end, there's a commonalty to all of these games. All you have to do is know what the fundamentals are and then think about how they apply to the game in question.

Here's my list of the top ten fundamentals of playing poker:

> ## FACT!
> The best players all have one thing in common: They have the most experience.

1. **The object of any game is to make better decisions than your opponents.**

   This means that you must be well-rested, free of distractions, have the time available to play, be focused on the game and have done your homework. You need to know what types of players you're playing against and you need to play your best throughout the entire game. Avoid players who you know make better decisions than you do.

2. **You must have a basic understanding of the odds.**

   By no means is knowledge of the odds all you need. You will not be guaranteed to be a winner just because you can quote any drawing or pot odds down to the nth degree; however, you can't be a winner if you don't know the odds. The odds are a good general guideline suggesting how you should usually play, but they are only one part of the game.

FACT!

Poker is all about making correct decisions. You're using cards and poker chips during the play of the game but what's going on is not really about poker. It doesn't actually matter if you win the pot or not. All that matters is that you consistently make the best decisions you can with the information you have available to you at the time. Winning pots and winning money are just by-products of cold, calculated, correct decision-making.

---

3. **You must understand the strategy of poker and the tactics used to employ those strategies.**

   You have to thoroughly understand how and why and when to make that first call, bet, raise, check-raise, semi-bluff, bluff, overcall and fold. More than that, you must understand why your opponents do these things.

4. **You must know your opponents.**

Anybody who plays at poker for a while can eventually learn to profit from his mistakes. If you want to become a great player, learn to profit from other people's mistakes.

I don't mean just knowing what their names are, I mean you must understand how and why they play poker and why they do what they do. You have to understand their style of play, what motivates them, what their goals are and how you would rate them using this Top Ten List.

5. **You must choose games you can beat.**

The profit and loss you have at poker comes from the quality of decisions you make. This means that you have to make better decisions than your opponents. If you are the 10th best poker player out of 500,000,000 poker players, it does you absolutely no good to be that good it you take a seat in a game with the 1st through 9th best poker players in the world. You don't have to avoid a game just because it might be tough, but you better stay away if the reason it's a tough game is because the players are all better than you.

6. **You must know your poker strengths and weaknesses.**

The old advice, "Know thyself," is good advice. A willingness and an ability to honestly evaluate your poker skills is the only way you will ever improve as a player. It's a good idea to ask another player whom you trust to offer some insight into your play. Besides looking at yourself from another's point of view, it's always a good idea to know what the opposition thinks of you.

7. **You must understand the importance of position.**

This is the one thing that you have to think about first when you decide to play each and every hand that you're going to play for the rest of your poker playing life. Your position at the table relative to the dealer has a profound impact on whether you should play a hand to begin with, and your position dictates how you should play the hand. If you don't understand position, you will be soundly beaten by players who do.

8. **You must have excellent beginning hand selection skills and you must play aggressively when you do play.**

There are two elements of this rule —hand selection and aggressiveness. This, in turn, produces four possible combinations:

A. Excellent hand selection/played aggressively

B. Excellent hand selection/played passively

C. Poor hand selection/played aggressively

D. Poor hand selection/played passively

All winning poker players are #1-type players. There is no such thing as a #2, #3 or #4 type player being a winning player. There are no exceptions and you cannot be a winning player without being a #1-type player, even if the rest of your game is perfect.

9. **You must keep records.**

How can this possibly affect your performance at the poker table? Winning players share many common attributes. They are all sharp, focused, self-aware, determined, self-reliant, quick studies and adaptable. They have the ability and desire to do what it takes to be a winner, and that includes learning from their mistakes. Records of past performance help reveal past mistakes. You can't learn, adapt, modify and improve on past performance unless you can reliably determine what that past is. A determination to keep accurate records stems from a determination to be a winning poker player.

10. **You must have the patience and discipline to do all of the above.**

It won't do to accomplish most of the above list. You have to be good at everything on this list. A big leak in any one of the above guidelines will keep you from being a winning poker player. A failure in any one category means an automatic failure in all categories. Look again at the list and see if there's an item you think you can ignore and still be a winning player. There isn't one.

SAID

"Uncorrected errors will multiply. Someone once asked me if there wasn't benefit in overlooking one small flaw. 'What is a small flaw?' I asked him."

— Don Shula

CHAPTER 26

POKER PERSONALITIES

"Never play poker with a guy named after a city or a guy named Doc."

— Poker Wisdom

Poker Legends of the Past

**Edmond Hoyle
(1672 – 1769)**

The name of Edmond Hoyle is inseparably and permanently linked with poker, even though the game of poker did not exist during his lifetime and he certainly never played poker. In 1742 Edmond Hoyle wrote a book entitled *A Short Treatise on the Game of Whist, containing the laws of the game; and also some Rules whereby a Beginner may, with due attention to them, attain to the Playing it well...* Incredibly, the book did not say a word about the game of Whist!

It was the first book of its kind to put into print the exact written rules of the game. Since card playing was very popular in England at the time, his book was the source for playing the game correctly and pretty soon, every game had to be played "according to Hoyle." The phrase was subsequently used to apply to all card games and soon rule books about card games used his name. *Hoyle's Games, American Hoyle* and *According to Hoyle* are some of the titles.

John H. "Doc" Holliday (1852 – 87)

Doc Holliday was born into a wealthy, genteel, aristocratic Southern family in Valdosta, Georgia not too long before the beginning of the Civil War. After the war he attended dental school in Baltimore, Maryland, where he earned a genuine medical degree and obtained a license to practice dentistry.

He was then immediately diagnosed with tuberculosis and decided to move to Dallas, Texas to take advantage of the dry and warm weather. His dental practice floundered because his illness scared off his customers and he quickly discovered that he preferred to spend his life in saloons and card rooms because the smoke-filled air provided a perfect cover for his constant coughing.

Within a few months he killed a popular city leader during a poker game in a dispute over a $500 pot. Later that night he abruptly, but cheerfully, moved to Jacksborough, Texas.

Shortly after opening his dental practice in Jacksborough, he killed a U.S. Union Army soldier during a poker game. Since this was the post-War Reconstruction era and he was a Southerner, he had a lot of help getting out of town that night. He moved to Denver, Colorado.

Discovering that Denver was one of those Western towns that did not allow firearms within the city limits, he checked his guns with the proper authorities. Later that night he nearly killed a poker player named Bud Ryan with a Bowie knife over a disputed pot. Ryan barely survived—minus three fingers and one eye.

This time Holliday moved on to Wyoming where he stayed a few short months and killed… nobody. After winning all the money he needed, he went back to Fort Griffin, Texas. There he met Wyatt Earp and Kate "Big Nose" Fisher. In short order, Doc Holliday killed a poker player over a $50 pot in a five-card stud game.

This time he was quickly arrested before he could get out of town and he was thrown in jail. Later that night, Kate Fisher set fire to a building near the jail and freed him while everyone else was distracted by fighting the fire. They then went to Dodge City, Kansas.

After a lover's quarrel with Kate, he headed off to Trinidad, Colorado. He won seven pots in a row in a poker game, then he shot "Kid" Colton and left him for dead after the subject of cheating was brought up. (The chances of winning seven hands in a row in a five-handed game are 78,124-1.) The pistol he used had an inscription on it that read, "To Doc from Kate." He then departed for Las Vegas, New Mexico.

Within a week, he killed a poker player named Mike Gordon and then returned to Dodge City. Once back in Dodge City, Wyatt Earp and Kate persuaded him to move to the dry, hot town of Tombstone, Arizona, where Earp was a federal Marshal. While passing through Santa Fe, New Mexico on the way to Tombstone, Doc Holliday killed three more of his fellow poker players who thought he was a bit too lucky.

Shortly after arriving in Tombstone, Doc killed one Bud Philpot and this time the murder was not poker-related. Philpot's crime was repeating gossip regarding Holliday and a certain stage robbery—gossip that was deliberately fabricated by his friend Kate Fisher.

Doc Holliday then participated in the famous shoot-out at the O.K. Corral and was found not guilty in a murder trial by reason of self defense. Now in the later stages of his disease and continuously coughing up blood, he rode the 800 miles back to Colorado on horseback—alone.

After arriving back in Colorado, the authorities tried to have him extradited back to Arizona to stand trial for the murder of Frank Stillwell. The Governor of Colorado refused to sign the extradition papers and Doc Holliday died in Glenwood Springs on November 8, 1887, at age 35.

His tombstone says, "He died in bed." No one knows where he's actually buried because his grave site had to be moved to allow for road construction and the records that would reveal where he's buried have been lost.

**James Butler
"Wild Bill" Hickock
(1837 – 76)**

Wild Bill Hickock is best know for the poker hand that is named for him, the "Dead Man's Hand." It's the poker hand he was holding when he was killed in a saloon in Deadwood, South Dakota.

At precisely 4:10 p.m. on August 2nd, 1876, Wild Bill Hickock was playing five-card draw at a table with Carl Mann, Charles Rich and Captain Massey, who was a retired Missouri riverboat captain. Hickock was sitting at a table with his back to the door instead of his usual seat on the opposite side of the table with his back to the wall.

He had just discarded three cards in his hand and as his replacement cards were being dealt to him, Jack McCall nonchalantly walked up behind him. Just as Hickock picked up his second card and as this third card was being slid across the table to him by the dealer, a bullet from an 1851 .36 Colt pistol entered the back of his head and exited from his right cheek. The bullet then went on to enter Captain Massey's arm.

Cards, cash, chips, cigars, chairs, tables and people went flying in every direction. McCall was apprehended and Doc Pierce, the town's undertaker, was called. When he arrived he found Hickock dead on the floor lying in the fetal position with four cards beside him—A♠ A♣ 8♠ 8♣.

Little known is the fact that McCall's gun was later tested and it was discovered that even though there were bullets in all six chambers, the only one that would fire was the one that killed Hickock. The other five bullets misfired.

McCall killed Hickock because he thought he had been cheated out of a twenty-five cent pot. This could be true because Hickock was a terrible poker player; he usually cheated when he did play and he was very blatant and open about it. He had a habit of drawing his guns and taking the pot whenever he felt like it and he had not yet had anyone object too strongly.

McCall was apprehended by the local citizenry and was found guilty of murder in a speedy trial and hanged on March 1st, 1877. President Ulysses S. Grant personally turned down a request to commute his sentence to life in prison. He was buried with the hangman's noose still tightly wrapped around his neck.

It has been variously reported through the years that Hickock's fifth card was either the Q♦, the J♦, the 9♦ or the Q♥, but these are all wrong. There never was a fifth card because Hickock never picked it up off the table and whatever it might have been, it was forever lost in the chaos caused by the shooting. This fact in incontrovertibly corroborated by Captain Massey and Harry Young, the bartender who witnessed the action.

It's ironic that Hickock has a poker hand named for him and that he is so closely associated with poker. That's because he was a lifelong Faro player and he actually played very little poker, relatively speaking. He just happened to be in a poker game when McCall found him.

Wild Bill Hickock was inducted into the Poker Hall of Fame in 1979.

William Barclay "Bat" Masterson (1854 – 1921)

If you really want to know who Bat Masterson was, you'll have to forget everything you learned from the popular television show of the 1950s. He spent most of his early adult life as a buffalo hunter and gambler while living alternatively in Denver, Colorado and Dodge City, Kansas.

In 1877, he was elected as a peace officer in Dodge City and from 1892 to 1893 he was the un-elected city marshal in Creede, Colorado. Up to this point in his life his reputation was that of a heavy gambler with a penchant for law and order. He also ran some casinos in Colorado and was a card dealer although everyone knew the real reason he worked as a dealer was because his mere presence helped ensure the peace in a gambling house.

He might have drifted into historical obscurity at this point in his life but for a major, watershed event that happened to him in Carson City, Nevada in 1897. He was an enthusiastic boxing fan and he went there to watch and to bet heavily on a fight between "Gentleman Jim" Corbett and Bob Fitzsimmons. Fitzsimmons knocked out Corbett in the fourteenth round. Boxing aficionados will recall that this was the famous "solar plexus punch" fight. Masterson was now forty-three years old and broke.

He migrated east and eventually became the sports editor of the New York Telegraph. He was very good at his trade and he became one of the world's boxing authorities. He died at work, falling dead onto his typewriter on October 25, 1921.

He was a legend in his own time and he did indulge himself in his unearned reputation as a prolific killer in one humorous way. He was still a heavy gambler late in his life, and whenever he needed a lot of money he would buy an old Colt .45 pistol for a few bucks, cut a lot of notches in the handle (he actually killed only two men in his life) and then sell the gun for hundreds of dollars.

George Devol (1829 – 1903)

George Devol left home and became a riverboat cabin boy at age ten. By the time he was seventeen, he was a professional riverboat gambler, plying his trade on the Mississippi and Ohio Rivers and at all points ashore between Cincinnati, Ohio and New Orleans, Louisiana.

He was a faro dealer, a three-card monte dealer, and a poker player. Or rather, that is to say, he was a crooked Faro dealer, a crooked Three-Card Monte dealer and an inveterate, professional cheat at cards. Before he turned eighteen, he could false-shuffle, false-cut, stack a deck, deal bottoms or seconds and run up a hand like a professional many years his senior.

Still a teenager at the time of the Mexican War, he won, or stole, tens of thousands of dollars from soldiers stationed near the Rio Grande River. He had numerous cheating partners during his lifetime and one of them, Pinckney Pinchback, a half African-American former slave, eventually became Governor of Louisiana.

George Devol never played an honest, fair game of anything in his life. He cheated, lied, and stole money from every person he ever came into contact with. He estimates that he won more than, and lost most of, two million dollars during his career, from which he retired at his wife's insistence in 1886. He died nearly penniless at his home in Hot Springs, Arkansas (boyhood home of President Bill Clinton) in 1903.

However, we do owe George Devol a huge debt of gratitude and that's why he's included in this list of poker legends of the past. Before he died, he wrote a book entitled *40 Years a Gambler on the Mississippi*. The book is not about poker or how to play poker but rather it is a book about his exploits as a riverboat gambler in the latter half of the 19th Century. The book contains 180 short stories taken from his life as a riverboat gambler.

It is one of the best gambling books ever written because he does a great job of describing poker, gambling and life in the 1800s. It is a must read for any serious student of poker or gambling who wants a historical viewpoint. The book is, of course, out of copyright but still in print and you can order a copy from the Gambler's Book Shop in Las Vegas at 1-800-522-1777 or on line at www.gamblersbook.com.

**Johnny Moss
(1907 – 1997)**

When Johnny Moss died in 1997, it was estimated that he had played over two million hands of poker in his lifetime. His career as a poker player began as a traveling professional throughout the south during the 1930s. In 1949 he participated in the now famous head-up match against Nick "The Greek" Dandalos, winning a reputed $5,000,000 in the five-month long five-card stud game.

Moss beat Dandalos because he was a pure poker player while Dandalos was a big-time gambler who played at poker. This match was the inspiration for what was to become the World Series of Poker tournament that began in 1970 and crowns a new world champion every year in April.

Johnny Moss has won the World Series of Poker three times and was inducted into the Poker Hall of Fame in 1979. He is affectionately known as "The Grand Old Man of Poker."

**Jack "Treetop" Straus
(1930 – 1988)**

He was called Treetop because he was 6'7" tall and usually sported a big beard. He's a much admired figure in the poker world because he's remembered for three important things:

1. He won the World Series of Poker in 1982.

2. He liked to carry thousands of dollars around in a small, brown paper bag, and he would sometimes lose the bag. He

took it philosophically and dismissed the loss with a "Such is life" comment.

3. During the 1982 World Series of Poker, which he won, he went all-in on one hand and lost the hand. But before he was forced to leave the table, a $500 tournament chip was discovered under his drink holder. It was ruled that he got to keep that chip and with that he went on to win the tournament. This is the inspiration for that poker saying that all a tournament player needs to win is "a chip and a chair."

Jack Straus died of a heart attack at the poker table while playing a high-stakes poker game. He was inducted in the Poker Hall of Fame in 1988.

Stuart "The Kid" Ungar (1953 – 1998)

Stu Ungar was a genius at cards. He was raised in New York City and was a world-class professional gin rummy player. He was so good that when he was a teenager he couldn't find anyone who would play rummy against him for money. He moved to Las Vegas, took up playing high-stakes poker and within three years he won the World Series of Poker for the first of three times ('80, '81 and '97).

He died in a Las Vegas hotel room of a drug overdose in 1998, at age forty-five. He was inducted into the Poker Hall of Fame in 2001.

Benny Binion (1904 – 1989)

Benny Binion moved to Las Vegas in 1946 to escape possible murder charges involving another gambler in Texas. He bought the El Dorado Casino and renamed it Binion's Casino. It was the site of the famous Moss-Dandalos match in 1949 and it is the site of the annual World Series of Poker tournaments held every year in March through April.

Binion's contribution to poker was that he helped popularize it by making it a game played in public by casual tourists instead of a game played by undesirables in smoke filled beer halls. Because of Benny Binion, live poker games are offered in almost every major casino in Las Vegas and Reno.

Binion's Casino in Las Vegas is a favorite of the locals because Binion knew how to treat a customer. His favorite saying was, "Treat people right and the rest will take care of itself." One time during a food service workers strike that hit most of the strip casinos, his son Jack came around to each slot machine player and filled their trays with free quarters from a big bucket carried by security guards. He died on Christmas Day, 1989, and was inducted into the Poker Hall of Fame in 1990.

Poker Legends of the Present

Doyle "Texas Dolly" Brunson (1934 –)

Doyle Brunson is a life-long high stakes poker player from Texas who won the World Series of Poker back-to-back in 1976 and 1977. While in high school, Brunson ran the mile in 4:18 and was picked as one of the ten best basketball players in the country.

His career as a professional athlete was all but assured. The Lakers were about to draft him until a ton of sheet rock crushed his leg while working at a part-time summer job. He took up playing poker full time and after years of playing the southern circuit, he ended up in Las Vegas in 1973. He won the world Series of Poker only three years later.

Brunson is the author of *Super/System, A Course in Power Poker,* a book that originally sold for $100 in 1978. Its subtitle is "How I Made Over $1,000,000 Playing Poker." Brunson is a voracious gambler, betting on anything on which he believes he has an edge. He has said that a revised subtitle to his book might be "How I Lost Over $1,000,000 Playing Golf."

Thomas "Amarillo Slim" Preston (1930 –)

Slim is another of the old-time Texas poker players who eventually wound up playing professionally in Las Vegas. He won the World Series of Poker in 1972 and his greatest contribution to poker has been his natural, down-home, soft-spoken, soft-sell, gentle manner that just makes everybody instantly like him.

Slim has appeared on *The Tonight Show with Johnny Carson* a dozen times and he has been on the television news show 60 Minutes three times. Being on television has enabled him to reach millions of potential poker players and that has helped spread the popularity of poker.

He was inducted into the Poker Hall of Fame in 1992.

**Johnny Chan
(1957 –)**

Johnny Chan won the World Series of Poker in 1987 and 1988 and came in second place in 1989. Nicknamed "The Oriental Express," Chan came to the United States from China when he was nine years old. He worked as a fry cook on Freemont Street in Las Vegas and soon quit his job to make a lot more money playing poker full time.

He is best known to the average poker player because of his role in the 1998 movie, *Rounders*, starring Matt Damon and Edward Norton.

**Scotty Nguyen
(1962 –)**

Of all of the eventual winners of the annual World Series of Poker, the route taken by Scotty Nguyen is probably the must unlikely and difficult. As a young boy in 1979, he left South Vietnam in a small boat and quickly found himself lost at sea in the South Pacific Ocean.

In an amazing stroke of luck, his vessel was spotted by a U.S. Naval ship and he was rescued. He and his family then settled in Chicago, virtually destitute, and there he stayed until he reached twenty-one years of age.

He then moved to Las Vegas to take a job as a poker dealer. He started playing in the small buy-in poker tournaments in town and then moved up in stakes as his skill increased. He went on to win the WSOP in 1997, at age thirty-five. He currently plays in most big tournaments and can be seen playing on television's Discovery Channel and ESPN2.

WORLD SERIES OF POKER

"Most players handle the winning side backward. They quit when they're winning, but stay when they're losing. Strange. When you're winning, it usually is because you're playing your best poker."

— Roy West

The World Series of Poker (WSOP) is a series of poker tournaments held each Spring at Binion's Horseshoe Casino in Las Vegas, Nevada. The Series began in 1970 when only 38 players competed in five events. Johnny Moss was voted the winner by the players and he was awarded a trophy to commemorate the event. The WSOP has steadily gained in popularity and prestige over the years and is now recognized as the premier event in the poker world. The winners of each tournament are recognized as the reigning world champion in their event.

The most recent WSOP featured 35 different tournaments with the biggest one being the $10,000 Buy-in No-Limit Texas Hold'em event. In 2003, novice poker player Chris Moneymaker won the world championship and took home the $2,500,000 first prize by defeating 838 other players. Let's take a look at the evolution of the WSOP and the winning hands that have taken place in the past 34 years.

1970 The First World Series of Poker (WSOP) was held in Las Vegas. Johnny Moss won all five events, defeating a field of thirty-seven other players, and was voted champion by the other players.

1971   The buy-in for the World Series of Poker was $5,000. It was a winner-take-all event.

The 2nd World Series of Poker was won by Johnny Moss. He defeated five other players to win the $30,000 first prize. The runner-up was Walter Clyde "Puggy" Pearson.

1972   The 3rd World Series of Poker was won by Thomas Austin "Amarillo Slim" Preston. He defeated seven other players to win the $80,000 prize. The runner-up was Walter Clyde "Puggy" Pearson.

1973   The 4th World Series of Poker was won by Walter Clyde "Puggy" Pearson. He defeated twelve other players to win the $130,000 prize. The runner-up was Johnny Moss. The last hand was:

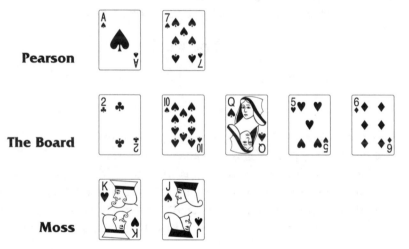

1974   The 5th World Series of Poker was won by Johnny Moss. He defeated fifteen other players to win the $160,000 prize.

1975 The 6th World Series of Poker was won by Sailor Roberts. He defeated twenty other players to win the $210,000 prize. The runner-up was Bob Hooks. The last hand was:

Roberts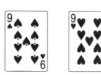

The Board [unknown]

Hooks

1976 The 7th World Series of Poker was won by Doyle "Texas Dolly" Brunson. He defeated twenty-one other players to win the $220,000 prize. The runner-up was Jesse Alto.

Brunson

The Board

Alto

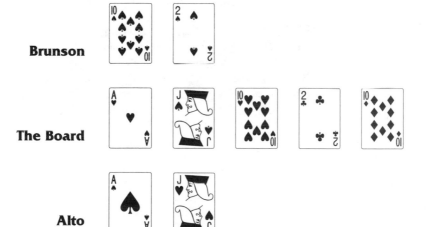

1977   The 8th World Series of Poker was won by Doyle "Texas Dolly" Brunson. He defeated thirty-three other players to win the $340,000 prize. The runner-up was "Bones" Berland. The last hand was:

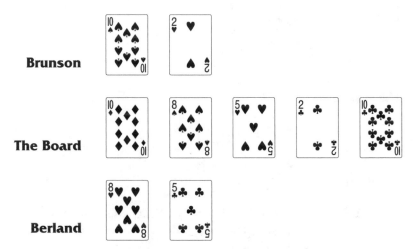

Brunson

The Board

Berland

Brunson won the World Series of Poker two years in a row by making a full-house while holding a 10 and a 2.

1977 Final Table		Hometown	Prize
1st	Doyle Brunson	Lubbock, TX	$340,000
2nd	"Bones" Berland	Las Vegas, NV	-0-
3rd	Milo Jacobson	Texas	-0-
4th	Andy Moore	Sarasota, FL	-0-
5th	Sailor Roberts	San Angelo, TX	-0-

1978 The 9th World Series of Poker was won by Bobby Baldwin. He defeated forty-one other players to win the $210,000 prize. This was the first year that the prize money was divided among the top five finishers. The runner-up was Crandall Addington. The last hand was:

Baldwin

The Board

Addington

1978 FINAL TABLE		HOMETOWN	PRIZE
1st	Bobby Baldwin	Tulsa, OK	$210,000
2nd	Crandall Addington	San Antonio, TX	$84,800
3rd	Louis Hunsucker	Houston, TX	$63,000
4th	Buck Buchanan	Killeen, TX	$42,000
5th	Jesse Alto	Houston, TX	$21,000

At age 27 Bobby Baldwin was the youngest-yet winner of the World Series of Poker.

1979   The 10th World Series of Poker was won by Hal Fowler. He defeated fifty-three other players to win the $270,000 prize. The runner-up was Bobby Hoff. The last hand was:

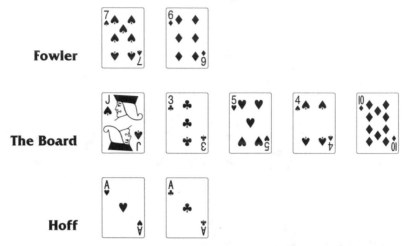

Fowler

The Board

Hoff

1979 FINAL TABLE		HOMETOWN	PRIZE
1st	Hal Fowler	Los Angeles, CA	$270,000
2nd	Bobby Hoff	Houston, TX	$108,000
3rd	George Huber	Las Vegas, NV	$81,000
4th	Sam Moon	Corpus Christi, TX	$54,000
5th	Johnny Moss	Las Vegas, NV	$27,000
6th	Sam Petrillo	Van Nuys, CA	-0-
7th	Crandall Addington	San Antonio, TX	-0-
8th	Bobby Baldwin	Tulsa, OK	-0-

Hal Fowler was the first amateur to win the World Series of Poker.

The Poker Hall of Fame was founded. The first seven inductees were: Johnny Moss, Nick "The Greek" Dandalos, Felton "Corky" McCorquodale, Red Winn, Sid Wyman, James Butler "Wild Bill" Hickock, and Edmond Hoyle.

1980 The 11th World Series of Poker was won by Stu Ungar. He defeated seventy-two other players to win the $385,000 prize. The runner-up was Doyle Brunson. The last hand was:

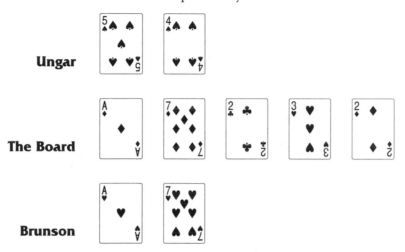

Ungar

The Board

Brunson

1980 Final Table	Hometown	Prize
1st Stu Ungar	Las Vegas, NV	$385,000
2nd Doyle Brunson	Lubbock, TX	$146,000
3rd Jay Heimowitz	Bethel, NY	$109,500
4th Johnny Moss	Las Vegas, NV	$73,000
5th Charles Dunwoody	Unknown	$36,500

1981 The 12th World Series of Poker was won by Stu Ungar. He defeated seventy-four other players to win the $375,000 prize. The runner-up was Perry Green. The last hand was:

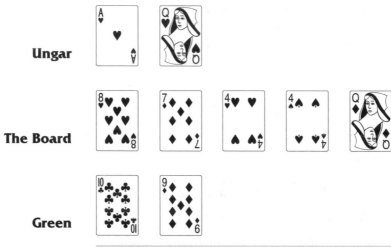

Ungar

The Board

Green

1981 FINAL TABLE		HOMETOWN	PRIZE
1st	Stu Ungar	Las Vegas, NV	$375,000
2nd	Perry Green	Anchorage, AK	$150,000
3rd	Gene Fisher	El Paso, TX	$75,000
4th	Ken Smith	Dallas, TX	$37,500
5th	Bill Smith	Roswell, NM	$37,500
6th	Jay Heimowitz	Bethel, NY	$30,000
7th	Bobby Baldwin	Tulsa, OK	$15,000
8th	Andy Moore	Sarasota, FL	$15,000
9th	Sam Petrillo	Van Nuys, CA	$15,000

The World Series of Poker awarded prize money to all nine of the players who made the final table.

1982   The 13th World Series of Poker was won by Jack "Treetop" Straus. He defeated 103 other players to win the $520,000 prize. The runner-up was Dewey Tomko. The last hand was:

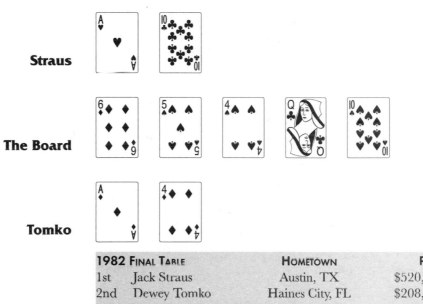

Straus

The Board

Tomko

1982 FINAL TABLE	HOMETOWN	PRIZE
1st Jack Straus	Austin, TX	$520,000
2nd Dewey Tomko	Haines City, FL	$208,000
3rd Berry Johnston	Las Vegas, NV	$104,000
4th Doyle Brunson	Lubbock, TX	$52,000
5th A.J. Meyers	Beverly Hills, CA	$52,000
6th Dody Roach	Stephenville, TX	$41,600
7th Buster Jackson	Texas	$20,800
8th Sailor Roberts	San Angelo, TX	$20,800
9th Carl Cannon	Mexia, TX	$20,800

1983   The 14th World Series of Poker was won Tom McEvoy. He defeated 107 other players to win the $540,000 prize. The runner-up was Rod Peate. The last hand was:

McEvoy

The Board

Peate

1983 FINAL TABLE		HOMETOWN	PRIZE
1st	Tom McEvoy	Grand Rapids, MI	$540,000
2nd	Rod Peate	Newport Beach, CA	$216,000
3rd	Doyle Brunson	Lubbock, TX	$108,000
4th	Carl McKelvey	San Jose, CA	$54,000
5th	Robbie Geers	Las Vegas, NV	$54,000
6th	Donnacha O'Dea	London, England	$43,200
7th	John Jenkins	Austin, TX	$21,600
8th	R.R. Pennington	Texas	$ 21,600
9th	George Huber	Las Vegas, NV	$ 21,600

1984   The 15th World Series of Poker was won by Jack Keller. He defeated 131 other players to win the $660,000 prize. The runner-up was Byron "Cowboy" Wolford. The last hand was:

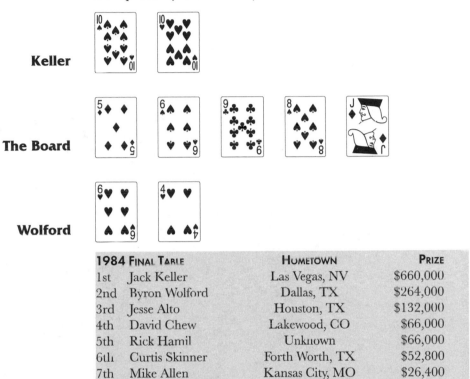

Keller

The Board

Wolford

1984 FINAL TABLE		HOMETOWN	PRIZE
1st	Jack Keller	Las Vegas, NV	$660,000
2nd	Byron Wolford	Dallas, TX	$264,000
3rd	Jesse Alto	Houston, TX	$132,000
4th	David Chew	Lakewood, CO	$66,000
5th	Rick Hamil	Unknown	$66,000
6th	Curtis Skinner	Forth Worth, TX	$52,800
7th	Mike Allen	Kansas City, MO	$26,400
8th	Howard Andrew	California	$26,400
9th	Rusty LePage	McAllen, TX	$26,400

1985   The 16th World Series of Poker was won by Bill Smith. He defeated 139 other players to win the $700,000 prize. The runner-up was T.J. Cloutier. The last hand was:

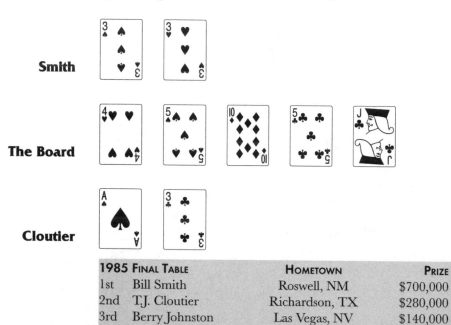

Smith

The Board

Cloutier

1985 FINAL TABLE		HOMETOWN	PRIZE
1st	Bill Smith	Roswell, NM	$700,000
2nd	T.J. Cloutier	Richardson, TX	$280,000
3rd	Berry Johnston	Las Vegas, NV	$140,000
4th	Scott Mayfield	Las Vegas, NV	$70,000
5th	Hamid Dastmalchi	England	$70,000
6th	Jesse Alto	Houston, TX	$42,000
7th	Johnny Moss	Odessa, TX	$42,000
8th	Mark Rose	Texas	$28,000
9th	John Fallon	Unknown	$28,000

1986   The 17th World Series of Poker was won by Berry Johnston. He defeated 140 other players to win the $570,000 prize. The runner-up was Mike Harthcock. The last hand was:

Johnston

The Board   [unknown]

Harthcock

1986 FINAL TABLE		HOMETOWN	PRIZE
1st	Berry Johnston	Las Vegas, NV	$570,000
2nd	Mike Harthcock	Winterhaven, FL	$228,000
3rd	Bones Berland	Las Vegas, NV	$114,000
4th	Jesse Alto	Houston, TX	$62,700
5th	Bill Smith	Dallas, TX	$52,300
6th	Roger Moore	Eastman, GA	$39,900
7th	Steve Lott	Victoria, TX	$34,200
8th	Jim Doman	Las Vegas, NV	$22,800
9th	Tom Jacobs	Denver, CO	$17,100

1987 The 18th World Series of Poker was won by Johnny Chan. He defeated 151 other players to win the $655,000 prize. The runner-up was Frank Henderson. The last hand was:

Chan

The Board

Henderson

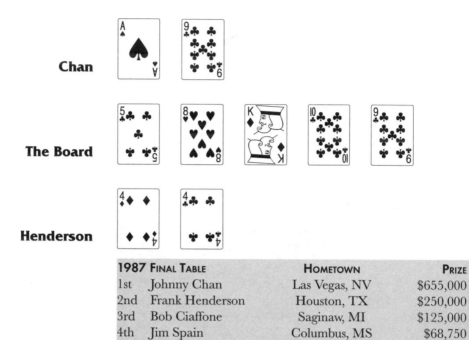

1987 FINAL TABLE		HOMETOWN	PRIZE
1st	Johnny Chan	Las Vegas, NV	$655,000
2nd	Frank Henderson	Houston, TX	$250,000
3rd	Bob Ciaffone	Saginaw, MI	$125,000
4th	Jim Spain	Columbus, MS	$68,750
5th	Howard Lederer	Las Vegas, NV	$56,250
6th	Dan Harrington	Las Vegas, NV	$43,750
7th	Eldon Elias	Palo Alto, CA	$35,500
8th	Mickey Appleman	New, York, NY	$25,000
9th	Jack Keller	Lake Cormorant, MS	$18,750

1988 The 19th World Series of Poker was won by Johnny Chan. He defeated 166 other players to win the $700,000 prize. The runner-up was Erik Seidel. The last hand was:

Chan

The Board

Seidel

1988 FINAL TABLE	HOMETOWN	PRIZE
1st Johnny Chan	Las Vegas, NV	$700,000
2nd Erik Seidel	New York, NY	$280,000
3rd Ron Graham	Las Vegas, NV	$140,000
4th Humberto Brenes	San Jose, Costa Rica	$77,000
5th T.J. Cloutier	Richardson, TX	$63,000
6th Jim Bechtel	Coolidge, AZ	$49,000
7th Quinton Nixon	Charlotte, TX	$42,000
8th Mike Cox	Unknown	$28,000
9th Jesse Alto	Houston, TX	$21,000

1989   The 20th World Series of Poker was won by Phil Hellmuth. He defeated 177 other players to win the $755,000 prize. The runner-up was Johnny Chan. The last hand was:

Hellmuth

The Board

Chan

1989 FINAL TABLE		HOMETOWN	PRIZE
1st	Phil Hellmuth	Madison, WI	$755,000
2nd	Johnny Chan	Houston, TX	$302,000
3rd	Don Zewin	Niagara Falls, NY	$151,000
4th	Steve Lott	Victoria, TX	$83,050
5th	Lyle Berman	Minneapolis, MN	$67,950
6th	Noel Furlong	Clifton Lodge, Ireland	$52,850
7th	Fernando Fisdel	New York, NY	$45,300
8th	Mike Picow	Las Vegas, NV	$30,200
9th	George Hardie	Bell Gardens, CA	$22,650

1990   The 21st World Series of Poker was won by Mansour Matloubi. He defeated 193 other players to win the $895,000 prize. The runner-up was Hans "Tuna" Lund. The last hand was:

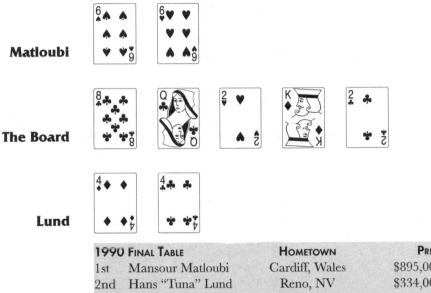

Matloubi

The Board

Lund

1990 FINAL TABLE		HOMETOWN	PRIZE
1st	Mansour Matloubi	Cardiff, Wales	$895,000
2nd	Hans "Tuna" Lund	Reno, NV	$334,000
3rd	Dave Crunkleton	Gastonia, NC	$167,000
4th	Jim Ward	Anchorage, AK	$91,850
5th	Berry Johnston	Las Vegas, NV	$75,150
6th	Al Krux	Syracuse, NY	$58,450
7th	Rod Peate	Long Beach, CA	$50,100
8th	John Bonetti	Houston, TX	$33,400
9th	Stu Ungar	New York, NY	$25,050

1991   The 22nd World Series of Poker was won by Brad Daugherty. He defeated 214 other players to win the $1,000,000 prize. The runner-up was Don Holt. The last hand was:

Daugherty

The Board

Holt

1991 FINAL TABLE		HOMETOWN	PRIZE
1st	Brad Daugherty	Reno, NV	$1,000,000
2nd	Don Holt	Henderson, NV	$ 402,000
3rd	Robert Veltri	Los Angeles, CA	$ 201,250
4th	Don Williams	Las Vegas, NV	$ 115,000
5th	Perry Green	Anchorage, AK	$ 69,000
6th	Ali Farsai	Reno, NV	$ 34,500
7th	Hilbert Shirey	Winterhaven, FL	$ 28,750
8th	Dan Hunsucker	Houston, TX	$ 23,000
9th	Donnacha O'Dea	London, England	$ 17,250

1992   The 23rd World Series of Poker was won by Hamid Dastmalchi. He defeated 200 other players to win the $1,000,000 prize. The runner-up was Tom Jacobs. The last hand was:

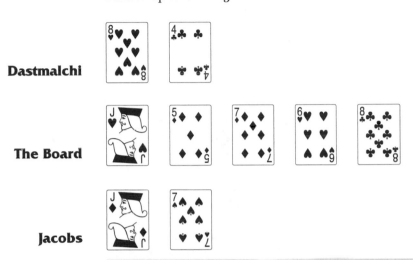

Dastmalchi

The Board

Jacobs

1992 FINAL TABLE		HOMETOWN	PRIZE
1st	Hamid Dastmalchi	San Diego, Ca	$1,000,000
2nd	Tom Jacobs	Denver, CO	$ 353,500
3rd	Hans "Tuna" Lund	Reno, NV	$ 176,500
4th	Mike Alsaadi	Las Vegas, NV	$ 101,000
5th	Dave Crunkleton	Gastonia, NC	$ 60,000
6th	Clyde Coleman	Marlowe, OK	$ 30,300
7th	Johnny Chan	Las Vegas, NV	$ 25,250
8th	Jack Keller	Lake Cormorant, MS	$ 20,200
9th	Christopher Goulding	Unknown	$ 15,150

1993   The 24th World Series of Poker was won by Jim Bechtel. He defeated 219 other players to win the $1,000,000 prize. The runner-up was Glen Cozen. The last hand was:

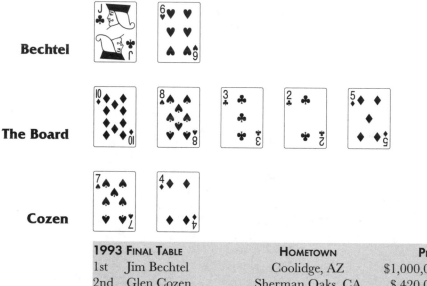

Bechtel

The Board

Cozen

1993 FINAL TABLE		HOMETOWN	PRIZE
1st	Jim Bechtel	Coolidge, AZ	$1,000,000
2nd	Glen Cozen	Sherman Oaks, CA	$ 420,000
3rd	John Bonetti	Houston, TX	$ 210,000
4th	Mansour Matloubi	Cardiff, Wales	$ 120,000
5th	Thomas Chung	Seattle, WA	$ 72,000
6th	Mick Cowley	Barnsley, England	$ 36,000
7th	Thomas Kreilein	Duncan, Canada	$ 31,200
8th	Al Korsin	Las Vegas, NV	$ 27,600
9th	Brad Daugherty	Las Vegas, NV	$ 24,000

1994 The 25th World Series of Poker was won by Russ Hamilton. He defeated 267 other players to win the $1,000,000 prize. The runner-up was Hugh Vincent. The last hand was:

Hamilton

The Board

Vincent

1994 FINAL TABLE		HOMETOWN	PRIZE
1st	Russ Hamilton	Las Vegas, NV	$1,000,000
2nd	Hugh Vincent	Palm Gardens, FL	$ 588,000
3rd	John Spadavecchia	Miami, FL	$ 294,000
4th	Vince Brugio	West Hills, CA	$ 168,000
5th	Al Krux	Syracuse, NY	$ 100,000
6th	Robert Turner	Downey, CA	$ 50,400
7th	John Aglialoro	Haddonfield, NJ	$ 43,680
8th	Don "Pilot" Pittman	Sapulpa, OK	$ 38,640
9th	Steve Lott	Downey, CA	$ 33,600

1995   The 26th World Series of Poker was won by Dan Harrington. He defeated 272 other players to win the $1,000,000 prize. The runner-up was Howard Goldfarb. The last hand was:

Harrington

The Board

Goldfarb

1995 Final Table		Hometown	Prize
1st	Dan Harrington	Downey, Ca	$1,000,000
2nd	Howard Goldfarb	Toronto, Canada	$ 519,000
3rd	Brent Carter	Oak Park, IL	$ 302,000
4th	Hamid Dastmalchi	San Diego, CA	$ 173,000
5th	Barbara Enright	Van Nuys, CA	$ 114,180
6th	Chuck Thompson	Santa Cruz, Ca	$ 86,500
7th	Tom Franklin	Gulfport, MS	$ 69,200
8th	Henry Orenstein	Verona, NJ	$ 51,900
9th	Dolph Arnold	Houston, TX	$ 39,970

1996   The 27th World Series of Poker was won by Huck Seed. He defeated 294 other players to win the $1,000,000 prize. The runner-up was Dr. Bruce Van Horn. The last hand was:

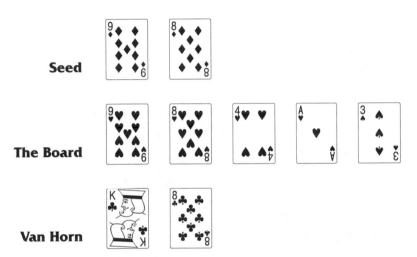

Seed

The Board

Van Horn

Huck Seed won the championship with the exact same hand that Dan Harrington won with the year before.

1996 FINAL TABLE		HOMETOWN	PRIZE
1st	Huck Seed	Las Vegas, NV	$1,000,000
2nd	Dr. Bruce Van Horn	Ada, OK	$ 585,000
3rd	John Bonetti	Houston, TX	$ 341,250
4th	Men Nguyen	Bell Gardens, CA	$ 195,000
5th	An Tran	Las Vegas, NV	$ 128,700
6th	Andre Boyer	Las Vegas, NV	$97,500
7th	J.P. Schmalz	Unknown	$78,000
8th	Fernando Fisdel	New York, NY	$58,500
9th	Steve Beam	Las Vegas, NV	$44,850

1997 The 28th World Series of Poker was won by Stu Ungar. He defeated 311 other players to win the $1,000,000 prize. The runner-up was John Strzemp. The last hand was:

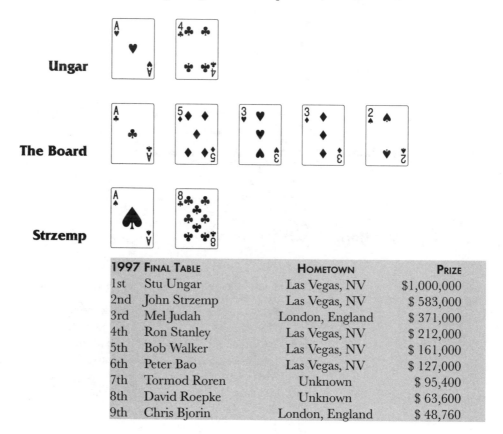

Ungar

The Board

Strzemp

1997 FINAL TABLE		HOMETOWN	PRIZE
1st	Stu Ungar	Las Vegas, NV	$1,000,000
2nd	John Strzemp	Las Vegas, NV	$ 583,000
3rd	Mel Judah	London, England	$ 371,000
4th	Ron Stanley	Las Vegas, NV	$ 212,000
5th	Bob Walker	Las Vegas, NV	$ 161,000
6th	Peter Bao	Las Vegas, NV	$ 127,000
7th	Tormod Roren	Unknown	$ 95,400
8th	David Roepke	Unknown	$ 63,600
9th	Chris Bjorin	London, England	$ 48,760

1998   The 29th World Series of Poker was won by Scotty Nguyen. He defeated 349 other players to win the $1,000,000 prize. The runner-up was Kevin McBride. The last hand was:

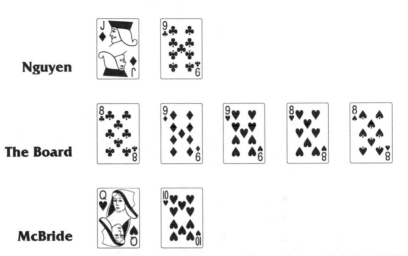

Nguyen

The Board

McBride

1998 FINAL TABLE		HOMETOWN	PRIZE
1st	Scotty Nguyen	Henderson, NV	$1,000,000
2nd	Kevin McBride	Boca Raton, FL	$ 687,500
3rd	T.J. Cloutier	Richardson, TX	$ 437,500
4th	Dewey Weum	Monona, WI	$ 250,000
5th	Lee Salem	San Diego, CA	$ 190,000
6th	Ben Roberts	London, England	$ 150,000
7th	Jan Lundberg	London, England	$ 112,500
8th	Mark Brochard	France	$ 75,000
9th	Paul McKinney	Princeton, WV	$ 57,500

1999   The 30th World Series of Poker was won by Noel Furlong. He defeated 392 other players to win the $1,000,000 prize. The runner-up was Alan Goehring. The last hand was:

Furlong

The Board

Goehring

1999 FINAL TABLE		HOMETOWN	PRIZE
1st	Noel Furlong	Clifton Lodge, Ireland	$1,000,000
2nd	Alan Goehring	New York, NY	$ 768,625
3rd	Padraig Parkinson	Dublin, Ireland	$ 489,125
4th	Erik Seidel	Henderson, NV	$ 279,500
5th	Chris Bigler	Fislisbad, Switzerland	$ 212,420
6th	Huck Seed	Las Vegas, NV	$ 167,700
7th	George McKeever	Dublin, Ireland	$ 125,775
8th	Paul Rowe	Las Vegas, NV	$ 83,850
9th	Stanley, "Ty" Bayne	Visalia, CA	$ 64,285

2000   The 31st World Series of Poker was won by Chris "Jesus" Ferguson. He defeated 511 other players to win the $1,500,000 prize. The runner-up was T.J. Cloutier. The last hand was:

Ferguson

The Board

Cloutier

2000 FINAL TABLE		HOMETOWN	PRIZE
1st	Chris Ferguson	Pacific Palisades, CA	$1,500,000
2nd	T.J. Cloutier	Richardson, TX	$ 896,000
3rd	Steve Kaufman	Cincinnati, OH	$ 570,500
4th	Hasan Habib	Bell Gardens, CA	$ 326,000
5th	Jim McManus	Kenilworth, IL	$ 247,760
6th	Roman Abinsay	Stockton, Ca	$ 195,600
7th	Jeff Shulman	Las Vegas, NV	$ 146,700
8th	Tom Franklin	Gulfport, MS	$97,800
9th	Mickey Appleman	New York, NY	$74,980

2001   The 32nd World Series of Poker was won by Carlos Mortensen. He defeated 612 other players to win the $1,500,000 prize. The runner-up was Dewey Tomko. The last hand was:

Mortensen

The Board

Tomko

2001 Final Table		Hometown	Prize
1st	Carlos Mortensen	Madrid, Spain	$1,500,000
2nd	Dewey Tomko	Haines City, FL	$1,098,925
3rd	Stan Schrier	Omaha, NE	$ 699,315
4th	Phil Gordon	South Tahoe, CA	$ 399,610
5th	Phil Hellmuth, Jr.	Palo Alto, Ca	$ 303,705
6th	Mike Matusow	Henderson, NV	$ 239,765
7th	Henry Nowakowski	Frankfurt, Germany	$ 179,825
8th	Steve Riehle	Lompoc, Ca	$ 119,885
9th	John Inashima	Pasadena, CA	$ 91,110

2002   The 33rd World Series of Poker was won by Robert Varkonyi. He defeated 630 other players to win the $2,000,000 prize. The runner-up was Julian Gardner. The last hand was:

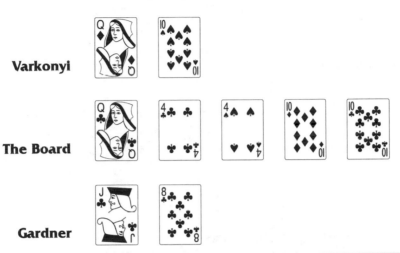

Varkonyi

The Board

Gardner

2002 FINAL TABLE		HOMETOWN	PRIZE
1st	Robert Varkonyi	Brooklyn, NY	$2,000,000
2nd	Julian Gardner	Manchester, England	$1,100,000
3rd	Ralph Perry	Las Vegas, NV	$ 550,000
4th	Scott Gray	Dublin, Ireland	$ 281,400
5th	Harley Hall	Capistrano, CA	$ 195,000
6th	Russell Rosenblum	Bethesda, MD	$ 150,000
7th	John Shipley	Solihull, England	$ 120,000
8th	Tam Duong	Los Angeles, CA	$ 100,000
9th	Minh Ly	Las Vegas, NV	$ 81,000

2003   The 34th World Series of Poker was won by Chris Moneymaker. He defeated 838 other players to win the $2,500,000 prize. The runner-up was Sammy Farha. The final hand was:

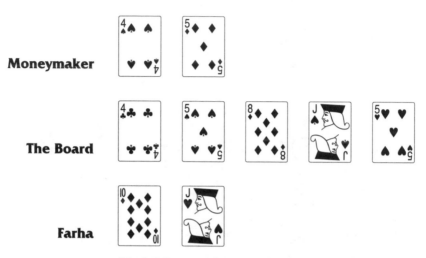

Moneymaker

The Board

Farha

Chris Moneymaker was the first World Series of Poker $10,000 Buy-in No-Limit Texas hold'em player to have won his entry fee through an on-line Texas hold'em tournament. His original buy-in was only $40. He was a 27-year old accountant from Spring Hill, Tennessee.

2003 FINAL TABLE		HOMETOWN	PRIZE
1st	Chris Moneymaker	Spring Hill, TN	$2,500,000
2nd	Sam Farha	Houston, TX	$1,300,000
3rd	Dan Harrington	Santa Monica, CA	$ 650,000
4th	Jason Lester	Las Vegas, NV	$ 440,000
5th	Tomer Benvenisti	Las Vegas, NV	$ 320,000
6th	Amir Vahedi	Reseda, CA	$ 250,000
7th	Young Pak	Bainbridge, WA	$ 200,000
8th	David Grey	Henderson, NV	$ 160,000
9th	David Singer	Mamaroneck, NY	$ 120,000

2004   The 35th World Series of Poker was won by 39 year-old corporate patent attorney Greg Raymer. He defeated 2,575 other players to win the $5,000,000 prize. The runner-up was David Williams. The final hand was:

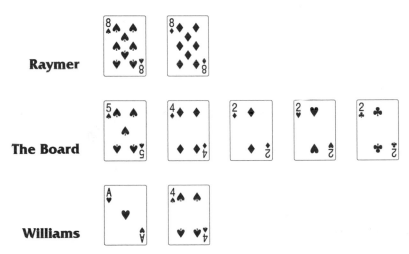

Raymer

The Board

Williams

Greg Raymer won his $10,000 entry fee into the WSOP by way of a $160 online shootout tournament. He bought his trademark glasses at the Disney World Tower of Terror gift shop. His nickname is "Fossilman" because he uses fossils as card protectors.

2004 FINAL TABLE		HOMETOWN	PRIZE
1st	Greg Raymer	Raleigh, NC	$5,000,000
2nd	David Williams	Dallas, TX	$3,500,000
3rd	Josh Arieh	Atlanta, GA	$2,500,000
4th	Dan Harrington	Santa Monica, CA	$1,500,000
5th	Glenn Hughes	Scottsdale, AZ	$1,100,000
6th	Al Krux	Syracuse, NY	$ 800,000
7th	Matt Dean	The Woodlands, TX	$ 675,000
8th	Mattias Andersson	Boras, Sweden	$ 575,000

2005   The 36th World Series of Poker was won by Australian chiropractor Joseph Hachem. He defeated 5,618 other players to win the record $7,500,000 first prize. The runner-up was Steve Dannemann. The final hand was:

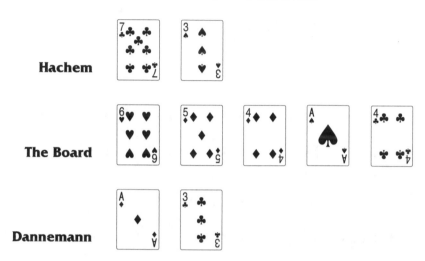

The final day of play was the longest in WSOP history, lasting more than 13 hours and 55 minutes and taking 232 hands to decide the winner.

2005 FINAL TABLE		HOMETOWN	PRIZE
1st	Joseph Hachem	Melbourne, Australia	$7,500,000
2nd	Steve Dannemann	Severn, MD	$4,250,000
3rd	Tex Barch	McKinney, TX	$2,500,000
4th	Aaron Kanter	Elk Grove, CA	$2,000,000
5th	Andrew Black	Dublin, Ireland	$1,750,000
6th	Scott Lazar	Studio City, CA	$1,500,000
7th	Daniel Bergsdord	Umea, Sweden	$1,300,000
8th	Brad Kondracki	Kingston, PA	$1,150,000
9th	Mike Matusow	Henderson, NV	$1,000,000

2006   The 37th World Series of Poker was won by 36 year-old Holly-wood talent agent Jamie Gold. He defeated 8,772 other players to win the record $12,000,000 first prize. The runner-up was Paul Wasicka. The final hand was:

Gold

The Board

Wasicka

A record total of $37,811,922 was paid to the nine players to make the final table. For the first time in WSOP history, each player at the final table was guaranteed to be a millionaire.

2006 FINAL TABLE		HOMETOWN	PRIZE
1st	Jamie Gold	Malibu, CA	$12,000,000
2nd	Paul Wasicka	Las Vegas, NV	$6,102,499
3rd	Michael Binger	Atherton, CA	$4,123,310
4th	Allen Cunningham	Las Vegas, NV	$3,628,513
5th	Rhett Butler	Rockville, MD	$3,216,182
6th	Richard Lee	San Antonio, TX	$2,803,851
7th	Douglas Kim	New York, NY	$2,391,520
8th	Erik Friberg	Stockholm, Sweden	$1,979,189
9th	Dan Nassif	St. Louis, MO	$1,566,858

2007 The 38th World Series of Poker was won by 39 year-old therapist and social worker Jerry Yang. He defeated 6,357 other players to win the $8,250,000 prize. The runner-up was Tuan Lam. The final hand was:

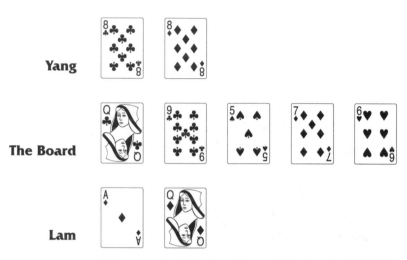

Yang

The Board

Lam

This was the first time since 1992 that the WSOP experienced a reduction in players, 2,415 fewer than 2006, due to the passage of the Unlawful Internet Gambling Enforcement Act (UIGEA), in the United States. This law restricted Internet gambling and reduced the number of players earning seats through online poker sites.

2007 FINAL TABLE		HOMETOWN	PRIZE
1st	Jerry Yang	Temecula, CA	$8,250,000
2nd	Tuan Lam	Ontario, Canada	$4,840,981
3rd	Raymond Rahme	Johannesburg, SA	$3,048,025
4th	Alex Kravchenko	Moscow, Russia	$1,852,721
5th	Jon Kalmar	Chorley, England	$1,255,069
6th	Hevad Khan	Poughkeepsie, NY	$956,243
7th	Lee Childs	Reston, VA	$705,229
8th	Lee Watkinson	Tacoma, WA	$585,699
9th	Philip Hilm	Cambridge, England	$525,934

GLOSSARY

A X suited　In hold'em, an ace and another card of the same suit.

Add on　In a tournament, the last additional chips that a player may buy, usually at the break.

Advertise　To make a loose play or an apparently bad play for the purpose of getting loose callers on a future play.

All-in　The act of putting all the remaining chips you have in the pot, usually before the hand is over. A player who is all-in can win only that part of the pot he was able to match, if he has the best hand at the end.

B & M　Stands for "bricks and mortar." Used to describe poker rooms that actually exist in buildings, as opposed to on-line poker rooms that exist only in cyberspace.

Baby　A 2, 3, 4, 5, or ace when playing for low or high-low split.

Backdoor　Making a hand that you originally weren't drawing to or trying to make. For example, you hold A♥ J♥ in hold'em and the flop is Q♥ 7♥ 3♦ and the turn is the K♦ and the river is the 10♠, giving you the straight, even though you were originally hoping for the heart flush after the flop.

Backraise　A re-raise from a player who originally just called on that round.

Bad beat　To lose with a great hand—usually aces full or better—to a player who made a longshot draw.

Banker　Usually applies only to home games. The one player who is responsible for selling the poker chips, keeping the cash, possibly providing credit and keeping the book work and accounting straight for that game.

Bankroll　The money you have set aside to put into a poker game. This money is physically, or at least mentally, segregated from other money used for non-playing expenses.

Bicycle　A 5-high straight: 5 4 3 2 A.

Big blind　The bigger of two blinds in a game; a mandatory bet posted by the player two places to the dealer's left.

Big flop　A flop that gives you almost everything you could hope for and helps your hand in more than one way. For example, you hold A♠ A♣ 2♠ 3♣ in Omaha High-Low Split and the flop is A♥ 4♠ 5♠. You have a set of aces, a wheel for high, an uncounterfeit-able low and the nut flush draw.

Big Slick　In a flop game (Texas hold'em, Omaha, and Pineapple), an ace and a king as your hole cards.

Blank　A card that is obviously of no help to a poker hand. Also called a brick.

Blockers　In Omaha, when the flop is three to a straight and you hold the open-end straight cards. For example, the flop is 9 8 7 and you hold 10 10 6 6.

Boxed card　A card that is accidentally turned face up during the shuffle and is then dealt to a player face up when it should be face down. It is treated as a blank piece of paper and is replaced with a new card after the deal is completed for that round.

Bluff　To bet a hand that is likely to lose if called.

Board　The cards that are turned face up in a flop game and belong to everybody. Also called community cards.

Broadway　An ace-high straight: A K Q J 10.

Bug　A fifty-third card in the deck that can, by agreement, be used only as a fifth ace or as any card needed to complete a straight, a flush or a low hand. It is not completely wild like a joker.

Burn or burn card　After the deal and before each betting round, the top card, which is mucked by the dealer. This is done to protect everyone in the event the top card is marked or somehow known to one player while the action is in progress and everyone is waiting for that card.

Button In casino games, a round, plastic disc with the word "Dealer" printed on both sides. It moves clockwise with each new hand to indicate who holds the dealer's position.

Buy-in The amount of money that it costs to play in a ring game or a tournament.

Call To match another player's bet without raising.

Calling station A player who calls way too much when folding or raising might be a better option.

Cards speak The concept that your poker hand is determined by what your cards actually are, and not by any remarks that a player may make about his hand. All casino games are played cards speak, and if you turn your hand face up at the end of the hand, the dealer will read the hand for you.

Carvee A player who is being carved up in a high-low split game. For example, Player A has the nuts for high and Player B has the nuts for low. Player C has what he thinks is a good hand but he cannot beat either Player A or B. When Player C calls the maximum number of bets on each round and then does not win any of the pot, he will have been carved up by Players A and B, and is therefore the carvee.

Case card The last card of a particular rank that has not been seen during the hand and believed to still be in the deck.

Change gears To change from loose to tight play, or from aggressive to passive, or vice versa.

Chasing Calling, or trying to make poker hands that are longshots or statistically improbable.

Check To not make a bet when it is your turn. It means, "I bet nothing." Checking is not allowed if there has been a bet in front of you.

Check-raise To not bet initially on a round, and then to raise when the action returns to you.

Chopping	When everyone but the two blinds have folded before the flop, chopping is an agreement they make to take their blinds back and end the hand right there, thus avoiding the rake.
Cold call	To call two or more bets at once as opposed to calling one bet then calling the other.
Community cards	See **board**.
Completed hand	A poker hand that requires all five cards to make the hand. That would be a straight, a flush, a full house, four-of-a-kind and a straight flush.
Counterfeited	To have made a low hand and then have one of the low cards in your hand pair on the board on the turn or river. For example, you hold A K 9 2 and the board is 3 6 8 J and the river is another 2.
Dangler	In Omaha, the one card in your hand that is not coordinated with the other three cards.
Dealer's choice	A game where the dealer has the right to name the game that will be played on his deal.
Declare	To indicate whether you're vying for a high or a low hand, or both.
Dominated hand	A hand that nearly always loses when competing against another particular hand. Dominated hands are typically 4 to 1 underdogs. Examples are A A vs. any smaller pair, A K versus any two smaller cards.
Door card	In stud games, the player's first up card.
Double belly buster	A straight draw that has eight outs, yet is not an open-end straight draw. For example, you have 8 6 and the board is 10 7 3 4 with one card to come. A 5 or a 9 will make your straight, yet your draw is not open-ended.
Draw light	When you run out of money and instead of going all in, you play on credit. The amount of credit is indicated by how much is in front of you. For example, when everyone puts $2 in the pot, you take $2 out. At the end of the game, the amount in front of you is what you owe the pot.

Drawing dead   Trying to make a particular poker hand that, even if you make it, is already beaten or cannot possibly win.

Ducks   Deuces. Two deuces is a pair of ducks. Four ducks is called Huey, Duey, Louie, and Uncle Donald.

Early position   To be in the first third of the players in a poker game to have to act on their hands.

Eight or better   When playing for low, the stipulation that your fifth highest card must be an 8 or lower to qualify as a low poker hand.

Emergency low   A low hand that you weren't trying to make, that you may not realize you have and certainly would not bet on if you knew you did have it. For example, in Omaha, you hold A♦ K♥ Q♦ 8♥ and the board is 7♦ 10♣ 5♦ 2♦, giving you the nut flush. When the board pairs on the river and your sole opponent shows you his K♦ K♣ 10♦ 10♥ to make a full house, you start to throw your hand away while not believing your bad luck. But wait! You also have A♦ 8♥ to go with the three low cards on the board, making an emergency low for half of the pot.

End   The fifth, and last, community card in hold'em. Also called the river.

Fifth street   The fifth card. In flop games, it is the river card. In stud games, it is the third up card each player receives.

Flop   The first three community cards turned face up in a hold'em or Omaha game.

Flop a set   To have a pair in the pocket and get one more of that rank on the flop to make three-of-a-kind, or trips.

Flush   A hand with five cards of the same suit that do not qualify as a straight flush or royal flush.

Flush card   A card of the suit that you need to make your flush or to pick up a flush draw.

Flush draw   To have four cards to a flush with one or more cards to come.

Fold   To throw your hand in the discard pile, or the muck, and to forfeit all interest and claims in the pot for that hand. A verbal declaration of your intent to fold, made in turn, is binding.

Four-of-a-kind   A hand with four cards of matching rank, plus a fifth card.

Fourth street   The fourth card. In flop games it is the turn card; in stud games it is the second face up card that everyone receives.

Free card   A card received on a betting round where there turned out to be no bet because everyone checked.

Freeroll   Whenever you have the nuts with more cards to come and you have a draw to an even better hand.

Freezeout tournament   A tournament where the only chips you get to play are the ones you buy-in with at the beginning of the tournament. You cannot rebuy or add on. Once you lose your chips, you are out of the tournament.

Full   When discussing a full house, the three-of-a-kind is what the hand is full of. 8 8 8 5 5 is "8s full of 5s."

Full house   A hand with three cards of matching rank, plus two cards of another matching rank.

Gutshot   An inside straight draw. For example, you hold A K and the flop is J 10 7.

Half-dangler   In Omaha, a card that is not that good, but does add a little something to the value of your hand. It is only marginally better than a blank.

Head-up   A game in which you have only one other opponent.

High wrap   In Omaha, when you have a straight draw and all four of your hole cards are higher than the cards on the board.

Implied odds   Money that is not yet in the pot but you believe will be in the pot after you make your hand. It is an educated guess of what your pot odds will be when the hand is over.

Inside wrap   To hold the three cards in a three-gap flop. For example, the flop is A 10 8 and you hold a K Q J in your hand. Any king, queen or jack on the turn or river will give you the nut straight.

Joker   A 53rd card in the deck that can, by agreement, be used as any other card in the deck. This makes five-of-a-kind possible.

Kicker	The highest card in your hand that does not help make a straight, flush, full house or pair.
Kill game	A game where the betting limits are increased—usually doubled—for the next hand only.
Late position	To be one of the last third of the players in the game to have to act on your hand.
Limp in	To call another player's bet when you might be thinking about raising.
Little blind	The smaller of the two blinds in hold'em, posted by the first player to the dealer's left before the hands are dealt.
Live cards	In stud, cards that you need to improve your hand and have not yet seen folded or in someone else's hand.
Low wrap	To hold four low cards and to get three more low cards on the flop without making a pair.
Maine to Spain	Two cards on the flop that—along with the four cards in your hand—give you a six-card straight. For example, you have 6 7 10 J and the flop is 9 8 2. A 5, 6, 7, 10, J or Q will give you a straight. This is a twenty-out draw. It occurs when, after the flop, any one of twenty cards will make your hand for you.
Middle position	To have an approximately equal number of players before and after you in the play of the hand.
Muck	To fold and throw your hand in the discard pile; the discard pile itself.
No-limit	A poker game where the players may bet any amount of money that they have in the game at any time.
Nut-Nut	In Omaha, said by the player at the showdown who makes the nut low hand and the nut high hand.
Nuts	The best possible hand that can be made after the flop, the turn, and especially after the river.
Off-Broadway	A king-high straight: K Q J 10 9.
On the button	To be in the dealer's position and therefore last to act throughout each betting round of that game.

Outs	The number of cards that will help your hand. For example, if you have two hearts and get two more hearts on the flop, then there are nine hearts (number of outs) that will make your hand.
Overcall	A call made after there has already been a bet and a call.
Overs, playing the	An agreement among any players in the game who want to raise the limits when only those players are left in the hand.
Overcard	A card on the board that is higher than either of your hole cards.
Overlay	Better pot odds.
Overpair	A pair in your hand that is higher than any card on the flop. Q♣ Q♥ is an overpair if the flop is J♦ 9♣ 5♠.
Padding the odds	Requiring grossly excess odds.
Pocket	The first two cards that you're dealt that constitute your private hand.
Pot limit	A poker game where the players can bet only up to the amount of money that is in the pot when it is their turn to bet.
Pot odds	The ratio of the amount of money in the pot compared to the amount of money that it costs to call a bet. For example, if the pot contains $42 and it costs you $3 to call, you are getting pot odds of 14 to 1. If it's $6 to call, you're getting pot odds of 7 to 1.
Rabbit hunting	Asking to see the next card after the hand is over so that you know how the rest of the hand would have turned out.
Rag	Usually a low card that appears not to have helped anyone's poker hand.
Rainbow flop	A flop with three different suits and no pair.
Raising in the dark	Raising before you get your cards.
Razz	Another name for seven-card stud low.
Represent	To play your hand in such a way that it is obvious to everyone what you have—except you don't have that hand.
Ring game	A poker game played for cash that is not a tournament.

River	See **end**.
Rock	A poker player who has a reputation for playing only premium starting hands and whose playing style is dull, boring and very low risk.
Rolled up	In stud, to start with three-of-a-kind in your first three cards.
Royal flush	A hand with five cards of consecutive rank, from ace to 10, all of the same suit, for example: A♦ K♦ Q♦ J♦ 10♦.
Rough	Used to describe a made low hand that is not very good, given the highest card. A player who has 8 7 4 2 A would say, "I have a rough 8." See **smooth**.
Runner-runner	Used to describe the turn and river cards when they were exactly what you needed to win, or what your opponent needed to beat you. Also called "perfect- perfect." Usually used to describe a made backdoor flush draw or double gutshot straight draw.
Rush	The experience of having won many pots close together in a short period of time.
Satellite	A one-table mini-tournament where the combined, total buy-in of all the players is exactly the buy-in needed for a larger tournament. For example, the buy-in for the World Series of Poker No-Limit Texas hold'em Tournament is $10,000. You can win that $10,000 by playing in and winning a satellite where ten players put up $1,000 apiece.
Scoop	To win both the high and low ends of the pot when playing a high-low split game.
Semi-bluffing	Betting with a hand that, if called, probably isn't the best hand at the moment, but has a chance to improve to the best hand with more cards to come.
Set	The exact situation of having a pair in the pocket and one of those cards on the board. Holding 9 9 with a board of 3 9 Q is a set of 9s, but holding 3 9 with a board of 9 9 Q is described as three 9s, but not a set.
Seventh street	In stud, the seventh, and last, card dealt.

Sheriff   A player who likes to always call on the river so that no one can ever get away with bluffing at that point in the game.

Sixth street   In stud, the sixth card. It is the fourth up card each player receives.

Slowplay   To play your hand in a much weaker manner than its strength would usually call for in order to disguise that strength for a future betting round.

Smooth   Used to describe a made low hand that is very good, given the highest card. For example, an 8 for low is not a very good low hand; however, if it is 8 4 3 2 A, a player would say, "I have a smooth 8." See **rough**.

Split pot   A poker game where the intention is to split the pot between the highest and lowest poker hands. The low hand will usually have to meet qualifying criteria, such as having an 8 or better for low.

Spread limit   A betting structure that allows you to bet any amount between the preset lowest and highest amounts. The most common spread limit used for seven-card stud is $1 to $4 or $1 to $5.

Steal   To raise on the first round of betting for the purpose of winning the blinds, regardless of the strength of your own poker hand.

Stop yourself   In Omaha, to have more than two cards of the same rank or same suit in your hand. For example, holding A♣ Q♣ 9♠ 4♣ or J J J 10. This is undesirable because it takes the cards you need to make your hand out of play.

Straddle   Occurs when the first player after the big blind raises before he receives his first two cards.

Straight   A hand with five ranks in sequence: A 2 3 4 5 through 10 J Q K A.

Straight draw   To have four cards to a straight with one or more cards to come.

Structured limit   A betting structure that forces you to bet only the amount specified as the small bet and the big bet. It's usually a 1:2 ratio.

Suited connectors	Two consecutive cards of the same suit, like Q♥ J♥, 9♦ 8♦, or 6♠ 5♠.
Swing	To declare for both high and low in a high-low split game.
Taking a book	In a draw game, to discard and replace your entire hand with new cards.
Tell	A clue from an opponent that helps you figure out what his poker hand is. That clue (or clues) can be made either voluntarily or involuntarily, and verbally or physically.
Three-of-a-kind	A hand of three cards of a matching rank and two other cards whose ranks don't match: 8 8 8 5 2.
Through ticket	A poker hand that you know you're going to play all the way to the river because it is either very good on the flop, has many outs to make, has the potential to make a monster hand, or the potential to win a huge pot. A flop that gives you a set of aces, the nut flush draw and the nut low draw in Omaha is a big flop and is therefore a through ticket.
Turn	The fourth community card in flop games.
Two pair	A hand with two cards of a matching rank and two other cards of a different matching rank.
Under the gun	In first position; first to act.
Up	Used to indicate two pair. A A 9 9 5 would be called "aces-up."
Wheel	See **bicycle**.
World Series of Poker (WSOP)	Approximately thirty-five tournaments held at Binion's Horseshoe Casino in Las Vegas every April-May. The winner of each event is crowned the World Champion in that event until the next WSOP.
Wrap	A straight draw that has more than eight outs.
Zero board	A board with which the highest possible hand is three-of-a-kind.

INDEX

FROM CARDOZA'S EXCITING LIBRARY
ADD THESE TO YOUR COLLECTION - ORDER NOW!

SUPER SYSTEM *by Doyle Brunson.* Jam-packed with advanced strategies, theories, tactics and moneymaking techniques, this classic work,widely considered to be the most important poker book ever written! Chapters are written by six superstars: Mike Caro, Chip Reese, Dave Sklansky, Joey Hawthorne, Bobby Baldwin, and Doyle—two world champions and four master theorists and players. Essential strategies, advanced play, and no-nonsense winning advice on making money at 7-card stud (razz, high-low split, cards speak, declare), lowball, draw poker, and hold'em (limit and nolimit). A must-read—every serious poker player must own this book. 628 pages, $29.95.

SUPER SYSTEM 2 *by Doyle Brunson.* The most anticipated poker book ever, SS2 expands upon the original with more games and professional secrets from the best players in the world. Superstar contributors include Daniel Negreanu, winner of multiple WSOP gold bracelets and 2004 Player of the Year; Lyle Berman, 3-time WSOP gold bracelet winner and founder of the World Poker Tour; Bobby Baldwin, 1978 World Champion; Johnny Chan, 2-time World Champion and 10-time WSOP bracelet winner; Mike Caro, poker's greatest researcher, theorist, and instructor; Jennifer Harman, the world's top female player; Todd Brunson, winner of more than 20 tournaments; and Crandell Addington, no-limit legend. 672 pgs, $34.95.

CARO'S BOOK OF POKER TELLS *by Mike Caro.* One of the 10 greatest poker books, this must-have classic should be in every player's library. If you're serious about winning, you'll realize that most of the profit comes from being able to read your opponents. This book reveals the the secrets of interpreting *tells*—physical reactions that reveal information about a player's cards—such as shrugs, sighs, shaky hands, eye contact, and more. Learn when opponents are bluffing, when they aren't and why—based solely on their mannerisms. Over 170 photos of poker players in action and play-by-play examples show the actual tells. These powerful eye-opening ideas can give you the decisive edge at the table. 320 pages, $24.95.

CARO'S GUIDE TO DOYLE BRUNSON'S SUPER SYSTEM *by Mike Caro.* Working with World Champion Doyle Brunson, the legendary Mike Caro has created a fresh look to the "Bible" of all poker books, adding new and personal insights that help you understand the original work. Caro breaks 36 concepts into the following categories: analysis, commentary, concept, mission, play-by-play, psychology, statistics, story, or strategy. Lots of illustrations and winning concepts give even more value to this great work. 86 pages, 8 1/2 x 11, $19.95.

CARO'S FUNDAMENTAL SECRETS OF WINNING POKER *by Mike Caro.* Learn the essential strategies, concepts, and plays that comprise the very foundation of winning poker play. Learn to win more from weak players, equalize stronger players, bluff a bluffer, win big pots, where to sit against weak players, and the six factors of strategic table image. Includes selected tips on hold'em, 7-card stud, draw, lowball, tournaments, more. 160 pages, $12.95.

MILLION DOLLAR HOLD'EM: Limit Cash Games *by Johnny Chan & Mark Karowe.* Learn how to win money at limit hold'em, poker's most popular cash game. You'll get a rare opportunity to get into the mind of the man who has won 10 World Series titles—tied for the most with Doyle Brunson—as the authors pick out illustrative hands and show how they think their way through the bets and the bluffs. No book so thoroughly details the thought process of how a hand should be played, how it could have been played, and the best way to consistently win. 368 pages, paperback, $29.95.

MY 50 MOST MEMORABLE HANDS *by Doyle Brunson.* This instant classic relives the most incredible hands by the greatest poker player of all time. Great players, legends, and momentous events in the history of poker march in and out of fifty years of unforgettable hands. Sit side-by-side with Doyle as he replays the excitement and life-changing moments of the most thrilling and crucial hands in the history of poker: from his early games as a rounder in the rough-and-tumble "Wild West" years—where a man was more likely to get shot as he was to get a straight flush—to the nail-biting excitement of his two world championship titles. Doyle brings to life the high stakes tension of sidestepping police, hijackers and murderers, competes for hands worth more than a million dollars, and sweats out situations where his last dollar relies on the outcome of a card. Engrossing, captivating, riveting, and ultimately educational, this is a momentous and thrilling collection of great stories and sage poker advice from the living legend himself. 168 pages, $14.95.

CARDOZA POKER BOOKS
POWERFUL INFORMATION YOU MUST HAVE

HOLD'EM WISDOM FOR ALL PLAYERS *by Daniel Negreanu.* Superstar poker player Daniel Negreanu provides 50 easy-to-read and right-to-the-point hold'em strategy nuggets that will immediately make you a better player at cash games and tournaments. His wit and wisdom makes for great reading; even better, it makes for killer winning advice. Conversational, straightforward, and educational, this book covers topics as diverse as the top 10 rookie mistakes to bullying bullies and exploiting your table image.176 pages, paperback, $14.95.

CHAMPIONSHIP NO-LIMIT & POT-LIMIT HOLD'EM *by T. J. Cloutier & Tom McEvoy.* This is the bible of winning pot-limit and no-limit hold'em tournaments. You'll get all the answers here—no holds barred—to your most important questions: How do you get inside your opponents' heads and learn how to beat them at their own game? How can you tell how much to bet, raise, and reraise in no-limit hold'em? When can you bluff? How do you set up your opponents in pot-limit hold'em so that you can win a monster pot? What are the best strategies for winning no-limit and pot-limit tournaments, satellites, and supersatellites? Rock-solid and inspired advice you can bank on from two of the most recognizable figures in poker. 304 pages, $29.95.

CHAMPIONSHIP HOLD'EM *by T. J. Cloutier & Tom McEvoy.* Hard-hitting hold'em the way it's played *today* in both limit cash games and tournaments. Get killer advice on how to win more money in rammin'-jammin' games, kill-pot, jackpot, shorthanded, and full table cash games. You'll learn the thinking process before the flop, and on the flop, turn, and river with specific suggestions for what to do when good or bad things happen. Plus 20 illustrated hands with play-by-play analyses, specific advice for rocks in tight games, weaklings in loose games, experts in solid games, how hand values change in jackpot games, when you should fold, check, raise, reraise, check-raise, slowplay, and bluff. Also tournament strategies for small buy-in, big buy-in, rebuy, add-on, satellite and big-field major tournaments. Wow! If you want to win at limit hold'em, you need this book! 392 pages, $29.95.

CHAMPIONSHIP OMAHA (Omaha High-Low, Pot-limit Omaha, Limit High Omaha) *by Tom McEvoy & T. J. Cloutier.* Clearly-written strategies and powerful advice from Cloutier and McEvoy who have won four World Series of Poker Omaha titles. Powerful advice shows you how to win at low-limit and high-stakes games, how to play against loose and tight opponents, and the differing strategies for rebuy and freezeout tournaments. Learn the best starting hands, when slowplaying a big hand is dangerous, what danglers are and why winners don't play them, why pot-limit Omaha is the only poker game where you sometimes fold the nuts on the flop and are correct in doing so, and, overall, how you can win a lot of money at Omaha! 296 pages, illustrations, $29.95.

CHAMPIONSHIP TABLE (at the World Series of Poker) *by Dana Smith, Ralph Wheeler, & Tom McEvoy. Championship Table* celebrates three decades of poker greats who have competed to win poker's most coveted title. This book gives you the names and photographs of all the players who made the final table, pictures the last hand the champion played against the runner-up, how they played their cards, how much they won, plus fascinating interviews and conversations with the champions. This fascinating and invaluable resource book includes tons of vintage photographs. 208 pages, $19.95.

HOW TO WIN THE CHAMPIONSHIP: Hold'em Strategies for the Final Table, *by T. J. Cloutier.* If you're hungry to win a championship, this is the book that will pave the way to success! T. J. Cloutier, the greatest tournament poker player ever—he has won 59 major tournament titles and appeared at 39 final tables at the WSOP, both more than any other player in the history of poker—shows how to get to the final table where the big money is made and then how to win it all. You'll learn how to build up enough chips to make it through the early and middle rounds and then how to employ T. J.'s own strategies to outmaneuver opponents at the final table and win championships. T. J. shows you how to adjust your play depending upon stack sizes, antes and blinds, table position, opponents' styles, and chip counts. You'll also learn the specific strategies needed for full tables and for six-handed, three-handed, and heads-up play. 288 pages, $29.95.

THE CHAMPIONSHIP SERIES
POWERFUL BOOKS YOU <u>MUST</u> HAVE

CHAMPIONSHIP HOLD'EM TOURNAMENT HANDS *by T. J. Cloutier & Tom McEvoy.* An absolute must for hold'em tournament players. Two legends show you how to become a winning tournament player at both limit and no-limit hold'em games. Get inside their heads as they think their way through the correct strategy at 57 limit and no-limit starting hands. Cloutier and McEvoy show you how to use skill and intuition to play strategic hands for maximum profit in real tournament scenarios and how 45 key hands were played by champions in turnaround situations at the WSOP. Gain tremendous insights into how tournament poker is played at the highest levels. 368 pages, $29.95.

CHAMPIONSHIP HOLD'EM SATELLITE STRATEGY *by Brad Daugherty & Tom McEvoy.* Every year satellite players win their way into the $10,000 WSOP buy-in event and emerge as millionaires or champions. You can too! Learn from two world champions, the specific, proven strategies for winning almost any satellite. Covers the 10 ways to win a seat at the WSOP, how to win limit hold'em and no-limit hold'em satellites, one-table satellites, online satellites, and the final table of super satellites. Includes a special chapter on no-limit hold'em satellites! 320 pages, $29.95.

CHAMPIONSHIP TOURNAMENT POKER *by Tom McEvoy.* Enthusiastically endorsed by more than five world champions, this is a *must* for every player's library. McEvoy lets you in on the secrets he has used to win millions of dollars in tournaments and the insights he has learned competing against the best players in the world. Packed solid with winning strategies for 11 games with extensive discussions of 7-card stud, limit hold'em, pot and no-limit hold'em, Omaha high-low, re-buy, half-and-half tournaments, satellites, and includes strategies for each stage of tournaments. 416 pages, $29.95.

HOW TO WIN NO-LIMIT HOLD'EM TOURNAMENTS *by Tom McEvoy & Don Vines.* Learn the basic concepts of tournament strategy and how to win big by playing small buy-in events, graduate to medium and big buy-in tournaments, adjust for short fields, huge fields, and slow and fast-action events. Plus how to win online no-limit tournaments. You'll also learn how to manage a tournament bankroll and get tips on table demeanor for televised tournaments. See actual hands played by finalists at WSOP and WPT championship tables with card pictures, analysis and useful lessons from the play. 376 pages, $29.95.

POKER TOURNAMENT TIPS FROM THE PROS *by Shane Smith.* Essential advice from poker theorists, authors, and tournament winners on the best strategies for winning the big prizes at low-limit rebuy tournaments. Learn the best strategies for each of the four stages of play—opening, middle, late and final—how to avoid 26 potential traps, advice on rebuys, aggressive play, clock-watching, inside moves, top 20 tips for winning tournaments, and more. Advice from McEvoy, Caro, Malmuth, Ciaffone, others. 160 pages, $19.95.

NO-LIMIT TEXAS HOLD'EM: The New Player's Guide to Winning Poker's Biggest Game *by Brad Daugherty & Tom McEvoy.* For experienced limit players who want to play no-limit or rookies who have never played before, two world champions give readers a crash course in how to join the elite ranks of million-dollar, no-limit hold'em tournament winners and cash game players. You'll learn the four essential winning skills: how to evaluate the strength of a hand, how to determine the amount to bet, how to understand opponents' play, and how to bluff and when to do it. 74 game scenarios and two unique betting charts for tournament play and sections on essential principles and strategies, show you how to get to the winners circle. Special section on beating online tournaments. 288 pages, $24.95.

CRASH COURSE IN BEATING TEXAS HOLD'EM *by Avery Cardoza.* Perfect for beginning and somewhat experienced players who want to jump right into the action and play cash games, local tournaments, online poker, and the big televised tournaments where millions of dollars can be made. Both limit and no-limit hold'em games are covered, along with the essential strategies needed to play profitably on the pre-flop, flop, turn, and river. The good news is that you don't need to memorize hands or be burdened by math to be a winner—just play by the no-nonsense basic principles outlined in this book. There's a lot of money to be made and Cardoza shows you how to go and get it. 208 pages, $14.95

POWERFUL POKER SIMULATIONS

A MUST FOR SERIOUS PLAYERS WITH A COMPUTER!
IBM compatible CD ROM Win 95, 98, 2000, NT, ME, XP

These incredible full color poker simulations are the best method to improve your game. Computer opponents play like real players. All games let you set the limits and rake and have fully programmable players, plus stat tracking, and Hand Analyzer for starting hands. MIke Caro, the world's foremost poker theoretician says, "Amazing... a steal for under $500... get it, it's great." Includes free phone support. "Smart Advisor" gives expert advice for every play!

1. TURBO TEXAS HOLD'EM FOR WINDOWS - $59.95. Choose which players, and how many (2-10) you want to play, create loose/tight games, and control check-raising, bluffing, position, sensitivity to pot odds, and more! Also, instant replay, pop-up odds, Professional Advisor keeps track of play statistics. Free bonus: Hold'em Hand Analyzer analyzes all 169 pocket hands in detail and their win rates under any conditions you set. Caro says this "hold'em software is the most powerful ever created." Great product!

2. TURBO SEVEN-CARD STUD FOR WINDOWS - $59.95. Create any conditions of play; choose number of players (2-8), bet amounts, fixed or spread limit, bring-in method, tight/loose conditions, position, reaction to board, number of dead cards, and stack deck to create special conditions. Features instant replay. Terrific stat reporting includes analysis of starting cards, 3-D bar charts, and graphs. Play interactively and run high speed simulation to test strategies. Hand Analyzer analyzes starting hands in detail. Wow!

3. TURBO OMAHA HIGH-LOW SPLIT FOR WINDOWS - $59.95. Specify any playing conditions, including betting limits, number of raises, blind structures, button position, aggressiveness/passiveness of opponents, number of players (2-10), types of hands dealt, blinds, position, board reaction, and specify flop, turn, and river cards! Choose opponents and use provided point count or create your own. Statistical reporting, instant replay, pop-up odds high speed simulation to test strategies, amazing Hand Analyzer, and much more!

4. TURBO OMAHA HIGH FOR WINDOWS - $59.95. Same features as above, but tailored for Omaha High only. Caro says program is "an electrifying research tool...it can clearly be worth thousands of dollars to any serious player. A must for Omaha High players."

5. TURBO 7 STUD 8 OR BETTER - $59.95. Brand new with all the features you expect from the Wilson Turbo products: the latest artificial intelligence, instant advice and exact odds, play versus 2-7 opponents, enhanced data charts that can be exported or printed, the ability to fold out of turn and immediately go to the next hand, ability to peek at opponent's hand, optional warning mode that warns you if a play disagrees with the advisor, and automatic mode that runs up to 50 tests unattended. Tough computer players vary their styles for a great game.

6. TOURNAMENT TEXAS HOLD'EM - $39.95
Set-up for tournament practice and play, this realistic simulation pits you against celebrity look-alikes. Tons of options let you control tournament size with 10 to 300 entrants, select limits, ante, rake, blind structures, freezeouts, number of rebuys, and competition level of opponents. Pop-up status report shows how you're doing vs. the competition. Save tournaments in progress to play again later. Additional feature allows